From the Sierras to the Pampas

By the same author

France and the Jacobite Rising of 1745
The Jacobite Army in England
The Jacobites
Invasion: From the Armada to Hitler
Charles Edward Stuart
Crime and Punishment in Eighteenth-Century England
Stanley: The Making of an African Explorer
Snow Upon the Desert: The Life of Sir Richard Burton

FRANK McLYNN

From the Sierras
to the Pampas

Richard Burton's Travels
in the Americas, 1860-69

CENTURY
LONDON   SYDNEY   AUCKLAND   JOHANNESBURG

First published in Great Britain in 1991 by Century
Random Century Ltd
20 Vauxhall Bridge Road, London SW1V 2SA

A catalogue record for this book is available from
the British Library

ISBN 0-7126-3789-3

Typeset in Imprint by SX Composing Ltd
Printed and bound by Mackays of Chatham

In memory of
Norah

Contents

Introduction   ix

I   NORTH AMERICA
1   To Salt Lake City   3
2   The City of the Saints   23
3   North American Impressions   46

II   BRAZIL
4   Imperial Brazil   73
5   Daily Life in Santos and São Paulo   86
6   Consul Burton   110
7   Liberation   119
8   Down the Rio São Francisco   139
9   Brazilian Finale   162

III RIVER PLATE
10   To the Paraguayan Front   175
11   Exploring Argentina   190
12   The Literary Legacy   209

     Conclusion   221

     Notes on Sources   224
     Appendix   251
     Index   259

Illustrations

Between pages 134 and 135

1   Isabel Burton

2   Richard Burton

3   Brigham Young and his family

4   Mormon Pioneer Company

5   Salt Lake City in 1864

6   The Temple at Salt Lake City

7   The Paulo Afonso Falls

8   Title page of *The Highlands of Brazil*

9   Burton on the Rio das Velhas

10   General Bartolomé Mitre

11   Marshal Francisco Solano López

12   The Argentine Infantry at Lomas Valentinas

13   The Paraguayan Army's retreat in August, 1869

The maps on pages 2, 72, 174 are reproduced by courtesy of the Royal Geographical Society

Introduction

Richard Burton was one of the most multitalented individuals in the nineteenth century – an epoch not notably short of talent. As an African explorer he joins a distinguished, select company containing himself,
Livingstone, Stanley, Speke and Baker. In addition, he possessed creative
and scholarly abilities far in advance of the other four. None of the others
had his intellectual abilities, his erudition, his scientific curiosity or his linguistic gifts. Additionally, he was one of the great pioneer anthropologists
and sexologists. In matters sexual he anticipated Havelock Ellis and
Freud, while his ethnological work on Dahomey was hailed for its insight,
accuracy, detail and imaginative perception by the modern anthropologist
Melville Herskovits.

As a linguist Burton was a true phenomenon. He mastered twenty-five
languages (forty, if we count the variant dialects) and could break the back
of any foreign tongue after two months' sustained study. He wrote a gram-
mar of the Jataki dialect in India, compiled dictionaries in Harar, Dahomey and Brazil, as well as making transliterations of proverbs in ten different West African *argots*. His translations are works of art: accurate,
vigorous, brilliant. He moved with ease from the Hindustani of *Vikram
and the Vampire* to Portuguese for Camoens and Lacerda, to Arabic for
the *Arabian Nights* and the *Perfumed Garden*; from Neapolitan Italian for
Il Pentamerone, to Sanskrit for the *Kama Sutra* and on to Latin for the
Priapeia and *Catullus*.

As a writer he was prolific, producing forty-three volumes on his travels
and explorations. The *Pilgrimage to El Medinah and Meccah* and the
Lake Regions of Central Africa are classics, but *First Footsteps in East*

Africa, Zanzibar, The City of the Saints (on the Mormons of Salt Lake City), and *Reports from the Battlefields of Paraguay* still are of some interest.

In his time Burton was soldier, swordsman, explorer, anthropologist, archaeologist, mining speculator, poet, translator, botanist, zoologist and dignified consul. He also played the roles (in costume) of Persian merchant in India, Indian doctor in Egypt and Arabia, Muslim merchant in Somaliland, and (*in propria persona*), London clubman, devoted husband, iconoclastic critic, raconteur, wit and world-weary cynic. He was a multitudinous man, in love with the exotic and the erotic, a permanent outsider, a man straddled between cultures, neither wholly British in sensibility nor wholly anything else.

After a peripatetic childhood on the Continent, Richard Burton went up to Oxford in 1840. He found the experience a grievous disappointment at all levels and was rusticated a year later for deliberate defiance of the Trinity College authorities. He persuaded a reluctant father (who had himself been a failed professional soldier) to allow him to enter military service with the East India Company. Burton spent the years 1842-9 in India, mainly in Sind and the Punjab; it was here that his awesome linguistic talents first fully manifested themselves. Invalided home after seven years, he spent three years in a limbo of illness, depression and indecision. Finally, in the autumn of 1852 he roused himself from his torpor and planned the exploit that made him a household name. In the summer of 1853 he undertook a pilgrimage in disguise to the holy cities of Mecca and Medina; entry to the sacred citadels of Islam was denied to infidels on pain of death. After this daring exploit, Burton turned his attention to Africa. He began by breaching the barriers of another 'forbidden' city – Harar in Somalia (1855). After service in the Crimea, he then headed an expedition sponsored by the Royal Geographical Society to find the sources of the Nile (1857-9). He discovered Lake Tanganyika but fell foul of his companion John Hanning Speke, who made a side trip to Lake Victoria and announced that *that* lake was the true fountain of the White Nile. 1859 saw Burton back in England embroiled in controversy with Speke. The Royal Geographical Society took Speke's part and sent him back to East Africa in command of a second expedition. By 1860, therefore, Burton was at a crossroads in his life.

I
NORTH AMERICA

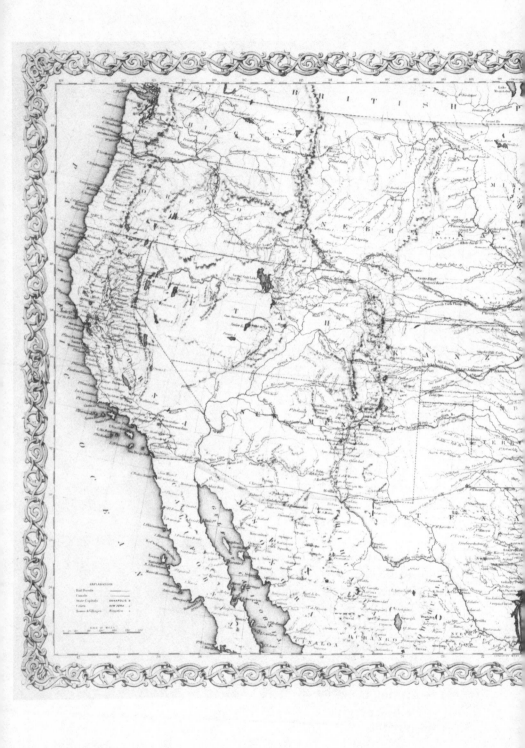

Chapter One

To Salt Lake City

Burton's decision to travel to the USA in 1860 was a product of two very different impulses. On his return to England in 1859 after discovering Lake Tanganyika, he found that his comrade on that expedition, John Hanning Speke, had claimed the major credit for the exploit, on the strength of a side trip to Lake Victoria, which he alleged to be the source of the Nile. The Royal Geographical Society had backed Speke and put up the money for a further African expedition under his command. Speke's treachery and the subsequent vitriolic recriminations, which sucked in friends and supporters on both sides, left Burton feeling listless and depressed. But when Speke departed for East Africa early in 1860, Burton found quiescence in England insupportable while his rival and erstwhile protégé garnered fresh laurels in the Dark Continent. He therefore requested convalescent leave from his employers, the East India Company, the furlough to be spent in North America.

On the other hand, the decision to depart for the New World solved a problem in Burton's personal life. For many years he had been conducting an on-and-off courtship of Isabel Arundell, scion of an old English Catholic family. Isabel's mother opposed the match on the grounds that Burton had no money and was not even a Christian. Burton suggested cutting the Gordian knot by elopement, but Isabel was too much under her mother's thumb to take such a precipitate step. Although she pleaded, cajoled and blustered with her mother, she drew back from a stark

3

choice of Richard against her family. Irritated by her apparent desire to have her cake and eat it, Burton departed for an extended tour of France. He was back in London for Christmas 1859, then settled in Boulogne for two months.[1] March 1860 found him back in London briefly. He avoided Isabel but spent time in the company of Alfred Bates Richards. Richards, a journalist and later editor of the *Morning Advertiser*, had been Burton's best friend during his ill-starred year at Trinity College, Oxford, in 1840-1. They had been athletic rivals: Richards was one of the few who could outbox Burton, but Burton was his superior with foil and broadsword. Together they obtained a ringside seat at the British heavyweight championship, as Richards later related: 'I saw Captain Burton at the fight for the championship, when we were both "brutal spectators".'[2]

It was during this visit that Burton booked passage to Canada. He then sped back to France and spent time in Paris before returning to England on 19 April ready for the Saturday sailing two days later.[3] His last task in England was to notify Isabel that she would not be seeing him for nine months. Burton clearly showed the pique he felt about her 'weakness' in not eloping when he ducked a personal interview and sent a letter instead. Isabel describes the sequel:

> One day in April 1860, I was walking out with two friends, and a tightening of my heart came over me that I had known before. I went home, and said to my sister, 'I am not going to see Richard for some time.' She said, 'Why, you will see him tomorrow!' 'No, I shall not,' I said. 'I don't know what is the matter.' A tap came at the door, and a note with a well-known writing was put into my hand. I knew my fate, and with a deep-drawn breath I opened it. He had left – could not bear the pain of saying goodbye; would be absent for nine months, on a journey to see Salt Lake City. He would then come back, and see whether I had made up my mind to choose between him or my mother, to marry me if I would; and if I had not the courage to risk it, he would go back to India, and thence to other explorations, and return no more. I was to take nine months to think about it.[4]

The shock of receiving this letter precipitated Isabel into nervous breakdown, from which she took a long time to recover. When she did, she 'repented' for her lack of courage by learning all the household and domestic arts, including the milking of cows, so as to make herself the perfect wife against the day Richard returned.

Burton embarked on the SS *Canada* on Saturday 21 April. Next day he posted his last letters from Cobh, the great sea port near Cork used by transatlantic vessels.[5] He told the world he was making the trip to add Salt Lake City to the list of 'holy cities' he had already visited, which included Memphis, Benares, Jerusalem, Rome and Mecca. But in his private diary he confessed that he had become slightly bored with the East and now wanted to try out the western hemisphere, in hopes that the experience would effect a radical change in him.[6]

His companion for the first part of the journey was Dr John Steinhaeuser, whom he had first met in 1844 when both men worked on General Napier's Sind survey.[7] Steinhaeuser was then a young surgeon, with a marked talent for languages and a collector of oriental art. One of Burton's half-dozen surrogate brothers, Steinhaeuser was originally to have joined Burton and Speke on the 1857-9 Tanganyika expedition but fell ill and had to remain in Aden. When the travellers returned to Aden in 1859, Steinhaeuser had a long talk with Speke while Burton was convalescing from fever. Following this talk, he went to Burton in some alarm to tell him that Speke's mind was already working along the lines of a 'double-cross'. Burton refused to take the warning seriously.[8] Steinhaeuser was therefore a trusted friend and Burton was delighted to have him along for the first part of the trip.

Indeed it seems that the initial impetus for the trip came from Steinhaeuser, for Burton says that the surgeon with whom he had been drinking 'on and off for fifteen years' pleaded with him to 'come with me and drink through America'. Steinhaeuser appealed to Burton's vanity by adding: 'I'll drink mint juleps, brandy-smashes, whisky-skies, gin-sling, cocktail sherry, cobblers, rum salads, streaks of lightning, morning-glory, and it'll be a most interesting experiment – I want to see whether after a life of three or four months, I can drink and eat myself to the level of the aborigines – like you.'[9]

With such a comrade in tow, it might be thought that Burton

would be in rare good spirits during the voyage across the Atlantic. But his diaries reveal him as a highly emotional and intense man, almost manic-depressive in his mood swings, which counterpointed the oceanic troughs and crests visible through the porthole. Burton seldom felt indifference towards anyone or anything. But initial enthusiasms could turn sour as the 'black dog' took the upper hand. The very first morning he awoke to a beatific vision of a lovely face, which turned out to be the reflection of the stewardess in the cabin mirror. But within days he had conceived a violent antipathy for the captain. On 24 April he wrote: 'The Captain is a d – d d – h of a d – l . . . I think he is a liar.' Later, when he suspected the master of making fun of him, he recorded: 'I *hate* that man.' The bile accentuated when the captain broke one of the laws of chivalry – which Burton, whatever his misogyny, always observed religiously – by commenting on the sexual desirability of a woman in her hearing. But rank has its privileges, however reprehensible the holder. At the May Day dance Burton was making good headway with the 'sweetest' of the girls on board until the captain whisked her away from under his nose. 'I could have cried with vexation,' he wrote, 'but I hope that I appeared calm.'[10]

The same uneasy relationship was in evidence with other people he met on the voyage. There was a Mr R, of whom his first impression was that he was 'a very handsome man though middle-aged and very polite'. By 3 May Burton was bored with him. '*I wish this journey was over.* Only imagine that wretch R is a widower with three children, one nearly grown up – how could I have thought him handsome. I refused to walk with him this morning and I thought he looked disappointed.' Part of Burton's oscillating moods is doubtless attributable to seasickness, for he had his invariable shipboard bad luck with the weather. From 25-27 April a full gale blew, and it was not until the 28th that Burton felt up to taking dinner. His attempts at wit, too, in this period, were below par. The diary entry for 23 April reads: 'Always had thought that a log was a piece of timber and now find that it is the captain's diary.'[11]

Burton also evinced a surprising degree of vanity and sensitivity in his private jottings. When he dressed for the May Day dance, the stewardess ruined things for him by remarking that his poplin jacket looked just like her wedding gown. 'My poplin *did* look ridiculous,' he admitted with mortification. Apparently this was not the only occasion when Burton did not receive the deference he considered his due, for when he landed at Nova Scotia he commented favourably on the locals' affability: 'Accustomed as a steamer passenger and tourist to the jeers and mockery of every woman and child . . . I could not detect in a single countenance an expression of contempt.'[12]

He was glad to disembark at Halifax and to begin his wanderings in the New World, which were to take him across 25,000 miles of territory.[13] First he toured Canada from Nova Scotia to Montreal. The countryside reminded him of the France of his boyhood: 'the interminable avenues of the old French roads, lined with parallel rows of poplars, which met at a vanishing point of the far distance.'[14] Then he crossed into Vermont and made his way to Salem. Evidently he ran into some difficulties here which caused him to move on quickly, for Speke's friends hastened to make black propaganda out of the incident. According to an absurd story recounted by Speke to his editor Blackwood, a newspaperman, whose feelings Burton was supposed to have 'abused' in one of his books, challenged him to a duel; at this the cowardly Burton decamped the very same night.[15] The absurdity of the story is palpable. The prospect of duelling with swords or pistols would have been a positive delight to the pugnacious and misanthropic Burton, and no man in his senses would ever have called him out. Besides, there *is* no American editor abused in Burton's books up to 1860, as a careful study will reveal. The entire fabrication is Speke's attempt at vengeance for the time Burton imputed cowardice to *him* during the desperate nocturnal fight at Berbera in 1855.

It seems that after Boston Burton headed west across New York state and Ohio before wheeling in a gigantic circle and coming back to New York city. One of his stopover points was at Niagara Falls, for he later tells us: 'I well remember not being able to sleep within earshot of Niagara, whose mighty orchestra, during the stillness of the night, seemed to run through a repertoire of oratorios and operas.'[16] New York city fascinated him for two main reasons: the influx of Irish immigrants and the numbers of prostitutes. The advent of the Irish was largely a result of the 'great hunger' of 1845-9 in the motherland. Burton, notoriously unsympathetic to the Irish, never expressed himself

7

on this subject, but there is something inhumanly cold in the way he deplores the thinning of population in Ireland simply because it deprives the English of a supply of 'comical Micks'. There was nothing comical about the New York Irishmen, as they proved three years later when rioting against the Federal draft. Curiously, their refusal to fight on behalf of 'the niggers' placed them at one with Burton, whose negrophobia was notorious. Typically, Burton was much more interested in New York's whores. Always fascinated by polygamy and its variations, he worked out that on Manhattan Island there was a polyandry of seventeen to one. He arrived at the figures by collating the 423,121 unmarried men with 3,000 officially registered prostitutes plus another 25,000 women who made an unofficial living by the sale of their bodies.[17]

In Philadelphia and Baltimore Burton remembered mainly the ornate furniture.[18] He proceeded to Washington, where he heard Senator Charles Sumner of Massachusetts denounce slavery and call for the admission of Kansas into the Union as a free state. Doyen of the radical republicans, Sumner had paid dearly for his fervent abolitionist beliefs. In 1856 in the Senate chamber he was struck on the head by Preston S. Brooks, a South Carolina congressman, and incapacitated for nearly four years. When Burton saw him speak, Sumner had only just resumed a full public life. Burton also called on the Secretary of War, John B. Floyd, and secured letters of introduction to the military commanders in the western territories, since all reports indicated an imminent Indian war on the frontier.[19]

From Washington Burton picked his way through the states which the following year would form the southern Confederacy. Burton liked the South, and found its ethos more congenial than that of the calculating Yankee. He noted the difference between the industrial North and the primary producing states south of the Mason-Dixon line and drew attention to the fact that virgin soil formed a considerable item in the real value of landed property in the South.[20] The prevalence of lynch law did not disturb him – he always felt the Rule of Law was too soft – and he was enchanted rather than irritated by certain typical Southern modalities: for example, the tendency for strangers to ask you at once, if seen with a woman, what was your relationship to her; the use of the vocative case ('O, Mr Smith') which Burton claimed to be unique in the English-speaking world.[21]

Yet any visitor to the South on the eve of the Civil War had perforce to address himself to the issue of slavery. Most British commentators of the time had an ambivalent attitude to the two contestants in the impending 'war between the States'. On the one hand, their sympathies and economic interests lay with the South. On the other, they largely abhorred the 'peculiar institution'. Burton wrestled with no such ambiguities. He had already gone on record as saying that the alleged horrors of slavery in Africa were overrated, that the typical East African slave lazed in the sun, that the attitude both of the British government and of missionaries and Exeter Hall liberals was humbug. Moreover, the starving British proletariat were slaves in all but name, and early Christianity was built on slavery. The Old Testament patriarchs and prophets had slaves, as did the early Christian kings and even some of the saints. Besides, the 'crusade' against the slave trade was mere disguised economic self-interest, as shown by the fact that slaves captured by Royal Navy ships were not freed but transported.[22] He summed up his feelings in the poem *Stone-Talk* (1865) as follows:

> Mr Legree in Maryland
> Lashes his own with sparing hand;
> Your fine East-Indian magistrate
> To free men deals far harder fate.

Burton felt his analysis held good *a fortiori* in the American South. Because of acquaintance since childhood, the Southerner knew the black man through and through; this was one of the reasons, incidentally, why in his opinion Southerners made ideal African explorers.[23] Burton made an extensive analysis of slavery, of which a few excerpts must suffice:

> The Northerner and the Canadian see, it is true, the negro in that debased state to which his race is condemned by climate about the Missouri Compromise line. Beginning in Pennsylvania, the Abolitionist traded his slaves down south – not liberated them – because they were not worth their hire. But he has ever kept those who live under his protection in their proper position, distinct from himself, in the

church as in the omnibus, whilst none but the extremest sectarian would admit them to the family circle, or marry daughters to them . . . [the Southerner, on the other hand] laments the existence of slavery, but he finds himself fast bound to it, by the law of self-preservation. Having wandered through every state of the Anglo-American republic, I can safely assert that in none of the richest, namely, the centres of cotton, tobacco and sugar, is white labour possible . . . the South is between the horns of the dilemma, slavery or ruin, and she necessarily prefers the former.[24]

There were only two circumstances in which Burton was prepared to condemn slavery. One was linked to his general negrophobia and sexual anxieties. This was the situation where miscegenation produced a 'mongrel' offspring. Burton was even prepared to attribute the failure of the Confederacy in the Civil War to this 'weakening' factor when he reflected on it in later years. 'Had the Southern States of America deported all the products of "miscegenation", instead of keeping them in servitude, the "patriarchal institution" might have lasted to this day (1882), instead of being prematurely abolished.'[25] Here was a case where two Burtonian hatreds cancelled out, or rather the greater (hatred of the black man) overcame the lesser (hatred of the 'do-gooder' or *bien-pensant* liberal).

The other context where Burton would introduce slavery to the discredit of North America was when he became irritated by 'Yankee' chauvinism. Echoing Dr Johnson's 'How is that we hear the loudest yelps for liberty among the drivers of negroes?' Burton produced this jibe in his autobiographical poem *Stone-Talk*:

Say! Have we not full right to gibe
That contradictious New World tribe
Whose fustian flag of Freedom waves
In mock'ry o'er a land of slaves.[26]

Whatever his feelings about slavery, Burton's sharp antennae picked up that by 1860 war over the ostensible issue of slavery was all but inevitable.[27] At the time, and throughout the early stages of the Civil War, he was convinced the South would win such a conflict. 'When do you expect the Northern States to sue for peace?' he asked his friend Monkton Milnes in December 1861.[28] When his expectations were frustrated, he wrote in some bitterness of the defeat of the better cause by the worse. He saw the triumph of the North as the victory of the cant cohorts of 'equality', of the most rebarbative aspects of industrial capitalism and of the pig-ignorant, know-nothing, lowest common denominator ochlocracy of the newer immigrants; in a word, 'the strong repulsive arm of the democracy, which enabled the Federal to beat down the Confederate.'[29]

By 1865 his distaste for many aspects of the USA led him to take up the posture of 'a plague on both your houses'. This is his gloomy version of the American Civil War in *Stone-Talk*:

Behold a brother-nation stand
Embattled on its mother-land –
This half for empire fights, the other,
That won't call Sambo man and brother,
For Freedom strikes; the twain appeal
To the old parent, who should feel
Bowels of pity yearn to see
The fury of his progeny.
A word in time had stayed the flood
That drenched the land in tears and blood.
'Tis money-loving cowardice,
'Tis slavish silence to be nice
When men's lives in the balance sway:
Outspeak it, men, come what come may.
But no! We wait what France may say.
France, being troubled with a throe
Abortive, called a Mexico,
For once sits deeply, deadly dumb;
So mumbles Bull with toothless gum,
'Oyez! ye great Confederates,
And Oyez! ye great Federal States;
Great are ye both! Considering this,
Considering that, and all that is
To be considered, I'm content
To call ye both belligerent,

11

To keep a strict neutrality,
Which means look out for self, ye see.
Bella debella belle! Belly
Will make ye soon knock off, I tell ye;
Meanwhile, fight on till all is red,
And grind your bones to make my bread.[30]

Burton arrived in New Orleans in early August. It seems that it was here that Steinhaeuser took his leave – the record is unclear but we know for certain that his friend did not accompany him to Salt Lake City.[31] Whereas Burton, emaciated and fever-ridden after his East African expedition, had been certified unfit for duty by the East India doctors, and needed only to get the occasional signature on a 'sick note' from whatever quacks and horse-doctors crossed his path in the USA, Steinhaeuser had a limited period of leave. If Steinhaeuser had left a record of his journey, we might be able to solve one of the great mysteries in Burton's life. When Burton returned to England in 1859, he found that his father had died and left him £16,000. Yet by the time of his marriage to Isabel in January 1861, only £4,000 of this remained, leaving a negligible income of £200 p.a. – not enough for the couple to live on. Where did all the money go? Even if Burton had been forced by the East India Company to pay the debts he repudiated in East Africa, these amounted only to £1,300. It was true that his brother Edward was by this time a hopeless psychotic in the Netherne Mental Hospital, Surrey, but his portion of the legacy would have sufficed to cover costs there. And even if Richard liquidated all the personal debts of a dowerless Isabel, these cannot have amounted to more than £2,000. At the most conservative estimate, then, some £9,000 vanished during Burton's time in North America. Not even the most staggering binges, coupled with nightly visits to brothels and bordellos could have consumed such a sum. A possible explanation is that Burton lost the money gambling; this was, after all, the golden age of the river-boat gambler. Certainly *something* happened in the three months May-July 1860 which Burton was anxious to conceal. This is the one area of his life that is virtually a blank in the records, and where Isabel's burning of the diaries is a catastrophic loss to the historian.

When Burton announced his intention to make for Salt Lake

City, the burghers of New Orleans were aghast. One of his friends there said to him, 'Going amongst the Mormons! They are shooting and cutting one another in all directions. How can *you* expect to escape?'[32] But tension between Mormons and the US Army was not the worst of it. In the West an Indian war was reported to be raging. Bands of hostile Cheyenne, Comanche and Kiowa were said to be 'out' across the line of the stagecoach from St Joseph, Missouri, to Salt Lake. Burton brushed aside such warnings and declared himself thirsty for action. 'If this chance failed, remained the excitement of the buffalo and the Mormon, both were likely to show better support than could be found in riding wildly around the country after runaway braves.'[33]

There were three possible routes from the United States to Utah territory. The northerly one took two to three months, so Burton ruled it out as too long. The southerly approach meant travelling through malarial climates and risking semi-starvation and poisoned wells. Burton therefore opted for the shortest route, from Missouri to Salt Lake City, where the fastest journey was twenty-one days. Burton had arranged to make the journey in company with a Lieutenant in the US Army, James J. Dana, who was travelling to Salt Lake City with his wife and small daughter to join the 4th US Artillery at the Utah garrison. Burton travelled up to St Louis to meet the family. The Danas then went ahead to St Joseph on 2 August. Burton followed two days later and put up overnight at the 5th Avenue Hotel, St Joseph, ready for an early start on the 7th.

Burton had taken great care with his equipment but, as it transpired, he had still not foreseen all eventualities. He took an India-rubber blanket as a poncho, but through ignorance spurned the far more efficacious buffalo robe. He wore a dark flannel shirt with a belt for a six-shooter and buckskin trousers tucked into his boots. Buckskin gloves, a pair of moccasins for warm weather, and a brown felt hat completed his wardrobe. His armoury comprised a buffalo rifle, a bowie knife and a pair of revolvers which never left his side. He prided himself on his prowess with handguns and was confident that he would acquit himself well in any showdown. In addition, he packed a supply of quinine, opium, citric acid and warburg drops and the inevitable cigars. His baggage also included sketching materials, pocket sextant, spirit level, day and night compasses, telescope, pocket thermometer and a copy of John Charles Fremont's account of his expeditions in 1842-9. He shaved his head to a close-cropped stubble, as had been his custom in India – in this case more a precaution against the hot, humid weather of the great plains than through fear of scalping – but neglected to bring one of the wigs he had worn for vanity's sake in Bombay. Burton displayed his fondness for children (provided always he did not have to assume the burdens of paternity himself) by taking a carved ivory image from his tobacco pouch and giving it to the Danas' child as a toy.

The stagecoach was a spring wagon, with a body shaped like a boxcart. Its wheels were five to six feet apart to prevent the conveyance from overturning and its tyres were of an unusual thickness. The wagon bed was supported by iron bands and was covered with stout osnaburg, supported by strong bars of white oak. There was a sunshade or hood in front where the driver sat, and a curtain behind, which could be raised or lowered at discretion. Teams of four mules pulled the stagecoach; they averaged five miles an hour but on good, downhill stretches could push this average up to eight.

The first task was to cross the Missouri river. Always fascinated by rivers, Burton 'took against' the 'Big Muddy'. 'Some geographers have proposed to transfer to the Missouri, on account of its superior length, the honour of being the real head of the Mississippi; they neglect, however, to consider the direction and the course of the stream, an element which must enter largely in determining the channels of great rivers. It will, I hope, be long before the great ditch wins the day from the glorious father of Waters.'[34] At first blush this sounds like typical dyspeptic, cross-grained Burtoniana. But Horace Greeley, travelling the same route the year before *en route* to the Mormons, felt exactly the same way.[35]

They now passed briefly through north-eastern Kansas and into the Nebraska territory. The endless prairies with their burnt-up aspect ('a part of hell with the fires burnt out' was General Custer's assessment) were monotonous, and their tints and colours reminded Burton of the Arabian desert.[36] It was too early in the season for prairie fires, so Burton could not look forward even to that dubious distraction. Yet Burton was ever the artist *manqué*, and the great plains evoked from him a 'meta-physical' response reminiscent of Herman Melville:

> Another peculiarity of the prairie is, in places, its seeming horizontality, whereas it is never level: on an open plain, apparently flat as a man's palm, you cross a long ground swell which was not perceptible before, and on its further incline you come upon a chasm wide and deep enough to contain a settlement . . . Over the rolling surface . . . lay a tapestry of thick grass already turning to a ruddy yellow under the influence of approaching autumn. The uniformity was relieved by streaks of livelier green in the rich soils of the slopes, hollows, and ravines, where the water gravitates . . . The silvery cirri and cumuli of the upper air flecked the surface of earth with spots of dark cool shade, surrounded by a blaze of sunshine, and by their motion, and as they trooped and chased one another, gave a peculiar liveliness to the scene; while here and there a bit of hazy blue distance, a swell of the sea-like land upon the far horizon gladdened the sight – every view is fair from afar. Nothing, I may remark, is more monotonous, except perhaps the African and Indian jungle, than those prairie tracts, where the circle of which you are the centre has but about a mile of radius; it is an ocean in which one loses sight of land. You see as it were the ends of the earth, and look around in vain for some object upon which the eye may rest: it was the sublimity of response so suggestive in the sandy deserts, and the perpetual motion so pleasing in the aspect of the sea.[37]

The travellers spent many nights in the wagon, very uncomfortably. After his fifth such night, Burton's joints ached with cramp, but he claimed his ordeal was a mere bagatelle when compared with 'the miasmatic and pestilential regions of Central Africa'. The only relief was at the staging posts, but the ability to sleep less uncomfortably was offset by the appalling food. At the lesser way-stations the travellers ate flyblown doughnuts and 'suspicious eggs in a greasy fritter, and rusty bacon, intolerably fat'. At the grander stations there were the horrors of Western 'cawfee' – three parts burnt beans, ground to a fine powder and exposed to the air – to contend with, plus ferruginous bacon cut in thick slices from a flitch and thrown on to a sizzling frying pan, and rancid antelope steaks hacked off a carcass hanging outside and permanently covered with flies. The only bread was an imperfectly cooked sourdough, kneaded with water and a pinch of salt; the raising was by means of a little sour milk or yeast powder. Whenever possible, Burton liked to mop up his meals with Mexican tortillas instead. 'Uncle Sam's stove, be it said, with every reverence for the honoured name it bears, is a triumph of convenience, cheapness, unwholesomeness and nastiness. It made everything taste like its neighbour; by virtue of it mutton borrowed the flavour of fish, and tomatoes resolved themselves into the flavour of greens.'[38]

Noisome food was not the only peril of the relay stations. To Burton the misogynist even more unpalatable was running the gauntlet of the Amazons and viragos the stations seemed to spawn:

One of these was a Bloomer. This, it is fair to state, was the only hermaphrodite of the kind that ever met my eyes in the States. The great founder of the Bloomer order has long since subsided into her original obscurity, and her acolytes have relapsed into petticoats. The Bloomer was an uncouth being, her hair, cut level with her eyes, depended with a graceful curl of a drake's tail around a fat and flabby countenance, whose only expression was sullen insolence. Her body dress, glazed brown calico, fitted her somewhat like a soldier's tunic, developing haunches which would be admired only in venison; and – curious inconsequence of woman's nature! – all this sacrifice of appearance upon the shrine of comfort did not prevent her wearing that kind of crinoline depicted by Mr Punch around 'our Mary Hanne'. The pantolettes of glazed brown calico, like the vest, tunic, blouse, shirt or whatever they may call it, were in peg-top style, admirably setting off a pair of thin-soled, Frenchified, patent-leather bottines, with elastic sides, which contained feet as large, broad and flat as a negro's in Africa. The dear creature had a husband: it was hardly safe to look at her, and as for sketching her, I avoided it. The other 'lady', though more decently attired, was like women in this wild

16

part of the world generally – cold and disagreeable, with a
touch-me-not air, which reminded me of a certain
    Miss Baxter,
    Who refused a man before he axed her.

One of the stage party was fiercely ejected from the kitchen when
he ventured to ask where the dormitory was and roughly informed that men had to sleep outside. The luckless males found
a barn 'hardly fit for a decently brought up pig'. After a terrible
night, Burton concluded, 'May the gracious heaven keep us safe
from all "ladies" in future! Better a hundred times the squaw,
with her uncleanliness and her civility!'[39]

On the fourth day out from St Joseph the travellers crossed
the Platte river, where Burton saw his first plains Indians. Ever
the eager anthropologist he began making notes on the tribes. At
Fort Phil Kearney Burton examined the military dispositions of
the US Army in the West and concluded they were all wrong.
The scattered garrisons were useless for the purpose of containing hostile Indians. Burton attributed the muddle to the
Anglo-Saxon political culture, with its excessive fear of a standing army and centralized authority. The French, he thought,
ordered matters far better. In Algeria they had abandoned the
idea of forts, extended lines, posts and block houses and provided instead a huge mobile centralized force, ready to move out
to deal with trouble at a moment's notice. He suggested the formation of a cavalry corps along the lines of General Napier's
camel corps in Sind, and the raising of native armies, so that
Indian could be pitted against Indian. This would be both
'divide and rule' and a way of channelling and diminishing the
ferocity and savagery of the tribes. In the light of the oft-re-
peated proposition that 'rugged individualism' was the essence of
the pioneer spirit, it is of more than passing interest to note that
Burton, a man of the extreme Right, prescribed communalism
and even French-style *dirigisme* as the remedy for the ills of the
frontier.

On pressed the travellers, over the limitless prairie, where the
passage from night to day was marked by the routing of the mosquito by the fly. On two different occasions, on 8 and 21 August,
their path crossed with that of the Pony Express despatch riders.
Burton was one of the few European travellers to see the famous

17

Pony Express in operation, for the service lasted less than two years. Inaugurated on 3 April 1860, the Express carried 34,753 items of mail in under ten days from St Joseph to Sacramento by a system of post horses. Despite its function as master propaganda for the West, the Pony Express carried too little mail and no passengers and was thus ruinously expensive. Two days after the even more speedy transcontinental telegraph was completed, on 26 October 1861, the service was abruptly terminated.[40]

The same dreary pattern of nights on the open prairie interspersed with the 'comforts' of the post houses continued. On one occasion it was 3.15 a.m. before the travellers heard the familiar 'yep, yep, yep' with which their driver was wont to announce a station. They sprang out in pitch darkness to find their 'hosts' deep in slumber. 'A heavy kick opened the door of the restaurant, when a wheezy, drowsy voice from an inner room asked in German-English, *"And how ze komen in?"* Without waiting to answer, we pulled the owner out of bed and ordered supper, refreshment and repose.'[41]

The food provided by the Germans was predictably bad. Burton's disillusionment with the 'pioneer spirit' found expression in a bitter fulmination against Frontier Man and all his works. 'The western man has been worked by climate and its consequences, by the huge magnificence of nature and the violent contrasts of scenery, into a remarkable resemblance to the wild Indian. He hates labour – which poet and divine combine to deify in the settled states – as the dire effect of a primeval curse; "loaf" he must and will; to him one hour out of twenty-four spent in honest industry is *satis superque*. His imagination is inflamed by scenery and climate, difficulty and danger; he is as superstitious as an old man o' war's man of the olden school; and he is a transcendental liar, like his prototype and origin, who in this point yields nothing to the African negro.'[42]

At only one station, called the 'Devil's Post Office', did Burton experience what he considered real hospitality. A model hostess was 'Miss' Moore (the appellation 'Miss' for 'Mrs' was widely used by Southern negroes and Westerners). Her rooms were spotlessly clean, her food good and – wonder of wonders for Burton – she actually washed his shirt, a labour he had had to perform on his own since leaving Missouri. Burton rated this encounter with an 'old world woman' his third novel sensation in

America. The first had been the bizarre assumption of equality by all classes. The second was black men employing the small change of polite intercourse (what Burton, always uncomfortable with emancipated blacks, typically called 'the equivalent of the African "Sambo" in European dress calling himself "Mr Scott"').

Burton salved his bitterness towards the white man (and woman) of the West by concentrating on the mores and folkways of the red man. An encounter with an armed band of Arapahos turned out badly. On the tenth day out they crossed the trail of an Arapaho war party and later caught up with them at the Platte Bridge station house. The Arapaho warriors were morose and irritable, as they were coming back empty-handed from an attempt to prey on Mormon caravans. Since the Mormons had put themselves outside the protection of the USA, it was common knowledge among the plains Indians that they could attack and kill migrating 'Saints' with impunity. The temper of the Arapahos was not improved when Burton started sketching them; they proved as hostile to the process as African tribesmen. Evidently, some kind of impassioned altercation arose, for Lieutenant Dana's great-nephew later claimed that the Arapahos attacked the station and were beaten off with heavy loss.[43] The story continues that the coach had to be escorted to the next station by 'sixteen of the most villainous cutthroats on the Plains,' followers of Wild Bill Hickok and the outlaw Joseph A. Slade, who had allegedly taken part in the repulse of the Arapaho. But it is likely that this tale had grown immeasurably in the telling by the time it came to Dana's great-nephew, Richard Hale.[44]

But it was when entering Sioux territory, after Horseshoe Station, that Burton's interest in the tribes reached white heat. Shortly after Scotts Bluff, an incredible rock formation dominating the plains, which for Burton excelled all the beauties of the Rhine, they passed the site of 'Grattan's massacre' in 1854, when an outburst of temper by a young Irish lieutenant from West Point, John Grattan, during a pow-wow with the Brûlé Sioux, led to the slaughter of thirty US cavalrymen.[45]

From Forts Kearny and Laramie the travellers headed west through South Pass, the watershed between the Pacific and Atlantic systems, and arrived at Fort Bridger, just 124 miles from Salt Lake City. Burton was a quick learner and throughout the journey had been cross-checking the observations of 'Path-finder' Fremont and his famous Indian scout Kit Carson against his own findings.[46] Burton had a pronounced fear of snakes ever since his unsuccessful attempt to handle cobras and become a snake-charmer in India in the 1840s. He therefore made careful notes on the threat to the prairie traveller from the rattlesnake, which he pronounced negligible in all normal circumstances. The bite of the serpent was rarely fatal, since a number of well-known folk remedies could be used as antidote: hartshorn drunk in dilution; dried and powdered blood of the turtle; ligature between the limb and the heart, followed by scarification and irrumation of the part; cauterization by gunpowder; and many others, all allegedly efficacious provided the remedy was immediately to hand and the snake did not strike an artery. Burton himself favoured the lighted end of a cigar applied as a moxa to the wound, followed by the consumption of a bottle of whisky and the assistance of a couple of men to keep the victim walking round and round.[47]

25 August 1860 was the last day on the journey to Salt Lake City. The travellers set out to cross the Wasatch, the last and highest of the mountain passes before 'the city of the Saints'. Slowly they wound their way up to the summit of the pass at 8,000 feet, just eighteen miles from their goal. The pass was so difficult that between November-February it was traversable only by sleigh, and then only provided there was no snow. Burton thus described the incomparable panorama:

From that eyrie, 8,000 feet above sea level, the weary pilgrim first sights his shrine, the object of his long wanderings, hardships and perils, the Happy Valley of the Great Salt Lake. The western horizon, when visible, is bound by a broken wall of light blue mountain, the Oquirh, whose northernmost bluff buttresses the southern end of the lake, and whose eastern flank sinks in steps and terraces into a river basin, yellow with the sunlit golden corn, and somewhat pink with its carpeting of heath-like moss. In the foreground a semi-circular sweep of hill top, and an inverted arch of rocky wall, shuts out all but a few spans of the valley. These heights are rough with a shaggy forest, in some places black-green, in others of brownish-red, in others of the lightest ash colour, based upon a ruddy soil; whilst a few silvery veins of snow still streak the bare grey rocky flanks of the loftiest peak.[48]

On the descent they reached a station at midday, run by the notable Mormon desperado Ephe Hawks, said to be the leader of the dreaded Danites, or death squads. Burton found him affable and sociable and concluded he was rather less black than painted. After dining at the station, the party wound down the narrow mountain shelf, creeping along precipitous ledges, to the valley bottom. It was 6 p.m. before they at last began to enter Salt Lake City. At a glance Burton could pick out the dwelling of the Mormon leader Brigham Young, for it was the only white-washed house; the rest were sun-dried adobe. He was at first surprised by the absence of churches and steeples, then as he concentrated his vision, it seemed that it was domes and minarets that were missing. 'At a little distance the aspect was somewhat Oriental, and in some points it reminded me of modern Athens – without the Acropolis . . . the number of gardens and compounds, dark clumps of cottonwood, locust or acacia, fruit trees – apples, peaches and vines – and, finally, the fields of long-eared maize, strengthened the similarity to an Asiatic rather than to an American settlement.'[49]

The stage pulled up at the Salt Lake House, a grander hostelry than any they had seen so far in the West. The hotel was a two-storeyed building, with a long veranda supported by painted posts, behind which was a large yard for coralling cattle. The proprietor, a Mormon who had married an Englishwoman, also ran contrary to the Western type Burton had encountered hitherto and was most civil and obliging. After a nineteen-day journey covering 1,136 miles, Burton felt that he had at last come to a civilized haven. Euphoria recollected in tranquillity found Burton at his most poetic:

The sublime and the beautiful were in present contrast. Switzerland and Italy lay side by side. The magnificent scenery of the past mountains and ravines still floated before the retina, as emerging from the gloomy depths of the Golden Pass – the mouth of Emigration Canyon is more poetically so called – we are suddenly in view of the Holy

Valley of the West.

The hour was about 6 p.m., the atmosphere was touched with a dreamy haze – as it generally is in the vicinity of the lake – a little bank of rose-coloured clouds, edged with flames of purple and gold, floated in the upper air, whilst the mellow radiance of an American autumn, that bright interlude between the extremes of heat and cold, diffused its mild soft lustre over the face of the earth. The sun, whose slanting rays shone full in our eyes, was setting in a flood of heavenly light behind the jagged outline of 'Antelope Island', which, though distant twenty miles to the north-west, hardly appeared to be ten. At its feet, and then bounding the far horizon, lay, like a band of burnished silver, the Great Salt Lake, that still innocent Dead Sea. South-westwards also, and equally deceptive as regards distance, rose the boundary of the valley plain, the Oquirh Range, sharply silhouetted by a sweep of sunshine over its summits, against the depths of an evening sky, in that direction, so pure, so clear, that vision, one might fancy, could penetrate behind the curtain into the regions beyond the confines of man's ken.[50]

Chapter Two

The City of the Saints

When Burton arrived in Salt Lake City, the Mormon experiment in Utah was just thirteen years old and the sect of 'Latter-Day Saints' the product of no more than three decades. Joseph Smith, the founder, born at Sharon, Vermont, in 1805, received his first 'revelation' at Manchester, New York, in 1820. Three years later an angel was said to have told him of a hidden gospel on golden plates, with two stones which should help translate it from the 'Reformed Egyptian'; and on the night of 22 September 1827 the sacred records were delivered into his hands. *The Book of Mormon* (1830) contained a highly fanciful history of America, allegedly written by a prophet called Mormon. America was said to have been first colonized during the period of 'confusion of tongues' in the fifth century AD. Despite ridicule, hostility and often overt violence, the new 'Church of the Latter-Day Saints' rapidly gained converts. In 1831 Smith set up his headquarters at Kirkland, Ohio. Meanwhile the search began for a new 'Zion' where the Mormons would be free from persecution. They began in Jackson County on the Missouri frontier. In 1833 the 'Saints' were banished across the river to Clay County. When there were signs of a mass withdrawal of the pioneers to Kirkland, Ohio, Smith moved the entire church to Far West, Missouri (1837). Continuing persecution led the community back across the Mississippi to Quincy, Illinois. Finally, in 1840, Smith established his last capital at Nauvoo ('beautiful place' in Hebrew), hard by the swampy village of Commerce, Illinois.

By 1844 there were 25,000 Mormons in Nauvoo and its environs. Nauvoo was designed on a grand scale as a model city and several imposing buildings were constructed. But a further wave of persecution swept over the 'Saints' as rumours grew, despite Smith's denials, that they practised polygamy. Smith and his brother Hyrum were arrested. On 27 June 1844, 150 masked men broke into Carthage jail, where the Smith brothers were being held, and shot them dead.[1]

Joseph Smith's last years had also seen the meteoric rise of Brigham Young. Also born in Vermont, Young was a 29-year-old carpenter, painter and glazier in Mendon, New York, when he first saw *The Book of Mormon* in 1830. Two years later he was converted by one of Joseph Smith's brothers, was baptized and began to preach. At Kirkland he was made an elder, then departed for a proselytizing tour in Canada in 1833. In 1835 he was appointed one of the twelve apostles of the Church. In 1840 he created a sensation by visiting England and making 2,000 converts. After Smith's death, Sidney Rigdon assumed the presidency of the Church, but following a brief but ferocious internal power struggle Young deposed Rigdon and cast him into anathema. He denounced Rigdon's prophecies as the work of the devil and handed over the unfortunate ex-president 'to the buffetings of Satan for a thousand years'.

After being elected president by a huge majority, Young decided to solve the problem of persecution of the 'Saints' by mass migration. On a bitterly cold night in February 1845 the Mormons crossed the frozen Mississippi, lighting their way by the glow of the Nauvoo temples they had put to the torch. They camped on the western edge of Iowa, where many succumbed to cold, starvation and want. Young meanwhile literally inherited the Prophet's mantle by dressing up in Smith's robes. Among his first 'revelations' was a direction to the faithful to practise polygamy, in line with a divine message supposedly made to Smith nine years earlier.

For two years the remnants of the Mormon Church huddled in Iowa while Brigham Young and an advance guard sought a refuge outside the jurisdiction of the hated USA. On 2 July 1847 Young saw the Salt Lake from the foothills of the Rockies and announced, 'This is the place.' Mass migration from Iowa to the promised land, comparable only with the Boers' Great Trek of

1836-8, ensued. But the US authorities were hot on his heels. The Treaty of Guadalupe Hidalgo which ended the Mexican-American war in 1848, ceded the Utah territory to the USA. 'That damned flag', as one Mormon elder called it, had caught up with them again.[2] For a while Washington marked time and appointed Brigham Young as the first governor of the Utah territory. But the seeds of future conflict were already sown.

Unlike Joseph Smith, Brigham Young was an organizer of genius. His grip on the Mormons tightened after being nominated First President of the Church of Jesus Christ of Latter-Day Saints (a title confirmed for life the following year). He was assisted by twelve counsellors, twelve 'apostles' and a growing bureaucracy. He now set out to prove, against all the odds, that the wilderness could be tamed; hitherto the inhospitable Great Basin area between the Rockies and the Sierras and Cascades had been deemed impossible to settle.

To consolidate the 'free and independent government of the State of Deseret' Brigham Young announced that the hereafter was his own personal heaven, into which the elect would be admitted. In this paradise social inequality would still prevail: a man's rank would depend on the number of wives and children he possessed. It was even possible for a man's friend to accumulate posthumous credits for him by marrying and begetting children for him after his death! Sustained with this vision, the Mormons resisted the blandishments of the passing wagon trains, which for years ploughed through Utah territory on their way to the California Gold Rush.

Farming the soil of the 'State of Deseret' taxed human ingenuity to its limits. Nearly half of Utah was sage-brush desert and enjoyed less than ten inches of rainfall a year. Brigham Young spoke dejectedly of 'these barren valleys, these sterile mountains where none but Saints can or could live'.[3] Uninhabited in 1846, Utah contained 11,380 persons in 1850 and 40,273 in 1860 when Burton visited. But to sustain even 11,000 souls in 1850 back-breaking toil was necessary, as well as masterly planning and execution. The very first thing Young's advance party did in July 1847 was to dam a stream and irrigate a field for the planting of potatoes.[4] Thereafter Young bent his energies to devising the first large-scale irrigation system in the USA and the most complex communal water scheme since the days of oriental despotism and Marx's 'Asiatic mode of production'. The first irrigation dam served a dual purpose, as many of the new arrivals in 1847 were rebaptized in it. As has been well said, 'The construction of water ditches was as much part of the Mormon religion as water baptism.'[5] When the transfer of 'Saints' from Iowa was complete, Young set to work on a wildly ambitious irrigation system. Mormon society defied any easy Right/Left classification. It was run as big business, but along the communalistic lines of an ant colony. However, Mormon organization was more typical of the collaborative effort of the true historical Western pioneers than of the mythical variety fuelled by Social Darwinism or 'rugged individualism'.[6]

It took the Mormons three years to learn the effective use of irrigation. Canals and ditches were built, water was divided. Water was diverted from a natural source into a general canal, and from that into 'laterals' and ditches which carried the water to the individual plots. 'Corngates' were cut next to each row to carry the precious liquid to the crops. 'Waste ditches' carried the water from one irrigated field to the next one below it. Each man got his water supply in return for a given amount of labour decided by the 'bishops'.[7]

Even with this titanic effort of organization, the 1850s saw the desert kingdom on the brink of collapse. First came the crop failures and famines of the 'grasshopper years', which ended in 1855-6 only with the incident enshrined in Mormon legend when a gigantic flock of seagulls devoured the marauding insects.[8] In 1857 economic recovery enabled Young to begin a Pony Express service, which carried monthly mail between Independence, USA, and Salt Lake City in twenty-six days. This was a signal example of Mormon entrepreneurship. But the US government cancelled their four-year mail contract on 10 June 1857, six months after it had been signed.[9] Then in 1857-8 came the declaration of war on the 'State of Deseret' by President Buchanan and the occupation of the territory outside Salt Lake City by federal troops. The abandonment of outposts even led to a brief exodus of the entire Mormon population from Salt Lake City itself.

Arguably the 'Saints' had only themselves to blame for this nemesis, since all officials sent out to Utah by Washington either became tame creatures of Brigham Young or decamped after a barrage of insults, threats, non-cooperation and civil disobedience.

The years 1857-60 witnessed two favourable developments for the desert kingdom. The first fillip for drooping morale was the handcart experiment. Apparently Brigham Young plucked out of the air, with no real conviction that his idea would work, the notion that the new Mormon converts who were trickling in from Europe should simply walk from Iowa City to Salt Lake, pulling their belongings in handcarts until they reached the promised land. Five handcart companies were formed, of which three got their people through safely. Two of them, however, ran into bad weather and lost about 200 dead in snowdrifts out of a total handcart exodus of 1,000 – a greater disaster than the most famous mortality to the Donner party in the Californian sierras. During the same period, additionally, another 5,200 immigrants arrived in Utah by wagon train.[10]

The other development was notable for swelling Brigham Young's coffers. The stationing of US troops at Camp Floyd led to economic symbiosis between Mormons and the Army. Salt Lake City's provisioners waxed fat, since every item eaten, drunk, worn or bought cost between three and ten times the price in the USA. Brigham Young made his money from timber and sawmills. He owned three sawmills in a choice valley which yielded a profit of $100 a day. His return on a consignment of lumber supplied at $70 per 1,000 feet was over $50,000. By 1859 it was estimated that he was already worth $250,000.[11] The shrewdest of the visitors to the 'City of the Saints' questioned the wisdom of maintaining an army in Utah, which the US government clearly never intended to use to extirpate the Mormons and whose main purpose seemed to be to enrich these declared enemies of the Union. Horace Greeley thought the real reason was the network of corruption in which the USA was already inveigled. Army suppliers in Leavenworth, Kansas, who furnished flour to Camp Floyd, got an allowance of twenty-two cents per pound for transportation costs to Salt Lake City. They simply sublet to Utah contractors at seven cents per pound and thus made $170,000 profit without lifting a finger. Another absurdity was the way the federal government sold mules at giveaway prices. At one auction 2,000 mules which cost $175 each were sold at knock-down prices (between $60 and $115) to

Mormons, who formed a 'ring' to keep the bidding down. In this way they acquired 2,000 mules which could be sold in California at 100% profit. As Greeley commented bitterly, 'Somebody's interest is subserved by this sale; but it is certainly not that of the Army nor of the people . . . Who issues such orders as this and for whose benefit?'[12]

Greeley's 1859 visit to Salt Lake City was merely the best-known to date. 'A modern Mecca', despite its clichéd redolence, describes the situation very well, for the 'City of the Saints' had by now become a magnet for foreign travellers in North America. William Chandless wrote a notably friendly account following a visit in 1855, at the height of the 'grasshopper years'. In the same year British naturalist Julius Brenchley passed that way, as did French botanist Jules Rémy, whose two-volume work it was fashionable to regard in the 1860s as a more balanced assessment than Burton's.[13] After Burton came Mark Twain (1861), Fritz Hugh Ludlow (1864), Ralph Waldo Emerson (1871) and, in the period after Brigham Young's death and the 'golden age', G.A. Sala, John Foster Fraser, Oscar Wilde, Rudyard Kipling and a host of others. But few of them had Burton's unrivalled eye for detail. It is true that Burton was strongly *parti pris* on behalf of the Mormons, but this should not distract us (as it has done with so many critics) from appreciating how shrewd an observer he was.

He began his visit by calling on the US governor of Utah territory. Alfred Cumming was the first genuine Washington-appointed official to be appointed to Salt Lake. He was the civil arm of Buchanan's pacification policy, the velvet glove draped over the mailed fist represented by 600 dragoons. Cumming had strict orders from the White House not to interfere with the institution of polygamy for the time being. By his justice and impartiality he won the grudging respect of the Mormons, but never their friendship, to Burton's disgust. Cumming confided to him the near impossibility of making the federal writ run. If a Mormon committed an offence against US law, none of his brothers would give evidence against him, nor would any Mormon jury convict, no matter how flagrant the wrongdoing. Even the fire-eating Judge John Cradlebaugh, associate justice of the Territorial Supreme Court, than whom 'no Gentile caused Brigham Young more trouble,' eventually had to throw up the sponge.[14]

On Monday 27 August the entire population trooped out to the outskirts of the city to welcome the arrival of a new wagon train of immigrants. Burton thought it significant that Brigham Young himself did not join the reception committee, thus giving the lie to the canard that he made a practice of reviewing the new arrivals to see if there were any pretty girls among them.[15] He began to ponder an alternative explanation: that the patriarch was afraid of assassination. An inspection of the leader's compound strengthened the inference. Surrounded by a high wall, and strengthened with semicircular buttresses, it contained as many dwellings as the inner kraal of an African chief. At the centre of the compound was a square or plaza. On the eastern side was the 'Lion House' occupied by Mrs Young, the 'chief wife' and his family. At the other side of the square was the great man's office. Here too was the historian's office – almost the only source of literary sustenance in a city that possessed not a single bookshop. Careful historical research has established that Burton spent the days of 3, 11 and 13 September, taking copious notes from the manuscript history of Brigham Young, which was the cynosure of the official Historian's office.[16] Beyond this was the 'Bee House', so called from the sculptured beehive in front. A large building, facing east and west, it contained Young's other wives and families. The association of ideas with a Sultan and his harem was not lost on Burton. 'There was a Moslem air of retirement about the Bee House; the face of woman was rarely seen at the window, and her voice was never heard without. Anti-Mormons declared the Bee House to be like the State Prison of Auburn, a self-supporting establishment, for not even the wives of the Prophet were allowed to live in idleness.'[17] Just how many wives Brigham Young had in 1860 Burton was not able to ascertain, but he inferred that the number was considerable from the fact that a private school was being built for his children.

Among the first social engagements Burton attended was a dance, which started at 4 p.m. and went through to 5 a.m., with a break for supper and an occasional interlude for amateur theatricals, of which the 'Saints' seemed exceedingly fond. Every man was allowed to lead out two women and dance with them, either together or alternately. Quadrilles only were allowed; the mazurka was considered sinful. By all accounts the standard of music-making was high, for another visitor in the 1860s reported, 'the orchestra in Brigham Young's theatre was quite equal to any in Broadway.'[18] The dancers were excessively polite, and called each other 'Brother' and 'Sister' with no use of Christian names. A man called Smith who had sons by a Miss Brown and a Miss Jones would thus have produced 'brothers' with the appellation 'Brother Smith-Brown' and 'Brother Smith-Jones' respectively.

As ever with Burton in any 'anthropological' situation, he took careful notes on the status and treatment of women. He was amused to find that the love of dress and finery was as pronounced among Mormon women as with others of their sex: 'the semi-nude savage, the crinolined *civilisée*, the nun and the quakeress, the sinner and the saint, the *biche* and the *grande dame*, all meet for once in their lives pretty much on a par and on the same ground.'[19]

Everywhere Burton wandered in the city, he was hospitably received. Religious dogma apart, the Mormons seemed remarkably tolerant, all the more so since opinion in the USA currently ran very high over the 'Mountain Meadows Massacre'. In 1857 Mormon fanatics in southern Utah, in alliance with the Indians, massacred a wagon train of 120 emigrants *en route* to California.[20] Although Brigham Young denied the atrocity, and Burton was disposed to accept his version of events, later evidence conclusively established that the carnage was every bit as horrific as first reports indicated. Burton was inclined to shrug the incident off, and then to attribute nearly *all* anti-Mormon prejudice to the massacre: 'Who, after the massacre of Cawnpore, would have admitted into his mind a shadow of an excuse for Nana Sahib?'[21]

Burton repaid the courtesy shown to him with a good-natured, ironical tolerance towards Mormonism and all its works. Ever afterwards he retained memories of the city's gutters gurgling with cool water and the civilized tree-planting propensities of Brigham Young (which he failed to connect with the Prophet's lucrative timber business).[22] He poked gentle fun at the Saints' supposed gift of glossolalia: 'Gentiles have observed that whatever may be uttered "in tongues", it is always translated into very intelligible English.'[23] His study of Mormonism convinced him that there was nothing sinister about the religion. Its practitioners spoke of 'error' with less vehemence than the Catholic Church treated of heresy. Freemasonry, for example, they characterized as 'like the Christian faith, founded upon truth, and originally of the eternal Church, but fallen away and far gone in error'. Basing himself on *quot homines, tot sententiae*, Burton argued that Joseph Smith 'had as good a right to establish a Church as Luther, Calvin, Fox, Wesley or even bluff King Hal'.[24]

Towards Smith, indeed, Burton bent over backwards to be fair. Rémy had described the founder as 'a mere impostor and speculator' but Burton thought the charge of charlatanry specious. Any deception involved had to be self-deception. Smith he took to be 'a man of rude genius, of high courage, of invincible perseverance, fired by zeal, of great tact, of religious fervour, of extraordinary firmness, and of remarkable talent in governing men'. But Burton did skate lightly over the 'unacceptable face' of Mormonism. Although he refers to the tripartite Mormon heaven, he does not mention the Lake of Fire, reserved for apostates. The greatest hatred was always reserved for those who had once accepted, then rejected, the gospel according to Joseph Smith. Burton contented himself with an amused reference to Smith's prophecy that Armageddon would come in 1890 (ironically that *was* the date of the end of the world for Burton).[25] And, as so often with Burton, there is a whiff of 'a plague on both your houses' about his conclusion: 'The Mormons declare that if they knew their prophet to be an impostor, they could still love, respect, and follow him in this life to the next. The Gentiles, I can see, would not accept him, even if he were proposed to them by a spirit from the other world.'[26]

Burton's love of paradox and aphorism sometimes led him into formulations which showed a shallow insight into Mormon motivations. 'The Mormons, having lost all hope of safety by isolation, now seek it in the reverse: mail communication with the Eastern and Western states is their present hobby; they look forward to markets for their produce and to a greater facility and economy of importing.' This was wildly overstating the case. It was quite clear that 'Zion' wished to remain aloof from 'Babylon' and traded with the Gentile world purely on its own terms. Burton also noted the high levels of apostasy and the fact that many of the new 'Saints' were an opportunistic floating population, but did not suggest a motive.[27] Shrewder was a later visitor, Charles Browne, who summed up the appeal of Mormonism thus: 'The agricultural labourer, who never earned more than ten shillings a week, finds himself in possession of a nice piece of land, a cottage and a cow . . . is it possible for any of them to disbelieve, looking at his or her present prosperity, and being taught to regard the cow, the cottage and the home as "the blessing of the Lord" in return for faith.'[28]

Burton described the Mormon form of government as democratic despotism 'with a leaven of true Mosaic theocracy'. He expected the theocratic element to predominate if, as he expected, the 'City of the Saints' became an independent state. 'Should this event ever happen, it will make the regions about Great Salt Lake as exclusive as Northern China or Eastern Tibet. The obsolete rigours of the sanguinary Mosaic code will be renewed in the middle of the nineteenth century, whilst the statute crime "bigamy" and unlimited polygamy will be legalized. Stripes, or at best fines, and imprisonment will punish fornication, and the penalty of adultery will be death by lapidation or beheading.'[29]

The Mormon penal code was indeed draconian. The two mortal sins – for sin and crime were conflated in Mormonism – were adultery and the shedding of innocent blood. Any man who killed his wife's lover was sure to be acquitted in Salt Lake City. The unwritten part of the Mormon law was that the man who seduced his neighbour's wife must die, the dolorous stroke to be dealt by her nearest male relation. The blood-feud and the vendetta were thus hallowed by law and custom, so that, far from being communistic, as the socialized irrigation schemes might be thought to imply, Mormonism was actually the apogee of individualism.

It always amazed Burton that he could walk home at night through the streets of Salt Lake City with more security than if he were in St James's Square. In the West in general lawlessness was endemic and crimes of violence were openly and blatantly committed; there was no need to murder by poison when the gun was sanctioned so overtly. While he was in Carson City, Burton witnessed three killings in three days but in Salt Lake there was not a single murder during his month's sojourn. There were only thirty policemen in the entire 'State of Deseret'. As in many later societies organized for co-operative economic endeavours (Mao's China being the obvious example), social control was by cultural sanction and taboo, by word of mouth and official rebuke. Brigham Young knew about any disloyal or dissentient word half an hour after it was uttered.

But rumour had it that there was more a sinister aspect to the virtually crime-free utopia of the 'City of the Saints'. Brigham Young was like the Old Man of the Mountain in that he could condemn a man to death simply by raising his hand. And, like the Old Man of the Mountain, he was rumoured to have his Assassins, who dealt with murderers, rapists and horse thieves in summary and surreptitious fashion. Although Mormon death squads were held by the 'Saints' themselves to be an invention of their enemies, Burton suspected that the dreaded Danites were indeed Brigham Young's assassination bureau, though their formation dated from the days of Joseph Smith.[30]

Officially, however, the Danites were merely Young's personal bodyguard. They acted as sentries at the gates of the Bee House and never left his side when he went about in public. Burton noticed that the Prophet never exposed his person to unnecessary risk and that, despite his powerful will and high moral courage, he was nowhere near as personally intrepid as Joseph Smith.[31] Burton, a physically courageous man himself, was remarkably uncensorious about this trait in the Leader. 'That such a mental anomaly often exists, those familiar with the biographies of the Brahmin officials at the courts of Poonah, Sattara and other places in India, well know: many a "Pant", whose reckless audacity in intrigue conducted under imminent danger of death argued the courage of a *coeur-de-lion*, was personally fearful as Hobbes, and displayed at death the terrors of Robespierre. A moment of fear is recounted of St Peter; Erasmus was not the stuff of which martyrs are made, and even the *beau sabreur* once ran.'[32]

The emphasis on armed force in the brief history of the Mormons convinced Burton that in future the 'Saints' would be formidable military adversaries. Compulsory military service for all males between the age of sixteen and fifty meant that by 1860 Brigham Young could put 6,000 men in the field, plus 30,000 Indian allies. On the other hand, the population of Utah at 40,000 in 1860 and its expected imminent quadrupling through philoprogenitive polygamy would soon enable Salt Lake City to outstrip New Mexico (pop. 93,000), Washington DC (75,000) and a string of minor states.[33] As it happened, Utah's population increase was nothing like as spectacular; it was still only 210,779 by 1890 after general demographic explosion in North America.

Burton was also convinced that the coming Civil War would lead to the establishment of Utah as a separate, independent state. It was notorious that the US Constitution of 1787 had not made clear whether participating states had the right to secede from a federal union. To Burton the question was absurd: 'What can be clearer than that the Constitution contemplated secession? If an adult citizen is allowed to throw off his allegiance, surely the body of citizens called a State have, *a majori*, a right to withdraw from a Federal Union?'[34] If the Southern states exercised their legitimate rights and seceded – as Burton expected them to do successfully – what chance was there of the adherence to the Union of a state that had never sought incorporation in the first place? As it turned out, the fall of Fort Sumter in April 1861 and the secession of Virginia – signalling the outbreak of the Civil War – was thought by the Mormons to be the harbinger of the eventual disintegration of the Union foretold by Joseph Smith.[35]

Mormon sympathies were entirely with the South in the war between the States. There were no blacks in Salt Lake City, since according to Mormon doctrine a black man could not enter heaven. Slavery was also practised, mainly, Burton alleged, to allow the 'Saints' to buy children who would otherwise be abandoned or killed by their starving parents. But this, typically Burtonian, apology for the Mormons was flimsy. In fact Brigham Young embraced the principle of slavery with much more avidity, as he told Horace Greeley: 'We consider it of divine institution, and not to be abolished until the curse pronounced on Ham shall have been removed from his descendants.' His sole regret was that slave labour was too expensive for Utah.[36]

Brigham Young was evidently flattered that such a world-famous traveller had come into his domain, for he arranged the earliest possible interview with Burton. It was 11 a.m. on Friday 31 August when the two – both great men in their own way, came face to face in Young's private office, a sparsely furnished room the main contents of which were a writing table and a money safe. A pistol and a rifle hung on the wall within easy reach. At fifty-nine, Young had the appearance of a man of forty-five. His thick, light-coloured hair was parted on the side. He had a calm and reserved expression, narrow forehead, thin eyebrows and grey-blue eyes. A slight droop in the left eyelid made Burton think he had suffered from paralysis, but Young explained the symptom as neuralgia. His fine and pointed nose was bent a little to the left; his teeth were imperfect and his lips, Burton thought, were the typical New Englander's. The cheeks were fleshy, chin peaked and face clean-shaven, except under the jaw, where he had allowed the beard to grow. His hands were well made, and his figure large and broad-shouldered. His dress was modest and ascetic. He wore a grey homespun Quaker's coat of an antique cut, with black buttons and baggy trousers. A necktie of dark silk, with a large bow, fringed a starchless collar. With black satin waistcoat and gold chain, Young looked for all the world like a New England gentleman farmer.

Burton took to him at once. 'He has been called a hypocrite, swindler, forger and murderer; no one looked it less.' Affable, impressive, unpretentious, undogmatic, even-tempered and cold-mannered were the epithets Burton used to describe Young's demeanour. Temperate, sober and ascetic, he neither smoked nor drank, disapproved of hard liquor and contented himself with a favourite 'luxury' of baked potato with a little buttermilk. A few minutes' conversation revealed that he was not an educated man. 'Men not books, deeds not words' was his motto. Burton noticed that he pronounced 'impetus' with the stress on the second syllable.[37] But Burton did not make the mistake of judging a man's stature purely by the level of his formal education. He was impressed by Young's general knowledge. When the Prophet called in some of the other elders to talk about Livingstone's missionary travels, Burton noticed that Young quickly corrected his followers' inept attempts to locate the Zambezi on a map. Burton commented, 'There are many educated men in England who could not have corrected the mistake as well.'

Since Brigham Young granted interviews on the strict understanding that the subjects of religious doctrine and polygamy were not to be raised, it was hardly surprising that after half an hour the conversation flagged. Burton took his leave, deeply impressed by the character of the Prophet. He was St Paul to

Joseph Smith's Jesus Christ, and the analogy held good down to the inspirational/wordly divide in each case. St Paul by his doctrine of Christology converted a Judaic sect into a world religion. Brigham Young largely eschewed the thaumaturgical and revelatory approach of Smith in favour of a hard-headed demonstration that Mormonism was universifiable as a prescription, simply because it worked, as demonstrated by the economic success of Zion.[38] Burton was prepared to give Young the benefit of most doubts:

> The first impression left upon my mind by this short *séance* was that the Prophet is no common man, and that he has none of the weakness and vanity which characterize the common uncommon man . . . His manner is at once affable and impressive, simple and courteous: his want of pretension contrasts favourably with certain pseudo-prophets that I have seen, each and every one of whom holds himself to be a 'logos' without other claim save a semi-maniacal self-esteem. He shows no signs of dogmatism, bigotry or fanaticism, and never once entered – with me at least – upon the subject of religion. He impresses a stranger with a certain sense of power . . . He has been so long used to power that he cares nothing for its display. The arts by which he rules the heterogeneous mass of conflicting elements are indomitable will, profound secrecy, and uncommon astuteness . . . He is the St Paul of the New Dispensation: true and sincere, he gave point and energy, and consistency to the somewhat disjointed, turbulent and unforeseeing fanaticism of Mr Joseph Smith; and if he has not been able to create, he has shown himself great in controlling circumstances.[39]

From winks and nods Burton also discovered what Young did with the tithes paid him by the faithful. The hostile canard at the time was that the Prophet pocketed the tithes, which was why he was a rich man. Burton's analysis was more subtle and more truthful. He saw clearly enough that Young was a highly talented entrepreneur and that the basis of his personal fortune was the timber business. The church tithes he used to bribe senators and newspaper editors in the USA and to maintain a network of spies and informers throughout the republic, so that he could be alerted of any moves to destroy Zion.

The favourable opinion Burton formed of Young was evidently reciprocated, for the British visitor was soon invited to another interview. It was well known that if Young did not like a man at the first meeting, he would never speak to him again.[40] This time the patriarch accompanied Burton on a tour of the city, ending with an ascent of a hill to the north whence all the principal landmarks could be clearly seen. Burton tentatively suggested that he might take postulant's orders as a 'Saint'. His intention was obvious: to get inside the Mormon culture as successfully as he had penetrated Muhammadanism during the famous journey to Mecca. Young treated the request as a joke. 'I think you've done that sort of thing once before, Captain,' he replied with a twinkle in his eye.[41]

When Young pointed out the Lion House, which contained many of his wives, Burton replied facetiously that he had come to Salt Lake City as a bachelor only to find all the women already appropriated by polygamous 'Saints'. Pointing to the lake with his right hand, he murmured 'Water, water everywhere' then jabbed his left hand towards the city – "and not a drop to drink". The quick-witted Young caught the allusion at once and laughed heartily.[42]

Burton's next self-appointed task was to attend a Mormon religious service, which Young would address. To prepare himself conscientiously, he began to read *The Book of Mormon*, which he found a farrago of millenarianism, eschatology, transcendentalism, freemasonry and chiliasm, with a leavening of Jewish mysticism and Islam. 'The mind of man', he concluded, 'most loves those errors and delusions into which it has become self-persuaded, and is most fanatic concerning the irrationalities and supernaturalities to which it has bowed its own reason.' As for the style of the book: 'surely there was never a book so dull and heavy; it was as monotonous as a sage prairie.'[43] Harsh as this judgement might seem, it was mild alongside that of Mark Twain: 'If Joseph Smith composed this book, the act was a miracle – keeping awake while he did it was at any rate . . . the book seems to me merely a prosy detail of imaginary history, with the Old Testament for a model; followed by a tedious plagiarism of the New Testament. The author laboured to give his words and phrases the quaint old-fashioned sound and structure of our King James's translation of the Scriptures; and the result is a mongrel – half modern glibness, and half simplicity and gravity. The latter is awkward and constrained; the former natural but grotesque by contrast. Whenever he found his speech growing too modern – which was about every sentence or two – he ladled in a few such scriptural phrases as "exceeding sore", "it came to pass" etc. and made things satisfactory again.'[44]

Having mastered the intricacies of *The Book of Mormon*, Burton one Sunday entered the Bowery – a large shed where the services were held. Containing a congregation of 3,000 souls, the Bowery had a roof of bushes and boughs supported by rough posts, and open for ventilation at the sides. The congregation sat on long rows of benches opposite the dais. Between the people and the platform was the 'orchestra', consisting of a violin and a bass and a choir of two women and four men. Burton remarked that they sang the 'sweet songs of Zion' tolerably well.

It took half an hour for the faithful to troop in, in their Sunday best. As this was a hot, sticky August, many of the men were in shirt-sleeves. The elders on the platform wore coats of black broadcloth. All kept their hats on until the service began, when they uncovered. Burton was astonished at the number of old people present, but his principal attention, as ever in an alien society, was focused on the women. 'There were a few specimens of the "Yankee woman", formerly wondrous grim, with a shrewd, thrifty grey eye, at once cold and eager, angular in body and mind, tall, bony and square-shouldered – now softened and humanized by transplantation and transposition to her proper place.'

The service opened with an address by 'bishop' Abraham Smoot: 'he made regular use of the regular Wesley organ – the nose.' In the middle of his sermon Brigham Young entered, dressed in his invariable grey homespun, in a tall steeple-crowned straw hat with a broad black ribbon. There was a long silence. Smoot hurriedly brought his speech to a close. Then, following another pregnant silence, Brigham Young removed his hat, advanced to the dais, expectorated into a spittoon, took a sip of water from a glass, then, leaning forward with both hands propped on the green baize of the tribune, began his address.

Burton was hoping for a rousing speech, full of the violent and flowery language appropriate to an Old Testament prophet for which Young was famed. In 1853 there had been the memorable, 'I will unsheath my bowie knife and conquer or die.' On another occasion the Prophet had warned food hoarders that their heads might be found 'wallowing in snow'. On yet another he had fulminated, 'If you are not heartily on the Lord's side, you will be hewn down.'[45] Alas for Burton's hopes, and doubtless because of the presence of his distinguished visitor, Brigham Young's address turned out to be low-key and conciliatory.

The manner and technique of the sermon convinced Burton that Young was a master of the art of public speaking. He was fluent and his gestures were easy and natural except for the New Englander habit of raising and shaking the finger, which elsewhere in the USA was considered a threatening gesture. The Prophet turned out to be a good mimic and during the sermon gave a droll impersonation of a Shaker. The content of the speech was anodyne. He told the faithful that there was a great future ahead for the 'Saints' but that the Earth would soon be visited by a tribulation. Burton commented that since the Earth had been suffering tribulations time out of mind, that was a safe enough prophecy. He enjoined the 'Saints' to show charity and good wishes to all: visitors, Gentiles, Indians, even the USA. Burton was less impressed by Young's tendency to lapse into rambling incoherence on doctrinal points and by his grammatical solecisms, such as 'he become' and 'for you and I'.[46]

When Young had finished speaking, Heber Kimball arose. Tall, powerful with dark-piercing eyes and clean-shaven face, Kimball was acknowledged as second only to Young in the Mormon hierarchy. Kimball was more of a hardliner than Young, and his theology harked back to the Joseph Smith days, being Judaic rather than Christian in tone. The year before he told Horace Greeley, 'I *do* pray for my enemies: I pray that they may all go to hell.'[47] Burton endorsed the judgment that Kimball's Mormonism was a more sinister variety than the Prophet's. 'He affected the Boanerges style . . . several of his remarks were loudly laughed at by the Congregation . . . he reminded me of Luther's description of Tetzel's sermons, in which he used to shout the words, "Bring! Bring! Bring!" with such a horrible bellowing that one would have said it was a mad bull rushing on the people and goring them with its horns.'[48]

After Kimball's sermon, an official adjourned the meeting until 2 p.m. As a finale two elders walked up and down the rows of benches, one carrying a pitcher, the other a plate of bread. Each 'Saint' partook of both, in a bizarre parody of the Christian Eucharist. Burton was never a patient man or one with a high boredom threshold, and the banality and bathos of the morning had stretched his tolerance to capacity. He did not return for the afternoon session.

The boredom was becoming more generalized. The longer he stayed, the more reserve he seemed to sense towards him among the 'Saints', who appeared to regard him as a federal spy because he consorted with Governor Cumming. In addition the 'Moslem gloom' from the austere manners of the Mormons and the semi-seclusion of the sexes began to affect him adversely. There was little change in the monotony of the days. He breakfasted between 6-9 a.m., dined at 1 p.m., enjoyed a siesta, then ate supper at 6 p.m. On 7 September he wrote to Norton Shaw at the RGS, 'I reached this place about a week ago and am living in the odour of sanctity – a pretty strong one it is too! prophets, apostles, *et hoc genus omne*.'[49] But a week later he was becoming irritable with ennui. Burton's usual solution for this was to take to the bottle, but Salt Lake City was virtually a 'dry' town. He was reduced to taking nips from a succession of rapidly emptying hip flasks.

Apparently on one occasion he did get his hands on a local brew, for Richard Walden Hale claims that Burton got into a brawl and was saved from imprisonment only through the intercession of 'bishop' John Lee. Like most of Hale's stories, this one lost nothing in the telling. Whatever minor incident may have occurred when Burton finally tasted locally distilled whisky, he clearly kept his reputation with the 'Saints' unsullied, for on 3 October 1860 the *Deseret News* bade him a cordial farewell. 'As far as we have heard, Captain Burton has been one of the few gentlemen who have passed through Utah without leaving behind him a disagreeable *Souvenir*. The Captain has seen Utah without goggles; we wish him a safe journey.'[50]

But finally Burton exhausted the potential of Salt Lake City and on 19 September set out for the Pacific coast. He spent 20-26 September at nearby Camp Floyd, trying to find onward transport. The tribes to the west were reported on the warpath, and fear of scalping meant that nobody was travelling that way; the regular stagecoach run had therefore ceased. Finally Burton persuaded a Dublin-born Californian called Kennedy to convey a stagecoach complement in his merchant's trotting wagon, provided each passenger paid $150. He asked the local commandant for Lieutenant Dana as his companion, and the arrangement was agreed. He had allowed his hair to grow while in the 'City of the Saints' but now once more had it "'shingled off", till my head somewhat resembled a pointer's dorsum'.

Burton spent the week while Kennedy made his preparations arguing politics and military strategy with the officers at Camp Floyd. Heated discussions took place over the militia, with the Americans citing the Bill of Rights in the Constitution which stated that the right of the people to bear arms should not be impaired. Burton soon realized that this doctrine was a sacred cow which foreigners criticized at their peril. However, when one pierced through the humbug and bombast that surrounded the subject, not to mention the dishonest conflation of quite separate (and professional) groups like the Texas Rangers, the fact remained that the militia cost far more in blood and money than the regulars. Burton's contempt for the militia revealed the typical posture of the professional soldier he still was. And as a detester of egalitarianism, he found loathsome the lack of deference to rank and position. 'You go to hell, Captain! I'm as good a man as you are!' was a typical militiaman's rejoinder to the officer who gave him orders.

> Mentally they are in many cases men ignoring the common restraints of society, profoundly impressed with insubordination, which displays equality, which has to learn all the wholesome duty of obedience, and which begins with as much respect for obedience as for the campaigns of Frederick the Great . . . In the field, like all raw levies, they are apt to be alarmed by anything unaccustomed, as the sound of musketry from the rear, or a threatened flank attack: they cannot reserve their fire, they aim wildly to the peril of friend and foe, and they have been accused of unmilitary cruelties, such as scalping and flaying men, shooting and killing squaws and children. And they never fail, after the fashion of such men, to claim that they have done all the

fighting.[51]

To while away the time until Kennedy was ready to start, Burton accompanied Governor Cumming and his wife on a trip to the great Salt Lake itself. 'The largest inland body of salt water, of no use, even for suicide,' as one wag dubbed it, intrigued Burton, as it did many British travellers after him.[52]

> That inland briny sea, which apparently has no business there . . . I had heard strange accounts of its buoyancy. It was said to support a bather as if he were sitting in an armchair, and to float him like an unfresh egg. My experience differs in this point from that of others. There was no difficulty in swimming nor indeed in sinking. After sundry immersions of the head, in order to feel if it really stang and removed the skin, like a mustard plaster, – as described – emboldened by the detection of so much hyperbole, I proceeded to duck under with open eyes, and smarted 'for my pains'. The sensation did not come on suddenly; at first there was a sneaking tinge, then a bold succession of twinges, and lastly a steady honest burning like what follows a pinch of snuff in the eyes. There was no fresh water at hand, so scrambling upon the rock I sat there for half an hour, presenting to nature the ludicrous spectacle of a man weeping flowing tears.[53]

At last, on 26 September, Kennedy was ready. They set out for San Francisco, 750 miles distant. On this stage of his North American journey, more than anywhere, Burton lived the life of a pioneer. Forever on the alert for Indian attacks, the travellers sighted many camp fires but made no contact with hostiles. Relations between white and red man in the Humboldt and Carson valleys had reached snapping point in recent years. Slaughtering braves, raping squaws and gutting villages, the human *canaille* who followed as the mining boom moved inland, had finally conjured up a bloody backlash. At Egan's Station they saw the results: the post had been reduced to ashes topped by a chimney stack – the revenge of the Gosh-Yuta Indians for the killing of seventeen of their number the week before. The ghoulish scene was made even more macabre by the excavations of wolves, who had dug up the Indian corpses, so that mutilated limbs and half-masticated torsos protruded above the snow.

Burton amused himself by compiling a glossary of Western usage from the mountain men they encountered; he noted the penchant for the phrase 'you bet', 'beeves' for 'cattle' and 'a beef' for 'a steer'. The roistering Burton was seen to best advantage in a meeting at American Fork with Porter Rockwell, the former bodyguard of Joseph Smith, and said to be the evil genius of the Danites or 'avenging angels'. Burton always relished encounters with larger-than-life personalities to match his own. The result was a glorious binge, in which each capped the other's tall stories and tried to drink the rival under the table with 'squar' tumblers of whisky. Rockwell liked Burton and advised 'the captain' that the worst danger to the party would come, not from the Indians, but from any whites they encountered on the way west – a route, said Rockwell, 'about as fit for travelling as hell for a powder magazine'.

On 5 October they emerged from the land of the hostile Gosh-Yuta Indians into that of the more friendly Shoshone. By 7 October, at Ruby Valley, 300 miles from Salt Lake City but still 300 miles distant from their first objective, Carson City, winter was beginning to send out its advance guard and the first flecks of snow started to fall. At least the cold weather cleared away the rattlesnakes, which grew to nine feet in this part of the West and were much feared. The mountain men hereabouts used ammonia as an antidote for snakebite, while the Indians favoured cauterization.

It was later a source of deep regret to Burton that he had not known about the Yellowstone Geysers in 1860[54] – they were not discovered until 1868 – but even had he been aware of their existence, Kennedy would surely not have taken a diversion in winter and with the threat from Indians ever-present. 17 October found the travellers at Carson Lake, then, two days later, they trailed into Carson City itself. The worst was now behind them, and Burton could relax and take in the impressions of his first large 'Wild West' town. Mark Twain remarked on the literal woodenness of the 'city'. The main street consisted of four or five blocks of white frame stores, all packed closely together as if land were scarce in the West.[55] 'Artemus Ward' remarked on the violence of the place: 'They shoot folks here somewhat, and the law is rather partial than otherwise to first-class murderers.'[56] In his impressions Burton synthesized these two salient features:

My informants declared that in and about Carson a dead man for breakfast was the rule; besides accidents perpetually occurring to indifferent or to peace-making parties, they reckoned per annum fifty murders. In a peculiar fit of liveliness an intoxicated gentleman will discharge his revolver in a ballroom, and when a 'shyooting' begins in the thin-walled frame houses, those not concerned avoid bullets and splints by jumping into their beds. During my three days' stay in Carson City I heard of three murders. A man 'heavy *on* the shoulder', who can 'hit out straight from the hip', is a valuable acquisition.[57]

From Carson City Burton explored nearby Virginia City, a gold rush town later to acquire fame from the writings of Mark Twain and 'Artemus Ward'.[58] It was an easy two days' ride by stagecoach from Carson to San Francisco, but Burton preferred to make his way there in a more leisurely manner. He visited Placerville and other diggings in the California gold country, then finally paid off Kennedy on 1 November at Sacramento – 'the newer name for New Helvetia – a capital mass of shops and stores, groggeries and hotels'. Then he took a boat on an eight-hour trip down the Sacramento river to San Francisco, the El Dorado of the West, where the visitor could get tolerable opera and a superior supper and company. 'Mr Consul Booke placed my name on the lists of the Union Club, which was a superior institute to that of the Leamington.'

After a thoroughly enjoyable ten days in San Francisco, Burton opted for a journey to the grandeur of Yosemite rather than the chance to visit Los Angeles or Vancouver Island. Then, on 15 November, with much regret he bade adieu to San Francisco, and steamed out of the Golden Gate on the *Golden Age*, Commodore Watkins. 'She was a model steamer with engines and engine rooms, clean as a club kitchen, and a cuisine whose terrapin soup and devilled crabs à la Baltimore will long maintain their position in my memory – not so long, however, as the kindness and courtesy of the ancient mariner who commanded the *Golden Age*.'[59]

On 28 November the steamer docked at Acapulco. Burton's hopes of being able to cross Mexico were dashed by the news that civil war made the road to the Atlantic port of Vera Cruz impassable. He continued on to the isthmus of Panama where he disembarked on 15 December and spent three days. The evenings there, he related, were 'made highly agreeable by a certain muscatel cognac'.[60] On 18 December he rode the Panama railway to Aspinwall, where he boarded a steamer next morning for St Thomas in the West Indies. There he embarked at once on the *Seine*, which made good progress all the way across the Atlantic to Land's End, 'where Britannia received us with her characteristic welcome, a gale and a pea soup fog which kept us cruising about for three days in the unpleasant Solent and the Southampton Water'.[61]

Chapter Three

North American Impressions

Burton's seven-month tour of North America in 1860 produced some of his most fascinating ethnological, anthropological and sociological observations. From the small-scale to the macrocosmic, Burton displayed his unique eye for detail. Almost nothing he ever said or did was uncontroversial. That he ran true to form in the territories of the then and future United States will become clear as we examine the reports he brought back in three salient areas: the American Indian, Mormon polygamy and the 'state of the nation' itself – his far from favourable conclusions on the 'land of the free'.

When Burton published *The City of the Saints*, the American Indian was going through a low in public esteem after the vogue earlier in the century for Fenimore Cooper's 'noble savages'. In his usual sardonic manner, Burton at first gave the impression that he too found the subject a bore. He remarked disdainfully that all the terms used in normal discourse were inaccurate: America, named after the impostor Amerigo Vespucci, should not be called America; the Indian should not be termed an Indian; 'red' Indians were not red, and so on.[1] But Burton's sardonic bark was always worse than his scholarly bite. It did not take him long to realize that the key tribe on the northern Great Plains was the Sioux or Dakota. His analysis of the Sioux was acute and profound. He did not make the mistake of more eminent anthropologists in thinking that the most interesting native Indians were all of the passé variety, such as the Iroquois and the

46

Cherokee. This emphasis on the eastern tribes, and the neglect of the western Indian, was particularly a feature of the influential work of Lewis Morgan, whose *Ancient Society* (1877) – ironically, written the year after the battle of the Little Big Horn – the principal source for Engels's *Origin of the Family, Private Property and the State* – severely downgraded 'the Dakota' in importance.

Burton's distinctive talent as an anthropologist was to work at three levels: of minute taxonomy, of structural analysis and of comparative sociology. He was a close observer of the minutiae of a given tribe and had a near genius for getting inside the idiom of the particular culture he studied. This held good whether the tribe in question was the Fon of Dahomey, the Danakil of Somaliland, the Gogo of East Africa or the Bedouin of the desert. Beyond this, Burton was a master at intuiting the overarching or 'structural' meaning of the mores and folkways he observed. Finally, he was able to relate his data to a mass of other ethnological and sociological material, the product of his own first-hand study. Thus Burton lucidly laid before his readers not only what was unique about a given tribe but also what the tribal culture had in common with others across the four corners of the globe.

The method of comparative sociology is evident in the very early pages of *The City of the Saints*; thereafter Burton often used the Plains Indians in his *oeuvre* as a buttress for one of his 'universalist' arguments. There is a comparison of African and Indian totemism, and a note on the similarity of the forms of expression used by Arabs, Australian aborigines and North American Indians.[2] Burton particularly favoured comparisons with the Bedouin, but he rated his beloved Arab higher than the Indian on three indices: general intellect, treatment of women, and place in history.[3] Most of all, he used the tribes of the West to 'prove' a favourite thesis. Following Montesquieu, Burton thought that a primary determinant of human social and political behaviour was climate. Levels of sensuality, lubricity and polygamy could even be correlated with climatic zones. Thus 'the voluptuousness and polygamy of the North American Indian under a temperature of almost perpetual winter is far greater than that of the most sensual tropical nations.'[4]

Burton had a keen eye for landscape, and his comparative method often embraces the peculiar terrain in which his 'similar' tribes operated. So the Indian reminded him of 'a Tartar or an Afghan after a summer march', or the Mongolians he had seen in Northern India. The Plains Indian rode his horse 'like the Abyssinian eunuch, as if born and bred to become part of the animal'. He likened the distant view of Scotts Bluff to the Arabian City of Brass, 'that mysterious abode of bewitched infidels, which often appears at a distance to the wayfarer toiling under the burning sun, but ever eludes his nearer search'. Independence Rock reminded him of *Jiwe la Mkoa*, the Round Rock in eastern Unyamwezi (in modern-day Tanzania); similarly the Devil's Gate recalled the Brèche de Roland in the Pyrenees. And the Sioux practice of 'cutting, or more generally biting off, the nose tip' of a woman taken in adultery was the identical practice he had witnessed in Hindustan in the 1840s.

Burton's method did not depend only on such homologies and analogies. When he narrowed the range and put the Indian villages under the microscope, his touch was just as sure. He laid out for the reader the dwellings, dress, weapons, martial traditions and sexual habits of the tribes. Their religion he saw as a kind of totemism; the medicine man acted as '*Mganga, Angekok*, sorcerer, prophet, physician, exorciser, priest and rain doctor'. The beliefs in a Great Spirit and the Happy Hunting Ground, widely known since the publication of Longfellow's *Hiawatha* in 1855, he construed as syncretism of ancient belief with the improperly digested soteriology of the missionaries. He observed the incidence of sodomy among the Sioux and the system of trial marriages – 'like the Highlanders before the reign of James the Fifth' – and polygamy – 'they prefer to marry sisters, because the tent is more quiet.' He mastered the rudiments of their sign language. He noted the Indians' custom of propitiating the spirits before setting out on a scalping raid, and gave details on the grisly results of such raids. Being Burton, he could not resist a stab at black humour: of a scalp he declared, 'set in a plain gold circlet, it makes a very pretty brooch'. It always amazed him that the Indians ran the gamut between heartless cruelty and sentimentality. On the one hand, he maintained that the North American aboriginal was imbued with furious and frantic vengefulness. On the other, they could never meet an acquaintance after a long separation without copious weeping for the mutual friends they had lost.[5]

Burton also disentangled the complex network of clans and septs hunting and fighting under the flag of the Sioux or Dakota. Dakota was what they called themselves: Sioux was a bowdlerization of *'Nadouessioux'* – the French transliteration of an Indian word meaning 'little snake' or 'enemy' – suggesting that the Sioux had been a thorn in the flesh of the white man from the earliest days. The Unkpapa Sioux, whose most famous scion was Sitting Bull, regarded themselves as an élite; their name signified 'They who camp by themselves'. The branch of the Sioux most involved in the famous campaigns against the US government in the 1870s were the Oglala, under their chief Crazy Horse. Oglala denoted a gesture of contempt, said to have been employed by the other Sioux when the Oglala in the eighteenth century made a brief attempt to be agriculturalists rather than nomads. The Oglala were a breakaway faction from the Brûlé, and played the Matabele to their Zulu. The Brûlé Sioux were said to have got their name when the clan was scorched by a prairie fire in 1763, which carried off a number of them. Bannock Sioux were literally 'the people who keep an untidy lodge'. The Wahpeton Sioux were experts in woodcraft and were said to live in the trees. The Two Kettle Sioux boasted of their prowess in hunting (they could fill two kettles of meat to any other tribe's one). The Miniconjoux were 'they who planted crops beside water'. Like the Oglala the Miniconjoux had once tried agriculture. Being more successful, they had stuck to it longer than the Oglala. The Blackfeet Sioux (*Sihasapa*) were said to be named for their black moccasins. They were utterly distinct from the Blackfoot tribe (*Siksika*), traditional enemies of the Sioux, who lived farther north and west and ranged into Canada. The Sans Arc Sioux were supposed in legend to have surrendered their bows on the promptings of an hermaphrodite seer. The resulting slaughter was only partly palliated by their being given the gift of prophecy.[6]

Burton was the first foreign observer to point up the gathering threat to the Sioux and all other Plains Indians from the gradual disappearance of the bison or 'buffalo'. While travelling in the Platte region in 1842, 'Pathfinder' Fremont found himself surrounded by two vast herds, each one extending several miles behind and ahead of him and so vast that no reasonable estimate was possible. In 1846 the historian Parkman reported: 'Far and near the prairie was alive with buffalo; now like black specks dotting the distant swells; now trampling by in ponderous columns or filing in long lines, morning, noon and night to drink at the river – wading, plunging, and snorting in the water – climbing the muddy shores and staring with wild eyes at the passing canoes.'[7]

But by 1860 Burton found the animal on which the Indian depended for his livelihood already in a parlous state. The bison was being caught between two fires and squeezed into a narrow enclave on the high plains. The animals retreated westwards from their habitat by an average of ten miles a year, taking losses from hunters of 20,000-30,000 a year. In 1830 they were still on the banks of the Missouri, but by 1860 could not be encountered until thirty miles farther west. At the same time the buffalo had become extinct west of the Rockies, in Yellowstone Valley, the headwaters of the Mississippi and in the prairie country between Arkansas and the Platte. The Indian consumed every part of the animal, which they killed in a manner reminiscent of Indian 'pig-sticking' by charging at full tilt with razor-tipped lances. They were such fine horsemen that they could swerve at the last moment and draw the missile from the victim's flanks before it fell. But the white hunter slaughtered the buffalo in thousands, not for food but for 'sport'. In England bison hunting had become a mania in aristocratic circles; every week English 'milords' crossed the Atlantic for a joust with the 'monarch of the prairies'. *The Times* actually ran advertisements for trips to Fort Wallace in Kansas for the shooting, at a cost of fifty guineas.[8]

Yet the threat to the bison was only the most serious threat to the future of the red man. Burton thought that the white man's whisky, diseases and 'culture' were doling out a kind of euthanasia of the tribes. Admiring the genuinely 'noble savage' he was at once distressed by and contemptuous of the degeneracy he observed among the tribesmen who aped the ways of the white or attempted symbiosis with him. Along the great emigrant routes west, he noticed that the Indians had become beggars, liars and horse thieves. 'Chastity is little esteemed amongst those Indians who have been corrupted by intercourse with the whites.' Hopes of 'civilizing' these outcasts were vain. 'I do not believe that an Indian of the plains ever became a Christian. He must first be humanized, then civilized, and lastly Christianized;

and, as has been said before, I doubt his surviving the operation.'

The US Bureau of Indian Affairs had a project for converting
the nomad hunters into a pastoral people. Burton applauded the
ambition, but thought it too was chimerical. 'The chiefs are still
bribed, and the people cheated, by white traders; and poverty,
disease, and debauchery rapidly thin the tribesmen.' He pointed
out that in two and a half centuries the inexorable pressure westwards by the white man had swept native Americans from the
East Coast to the Mississippi 'as the grey rat in Europe expelled
the black rat'. He predicted, accurately enough, that in the end
the Indians would all be settled on reservations far from their
ancestral territories and on inhospitable land of no commercial
value. The final stage would be extinction. As he put it in *Stone
Talk*:

Of old, the Red Man in the West
How different his lot, how blest,
How happy in his wigwam home!
By Saxon's poisonous pox and rum
Now what a vile and ruined race!
A few years more its every trace
Will vanish clear from Earth's fair face,
Except in books, and by-gone tales,
Of squaws, scalps, tomahawks, and trails.[9]

Yet of all the subjects Burton broached in his book on his North
American travels, it was Mormon polygamy which most held his
readers in thrall. As he himself remarked, Salt Lake City without plural wives was like *Hamlet* without the Prince. Brigham
Young's contribution to the doctrine of the 'Saints' was an ex-
hortation to the 'selfish gene' to 'go forth and multiply'. At his
death in 1877 it was not his personal fortune of $2,500,000 that
excited comment so much as his seventeen 'official' wives (and
fifty-six children) and fifty-four concubines.[10] Young's philoprogenitive mania was pronounced. In 1855 Jules Rémy heard him
pronounce in a sermon to the faithful, 'Make haste and get married. Let me see no more boys above sixteen and girls above
fourteen unmarried.'[11]

Burton strongly supported the Mormon case for polygamy,

which he analysed as threefold: a vast population increase among the 'Saints' was required; excessive expenditure was an obstacle to freehold property; and since servants were rare and costly, it was cheaper to marry them. Burton endorsed the Mormon claim that the aim of polygamy was eugenic, not licentious; all sensuality other than what was necessary for procreation was forbidden. Polygamy, in Burton's view, produced population growth, since it was one of his favourite axioms that a plurality of wives resulted in more girl babies than boys, while polyandry produced a surplus of males. The eugenic factor was clearly uppermost in the mind of the Prophet when he laid down his rules for women. During gestation and nursing, the strictest chastity was ordained; lactation was prolonged for two years, as this was said to produce a splendidly sturdy race.

So much for expediency. But Burton also supported the wider Mormon arguments for polygamy. The received opinion was that anything other than monogamy led to the exploitation of women. On the contrary, argued Burton and Brigham Young.

> Mormons claim that they have removed their ways from those 'whose end is bitter as wormwood and sharp as a two-edged sword' . . . They boast that if it [polygamy] be an evil they have at least chosen the lesser evil, that they practise openly as a virtue what others do secretly as a sin – how full is society of these latent Mormons! – that their plurality has abolished the necessity of concubinage, cryptogamy, contubernium, celibacy, *mariages du Treizième arrondissement*, with their terrible consequences, infanticide, and so forth . . . like its sister Institution, Slavery, the birth and growth of a similar age, Polygamy acquires *vim* by abuse and detraction; the more turpitude is heaped upon it, the brighter and more glorious it appears to its votaries.[12]

Not content with this, Burton boldly asserted that polygamy was actually in women's interest. He claimed, in the teeth of most other observers, that the women of Salt Lake City were well above average in prettiness and that polygamy agreed with them. He singled out a certain Miss Sally, a judge's daughter, as the belle of the 'City of the Saints'.[13] Divorce was rare, since the only escape route from marriage for a woman was via adultery, against which the social sanctions were severe. Whereas a woman could divorce for cruelty, desertion or neglect, the only grounds open to a man were adultery. The consequence was that he was forced to take his marital responsibilities more seriously. A man with five wives had to inure himself to a fixed life; there could be no such backsliding as was available to the bachelor or monogamic male. For this reason, Burton asserted, women were actually more in favour of polygamy than men.[14]

Moreover, 'sisterhood' actually had a real meaning in Salt Lake City, unlike in the American feminist associations. The first wife assumed the husband's name and titles; the next wives then became her 'sisters' and aunts to her children. The widows of the Prophet were married to his successor just as David took unto himself the wives of Saul. Additionally, because of the high rates of apostasy from the 'Saints', the church elders concentrated a good deal of attention on women. According to strict Mormon doctrine, a woman could not enter heaven without a husband to introduce her – 'a virgin's end is annihilation or absorption' – but Brigham Young and his acolytes bribed their females with 'indulgences' or browbeat them with threats of damnation. Ever-present was the fear of apostasy, which Young tried to avert by prescribing the most dire penalties. A Mormon woman marrying a Gentile man was ostracized from the 'Saints'; whereas an apostate male was regarded as a knave, an apostate female was considered a veritable Jezebel. Polygamy thus contained a subtle element of social control by tying a man to Mormonism for life. Because apostasy was common in the early era of Mormon conversion, the young were rigorously tested for 'soundness' before being married. Girls in particular put their prospective husbands through a series of theological and doctrinal hoops, since later backsliding by their consorts would debar their own entry into heaven.

Further arguments adduced by Burton in favour of Mormon polygamy were that the brittle relations between the sexes which he found elsewhere in North America were here harmonized. Like many other visitors, Burton commented on a bitter war between the sexes in nineteenth-century USA, which he attributed to a neurotic fear of maternity, aggravated by 'a highly nervous temperament, small cerebellum, constitutional frigidity and extreme delicacy of fibre'.[15] Furthermore, Mormonism provided extreme financial security: Burton remarked that, in his experience, a woman would rather be the fiftieth wife of Dives than the toilsome single wife of Lazarus. Commentators have sometimes been misled into thinking that Burton ultimately condemned Mormon polygamy as inadequate on the strength of the statement, 'A *ménage à trois*, in the Mormon sense of the phrase, is fatal to the development of that tender tie which must be confined to two.' But, read in context, the remark suggests that Burton did not anyway think much of so-called romantic love. In its place in Salt Lake City he found comfort, affection, circumspection, friendship and domestic discipline, which seemed to him superior virtues. 'Womanhood is not petted and spoiled, as in the Eastern States; the inevitable cyclical revolution, indeed, has rather placed her below par, where, however, I believe her to be happier than when set upon an uncomfortable and unnatural eminence.'[16]

But, most of all, Burton thought Mormonism appealed to women and made them converts because it offered the certain prospect of becoming wives. No girl ever remained single past the age of sixteen, as against an average age of marriage at thirty for an English spinster. 'The old maid is, as she ought to be, an unknown entity. Life in the wilds of Western America is a course of severe toil: a single woman cannot perform the manifold duties of housekeeping, cooking, scrubbing, washing, darning, child-bearing and nursing a family. A division of labour is necessary, and she finds it by acquiring a sisterhood. Throughout the States, whenever a woman is seen at manual or outdoor work, one is certain that she is Irish, German or Scandinavian. The delicacy and fragility of the American female nature is at once the cause and the effect of this exemption from toil.'[17]

There is some slight support for Burton's arguments in history. For example, Eliza 'Sister' Snow, once a wife of Joseph Smith, headed many of Brigham Young's anti-luxury 'retrenchment' campaigns and contrived to be at once plural wife and feminist. And it was true that sensuality was not the overriding motive for polygamy. An earlier British traveller, William Chandless, wrote, 'They are not a specially sensual people, the wretchedness of wives in Utah has been greatly exaggerated.'[18] Jules Rémy concurred, 'The Mormons appeared to us less licentious than we were naturally inclined to suppose.'[19]

But the overwhelming consensus of travellers' reports is against Burton. 'Artemus Ward' (Charles F. Browne) cited Young's own words in the *Deseret News* of 21 September 1856 to show that Mormon women were unhappy.[20] Burton's argument that anti-Mormon propaganda along the line of the 'rights of women' was so much cant and humbug, since none of the 'advanced' societies allowed women the vote, failed to meet the objection that Mormonism did not even permit the female the famous 'behind the scenes influence' which was supposed to be her consolation for political powerlessness. This point emerged very strongly during Horace Greeley's interview with Brigham Young in 1859. Greeley attacked 'the degradation . . . of woman to the single office of child-bearing and its accessories . . . I have not observed a sign in the streets, an advertisement in the journals of this Mormon metropolis, whereby a woman proposes to do anything whatever. No Mormon has ever cited to me his wife's or any woman's opinion on any subject; no Mormon woman has been introduced or has spoken to me.' Brigham Young told him, 'If I did not consider myself competent to transact a certain business without taking my wife's or any woman's counsel with regard to it, I think I should let that business alone.'[21]

The most effective rebuttal of Burton's position comes from his own mouth. The 'Miss Moore' whom he had met at the 'Devil's Post Office' had married a man who converted from the Church of England to Mormonism. Burton takes up the story: 'But when the serpent came and whispered in "Miss" Moore's modest, respectable, one idea'd ear that the Abrahams of Great Salt Lake City were mere "shamabrams", and, not content with Sarahs, but added to them an unlimited supply of Hagars, her power of endurance broke down. Not an inch would she budge, not a step nearer to the "City of the Saints" would she take. She fought against the impending misfortune, and she succeeded in reducing her husband to submission and making him earn a good livelihood as stationmaster on the waggon line – he who might have been a Solomon in the "City of the Saints".'[22]

On the subject of polygamy Burton was not a dispassionate student but a propagandist and exponent of *parti pris*. He claimed to know better than his *bien-pensant* critics what was actually involved in the institution, since he had observed its working in many different societies in three continents. 'The Mormon houshold has been described by its enemies as a hell of envy, hatred and malice – a den of murder and suicide. The same has been said of the Moslem harem. Both, I believe, suffer from the assertions of prejudice or ignorance. The temper of the new is so far superior to that of the old country that, incredible as the statement may appear, rival wives do dwell together in amity . . . I believe that many a "happy English home" is far stormier, despite the holy presence of monogamy.'[23]

Burton advanced a number of different theses for the desirability of monogamy outside western Europe. The first of these was that Mormonism tapped into an archetypal wisdom, as shown by the similarity of its treatment of women during pregnancy and lactation to that of other polygamous societies. 'The same custom is practised in part by the Jews, and in whole by some of the noblest tribes of savages; the splendid physical development of the Kaffir race in South Africa is attributed by some authors to a rule of continence like that of the Mormons, and to a lactation prolonged for two years. The anomaly of such practice in the midst of civilization is worthy of a place in De Balzac's great repertory of morbid anatomy; it is only to be equalled by the exceptional nature of the Mormon's position.'[24]

Another Burton thesis was that polygamy was required to fill up the sparsely populated areas of the world; this was a truth that could be appreciated only by one who had travelled widely and sampled many different cultures.[25] 'To the unprejudiced traveller it appears that polygamy is the rule where population is required, and where the great social evil has not had time to develop itself. In Paris or London the institution would, like slavery, die a natural death; in Arabia and in the wilds of the Rocky Mountains it maintains a strong hold upon the affections of mankind. Monogamy is best fitted for the large, wealthy, and flourishing communities in which man is rarely the happier because his quiver is full of children, and where the Hetaera becomes the succedaneum of the "plurality-wife".'[26]

The most obvious argument was that of cultural relativism (*autres lieux, autres moeurs*). He pointed out that he had seen African chiefs with 300 wives; had visited peoples where polygamy was unlimited; while in the Lake Regions of East Africa he had encountered a tribe where the pecking order of the farmyard prevailed with a vengeance – the chief alone was allowed plural wives, and his subjects were punished for the slightest infraction of a draconian sexual code by having their eyes gouged out.[27] Moreover, until fairly recently in history, Christian kings maintained harems: he instanced the case of Charlemagne.[28] As for critics of Arab polygamy, such as Harriet Martineau, they were calculated to bring out the most robust defence from Burton. In the first place, in their ignorance they thought polygamy was more widespread than it really was. In so far as the harem culture did exist, it prevented the social ills of the West. Woman's role in the harem was more assured than in the marriage markets of London and New York. Burton added to this the curious theory that when barbarism ascended to semi-barbarism (as in the Ancient World), women lost their place in society. When they regained it under 'civilization', their sensibility was shot through with frivolity and neurosis.[29] Monogamy was always the worst of all possible worlds. 'As far as my limited observations go, polyandry is the only state of society in which jealousy and quarrels about the sex are the exception and not the rule of life. In quality of doctor I have seen a little and heard much of the harem. It very much resembles a European home composed of man, his wife, and his mother . . . I have seen in the West many a "happy fireside", fitter to make Miss Martineau's heart ache than any harem in grand Cairo.'[30]

Ingeniously, Burton sometimes works in an argument from the division of labour, showing once again that the sociological imagination is not necessarily the preserve of persons of Leftish persuasion. 'Another instance that the plurality system of patriarchal marriage does not make a "bleak house". In semi-civilization, as in the "East", disorders may result from it; but amongst savages and barbarians, it produces a division of labour which tends to the comfort and happiness of woman. The same is the case in communities on the borderlands of old and settled societies. It is curious to see the women of the "Saints" persisting against being subjected to monogamy; but, though it is an anachronism, it is not an anachorism. The petitions for permissive polygamy in Massachusetts must be explained on different motives.'[31]

Yet another distinct Burton argument about polygamy is that

concerning climate, a view mentioned earlier in connection with the Sioux. Since libido is dampened down in hot climates – or so Burton thought – polygamy was essential to outweigh the natural disadvantages of climate. 'Man in hot and enervating climates, coming to maturity early and soon losing his powers . . . would never raise up a large family as the husband of only one wife.'[32] Also, he believed in the old adage about man being naturally polygamous and woman monogamous, subject to a gloss of his own: 'Man is by nature polygamic, whereas woman, as a rule, is monogamic, and polyandrous only when tired of her lover. The man loves the woman, but the love of the woman is for the man.'[33] Yet arguably under all these discrete theses lurks the spectre of a 'hidden agenda'. At root, Burton's misogyny fuelled his arguments for polygamy. He thought the happiest society was the one which exercised tightest control over female libido and, Nietzsche-like, advocated the whip or the method of Petruchio in *The Taming of the Shrew*. He spoke with approval of marital customs in Somaliland: 'On first entering the nuptial hut, the bridegegroom draws forth his horsewhip and inflicts memorable chastisement upon the person of his fair bride, with the view of taming any lurking propensity to shrewishness.'[34]

Thus Burton assembled both *general* arguments for polygamy, based on comparative sociology, and *particular* ones geared to the exigencies of life in Salt Lake City and designed to support the ideology of Brigham Young. Burton was always deadly serious in his scepticism about western monogamy and other 'superior' institutions. He had, however, always to look over his shoulder at a Victorian readership, so sometimes had to carry on his advocacy in a jokey or facetious mode. It is important to realize that when Burton appears to be writing with tongue in cheek, he is actually 'joking but serious', as in the following peroration: 'Without cannibalism how could the Zealander have preserved his fine physical development? Certainly not by eating his bat and his rat. Without slavery how could the Antilles and the southern states of the American Union have been cleared of jungle? White men could not, and free black men would not have done it. Without polygamy how could the seed of Abraham have multiplied exceedingly?'[35]

Burton's praise for aspects of the Mormon system and his arguments in favour of polygamy seriously ruffled Establishment feathers in England. The *Athenaeum*, reviewing *The City of the Saints*, complained: 'Captain Burton is one of the best travellers we have. One would like him better if he had a little more faith and a little less credulity.'[36] But Burton was the least naïve man imaginable and his *obiter dicta* on Mormonism certainly do not come from the pen of an ingenuous or credulous man. 'The mind of man most loves those errors and delusions into which it has become self-persuaded, and is most fanatic concerning the irrationalities and the supernaturalities to which it has bowed its own reason,' he wrote. Those are not the words of a man likely to have been convinced by *The Book of Mormon*. In fact, Burton spent much time in the literary circle of Monkton Milnes (Lord Houghton), having a good laugh at the 'Saints'' expense.[37] His later remarks are no more sympathetic. He commented waspishly that since Muhammad no man had claimed to be a great prophet and got away with it; the most signal failure in this field was Joseph Smith.[38] In old age his cynicism increased, and the final reference to the 'Saints' in his *oeuvre* talks of 'the shallow imposture of Mormonism'.[39]

Burton's impressions of the United States revealed a sharp disjuncture between his generally favourable view of individual Americans and his distaste for the political and social system they represented. Writing the following year (1861) he summed up this dichotomy in the American: 'He is a favourite wherever he goes, by reason of a certain freedom of manner which is liked everywhere save in England. The only pity is that he should ever appear in print. Then he is compelled by Public Opinion – that tyrant which renders the Free Republic the worst of despotisms – to introduce some fustian "bunkum" and *ad captandum* sneers concerning kings and queens, lords and landlords, the decadence of England, the oppressively brilliant prospects of the United States, the blessings of a democracy, and the curses of limited monarchy, till every New World reader thinks himself, very vainly, a shining light to those who dwell in the outer darkness of European civilization.'[40]

Burton's views on the United States cannot be fully understood without an awareness of chronology. His emphasis on the dark side of North America deepened as the years went on, culminating in a vitriolic outburst against those critical tormentors in the New World who could not see the merits of his translation of the *Arabian Nights*.[41] Even less can his views be appreciated unless they are placed in the general context of British reservations about life in the United States in the nineteenth century.

Anti-American sentiment has taken many different forms over two centuries. In the twentieth century political and economic critiques have predominated, with the United States in the dock over its global economic empire and its use of the Third World as 'international proletariat'. Another strand has been the cultural criticism that derives from psychoanalysis (surprisingly so, in view of the avidity with which that dispensation has been embraced by Americans). It is a view associated particularly with Freud, Jung and Otto Rank, that the USA is the repressed and alienated society *par excellence*. The criticisms made by British travellers in the nineteenth century were a world away from such concerns and at heart centred on the anomaly of 'two nations divided by a common language', to use the Shavian formulation.

Critical perception of the USA among Britons sharpened after about 1825. Up to that time most travellers from the sceptred isle had been emigrants from the middle or working classes, in search of work. As the great peace of the post-Waterloo years made its impact, there arose a new breed of traveller from the upper and professional classes, seeking new sights and experiences. By this time the frontier had moved on. In the Jacksonian period the cultivated manners of New England and the eastern seaboard – the main experience of Britons of the pre-1825 generation – gave way to the rougher mores of the expanding frontier. Culture shock was thus bound to be greater. At the same time, fearful of Chartism and other radical manifestations, the Tory élite began a sustained campaign in their reviews such as *The Quarterly* and *Blackwood's* to discredit egalitarianism at its imagined source in the USA.

The result of these changed circumstances was a wave of British travellers profoundly critical of their hosts. Broadsides were directed at American culture and folkways along a wide spectrum, from eating habits to slavery. Each traveller found his or her own special target for ridicule: the endemic violence, the fondness for nostrums and quack medicines, the cynicism of the yellow press, the emancipation of women. For some it was the maniacal taste for luxury that most offended; others professed incredulity at the American tendency to live in hotels and boarding houses. From some of these animadversions Burton dissociated himself. But in other cases he pitched in with sufficient vehemence to be regarded as the pack leader, or at any rate the most vehement and articulate spokesman of those who regarded the USA as, in George Borrow's words, 'the home of all cant and humbug'.

Slavery was a burning issue especially for female travellers.[42] As has been seen, the 'peculiar institution' failed to move Burton deeply. He was more concerned to attack the 'cant' of abolitionists and philanthropists. Nor did the rough ways of the South bother him. He related with amusement, but no particular sympathy, how an unmarried woman was run out of town with her lover simply because of the 'moral turpitude' of 'living in sin'.[43] As a man of the Right who believed in 'that good old remedy, the sword', Burton was undisturbed by the prevalence of lynch law, and he agreed with an earlier traveller, Captain Frederick Marryat, that summary justice was justifiable on the frontier, where the only law was the gun, or in other cases where the law had proved itself an ass.[44]

The rough ways of Americans never ceased to amaze their transatlantic cousins. Even veteran 'trenchermen' professed themselves amazed at the way food was bolted: one famous instance dealt with the despatch of an entire dinner in twenty minutes.[45] Far more objectionable was the near-universal habit of tobacco chewing among American males. When the railways made their debut, the floods of tobacco juice squirted all over the 'cars' frequently forced travellers to take refuge on the observation platforms. Even Burton, used to the strange customs of the Gogo and Danakil, found this aspect of American culture hard to take.[46] The problem was compounded by the fashion, as in modern China, for spitting; passengers on trains could expect to find missiles of phlegm flying over their shoulders or plopping at their feet. 'America is one long expectoration,' said Oscar Wilde in a newspaper interview during his visit to the USA in 1882. G.A. Sala, travelling during the Civil War, had similar feelings: 'To attempt to describe any phase of American manners without frequent reference to the spittoon is impossible. It would be like the play of *Hamlet* with the part of Hamlet omitted.'[47]

Another source of amazement to travellers was the American

partiality for strong liquor. De Tocqueville pointed out that whereas in Europe a young man might go out to a dance or some public entertainment to spend a leisure hour, his American counterpart would go home and shut himself up for some private drinking.[48] Captain Marryat took his hosts to task for this:

> The 4th of July, the sixty-first anniversary of American independence. Pop-pop-bang-pop-pop-bang-bang-bang! Mercy on us! how fortunate it is that anniversaries come only once a year. Well, the Americans may have great reason to be proud of this day, and of the deeds of their forefathers, but why do they get so confoundedly drunk? Why on this day of independence, should they become so *dependent* upon posts and rails for support? . . . There is something grand in the idea of a national intoxication. In this world, vices on a grand scale dilate into virtues: he who murders one man is strung up with ignominy; but he who murders twenty thousand has a statue to his memory, and is handed down to posterity as a hero. A staggering individual is a laughable, and sometimes a disgusting spectacle; but the whole of a vast continent reeling, offering a holocaust of its brains for mercies vouchsafed, is an appropriate symbol of gratitude for the rights of equality and the *levelling spirit* of their institutions.[49]

Burton, a hardened drinker himself, was not worried by this manifestation of the spirit of the 'land of the free'. Indeed, there is a strong circumstantial case that he ate up his patrimony in just such debauchery.

Nor would the absence of 'culture' in the European sense have affected Burton as it affected other eminent Victorians. Ruskin declared that he could not bear to visit a country devoid of castles; Matthew Arnold found America 'so uninteresting, so without savour and without depth'; while Henry James found his native land suffused with ignorance and a grudging, stingy, defiant attitude towards everything European: 'The Englishmen I have met not only kill but bury in unfathomable depths the Americans I have met. A set of people less framed to provoke national self-complacency than the latter it would be hard to imagine. There is but one word to use in regard to them – vulgar, vulgar, vulgar.'[50] But this scarcely affected the man who had witnessed so many different civilizations in four continents. The absence of cathedrals, Norman ruins and Roman remains was a trifle to the man who had experienced despair in the deserts of Harar, hunger and thirst in the Hejaz, and the horrors of a small-pox epidemic at Kilwa in East Africa.

Much the same consideration applies to the other 'horrors' pointed to with contempt by the most anti-American of the travellers of this hemisphere. The wooden architecture, free lunches, rocking chairs, the mania for ice and seafood, the quick-bolting 'heavy grubbers' of the inns, the tavern keepers who could not understand a man who objected to sleeping two to a bed, the emotional excesses of 'camp meetings', the sharp prac-tice in business, the philistine lack of interest in the arts, all these he could shrug off as quaint folkways, but not as interesting to the anthropologist as the circumcision, infibulation and clitori-dectomy of savage tribes. Moreover, Burton had a blind spot when it came to sophisticated analysis of advanced political structures. The corruption and latent anti-democratic tenden-cies analysed by de Tocqueville or, at a slightly later date, by Walt Whitman in *Democratic Vistas*, were matters that passed him by or in which he had no interest.

Thus far at least Burton dissociated himself from the main currents of anti-American sentiment. But there were two in-fluential travellers with whose views he had a strong affinity. Perhaps the most notorious of all nineteenth-century British critics of the USA was Mrs Frances Trollope, who swept into her net almost every conceivable aspect of American behaviour. 'I do not like their principles, I do not like their manners, I do not like their opinions . . . I never saw an American man stand or walk well . . . In England the laws are acted upon, in America they are not,' such were merely warm-up remarks before Mrs Trollope hit her stride.

She denounced the boorishness and absurd prudery of North Americans. At Pennsylvania Academy in Philadelphia, for example, the gallery of antique statues was never visited by both sexes together: it was either all men or all women. She made fun of the alleged inability of Americans to speak or pronounce words properly. She exposed in hilarious detail the impertinence of strangers and their rank inquisitiveness about another's business. She pointed to religious persecution and the poor health of the inhabitants. She excoriated their rudeness, to such biting effect that after the appearance of her volume it was said that the easiest way to silence a loud-mouthed lout in the theatre was to raise the cry, 'A Trollope! A Trollope!' The flavour of Frances Trollope's writings can be gauged from this remark on the town of Avon in New York State: 'It is a straggling ugly little place, and not any of their "Romes, Carthages, Ithacas or Athenses" ever provoked me so much. This Avon flows sweetly with nothing but whisky and tobacco juice.'[51]

But Mrs Trollope decisively joined hands with Burton in her denunciation of American women. She described them as the least attractive in the world, in poor health, of highly nervous disposition, and with no middle period of womanhood between infancy and marriage.[52] This was very much grist to Burton's mill, for he was firmly convinced that the American female was neurotic to the highest degree, with a morbid fear of pregnancy. Many years after *The City of the Saints* he repeated the charge: 'Especially in the case of highly nervous temperaments – and these seem to be increasing in the United States and notably in New England – the fear of nine months' pains and penalties makes the sex averse to the "deed of kind".'[53] *The City of the Saints* itself teems with Burton's pseudo-scientific or 'sociological' asides on 'the sex', none of them favourable. 'I remarked to my companion the change from the lymphatic and the sanguine to the bilious-nervous, and the purely nervous temperament, and admired its results, the fining down of redundancy in wrist, ankle and waist . . . Men protect their women in two ways. Either, as Orientals, they keep them out of temptation; or, as we do, they expose them freely, but with the gaslight of publicity turned full upon them . . . In Canada the freedom is carried to excess, quite as much perhaps as in the United States, but in the latter women are accompanied by the revolver and the bowie knife.' Here we notice the perennial conviction in Burton that women have to be rigidly controlled and protected from their own 'weakness'.

Burton's conviction that relations between the sexes were more difficult in North America than in Europe, chiefly because of 'female neurosis', has been repeated by many critics right into the twentieth century. In the nineteenth he had many allies among British observers. Harriet Martineau denounced the inability of her American sisters to articulate any other sound except a whine or a twang; de Tocqueville referred to the 'strange restlessness' of the US female; William Baxter claimed to have seen few beautiful girls in the entire continent; James Silk Buckingham remarked the especial failure of young women to take exercise or care for their health.[54] Perhaps the most biting criticism came from Anthony Trollope. He indicted the American male for excessive chivalry and deference to the female. He thought excessive the ubiquitous provision of 'ladies' rooms': in hotels, on steamers and ferries, and even at the Post Office. In New York he noticed with bitterness the way women pushed themselves into public vehicles, accepting seats as of right and without a word of acknowledgment to the men who proffered them. He thought the American female 'uppity' and 'out of line': 'the best right a woman has is the right to a husband, and that is the right to which I would recommend every young woman . . . to turn her best attention.' There is a Burtonesque ferocity about the following: 'For myself I have entertained on sundry occasions that sort of feeling for an American woman which the close vicinity of an unclean animal produces . . . If there be two of them they talk loudly together, having a theory that modesty has been put out of court by women's rights.'[55]

The other notable critic of the USA whose findings Burton echoed was Charles Dickens. Burton was indifferent to the three main targets of Dickens's *American Notes*: slavery, the penal system and copyright piracy, but wholeheartedly endorsed the strictures in *Martin Chuzzlewit* on the peculiar American combination of boastfulness and thin-skinned intolerance for the mildest criticism from outsiders. As Dickens wrote in his private correspondence: 'I am quite serious when I say that it is *impossible*, following them in their own direction, to caricature that people. I lay down my pen in despair sometimes when I read what I have done, and find how it halts behind my own recollection.' And again: 'I believe there is no country, on the face of the earth, where there is less freedom of opinion on any subject in reference to which there is a broad difference of opinion, than in this.'[56]

This was an uncanny echo of de Tocqueville on the same subject. Describing the impatience with the smallest censure and the insatiable desire for praise from strangers, the great French historian hit the nail on the head: 'Nothing is more embarrassing in the ordinary intercourse of life than this irritable patriotism of the Americans. A stranger may be well inclined to praise many of the institutions of their country, but he begs permission to blame some things in it, a permission that is inexorably refused. America is therefore a free country in which, lest anybody should be hurt by your remarks, you are not allowed to speak freely of private individuals or the state, of the citizens or of the authorities, of public or of private undertakings, or, in short, of anything at all except, perhaps, the climate and the soil; and even then Americans will be found ready to defend both as if they had co-operated in producing them.'[57] Mackay explained this as the peculiar American loyalty to institutions rather than places; the boastfulness could then be explained as the reflex action of each man who considered himself bound up in the success of the political system. But it is true that this trait in the American character was underlined by virtually every British traveller in the New World.

This takes us to the heart of Burton's misgivings about the USA. He found it suffused with cant, intolerant, shallow, dedicated to the lowest common denominator and bewitched by a 'rage for equality'. In 1860 he was prepared to exempt a few noble souls like Emerson from his general strictures. 'The American character mixes transcendentalism with the purest literalism, as Mr Emerson, the Sufi, contrasts with the Pilgrim Fathers and Sam Slick.' But as the years went on, Burton's attitudes hardened as he saw the triumph of 'mobocracy' consolidated. 'Few Anglo-Americans can afford to confront the crass and compound ignorance of a "free and independent majority",' he remarked scathingly. No one in America could resist the remorseless levelling down of all tastes and standards 'unless he can afford the luxury of telling unpopular truths, and of affronting Demos, the hydra-headed.' He detested 'the glorification of mediocrity, of the average man and woman, whose low standard must be a vow to statesman and publicist.'[58] Like many other commentators he saw American 'liberty' as mere licence and the much-vaunted 'freedom' as merely the substitution of the tyranny of the majority for the tyranny of kings and aristocrats.[59] 'This disposition of mind, whose favourable and laudable presentations are love of liberty and self-reliance, began with the beginnings of American history. The "Fathers", pilgrim and puritan, who left their country for their country's good and their own, fled from lay tyranny and clerkly oppression only to oppress and tyrannize over others in new and distant homes.'[60]

The triumph of the lowest common denominator seemed to Burton evident from the dearth of great writers produced by the USA. 'The vast country has produced a few men of original genius, such as Emerson and Theodore Parker, E.A. Poe and Walt Whitman, but the sum total is as yet too small to leaven the mighty mass.'[61] To Burton this was a mere actualization of the latent tendencies in American society first adumbrated by John Keats when he wrote, 'Dilke, whom you know to be a Godwin perfectibility Man, pleases himself with the idea that America will be the country to take up the human intellect where England leaves off – I differ there with him greatly – A country like the united states [sic] whose greatest Men are Franklins and Washingtons will never do that – They are great men doubtless but how are they to be compared with those of our countreymen Milton and the two Sidneys – The one is a philosophical Quaker full of mean and thrifty maxims, the other sold the very Charger who had taken him through all his Battles. Those Americans are great but they are not sublime Men – the humanity of the United States can never reach the sublime.'[62]

A similar judgment was entered by Samuel Butler: 'I do not think America is a good place in which to be a genius. A genius can never expect to have a good time anywhere, if he is a genuine article, but America is almost the last place in which life will be endurable at all for an inspired writer of any kind.'[63]

For Burton the root cause of all the ills of the United States was a kind of mindless egalitarianism which insisted on the equality of all at all levels, spiritual, intellectual, creative, aesthetic, but significantly excepted the most important equality of all: money. It was held to be 'élitist' to claim superior knowledge, education, intellect or understanding, but it was considered a concomitant of 'freedom' that the most glaring inequalities of wealth and income should persist. For Burton this was the profoundest of all fallacies: as he put it, 'we all row in the same boat but not with the same sculls.'[64] He facetiously recommended a sound flogging for all Americans, to remind them that all men were *not* created equal.[65]

It was not surprising, then, to find him pitching into the 1776 Declaration of Independence with rare gusto. 'It is regrettable that so trenchant a state paper should begin with so gross and palpable a fallacy. Men are not born equal, nor do they become equal before their death days even in condition, except by artificial levelling, and in republics and limited monarchies, where all are politically equal, the greatest social inequalities ever prevail. Still falser is the shibboleth-crow of the French cock: *Liberté, Egalité, Fraternité*, which has borrowed its plumage from the American Bird O'Freedom.'[66]

Burton's irritation with the United States led him to many a self-righteous smirk during the Civil War. His position was very like that of Walter Bagehot who wrote in *English Feelings Towards America* at the beginning of the Civil War, 'We rejoice that they are weakened, not because we derive gratification from their mortification, or desire to take advantage of their misfortunes, but because they both over-estimated and abused their strength, and because this over-estimate and this abuse were bad for them as well as disturbing to us.'[67] Characteristically, Burton expressed this point of view with more force in *Stone Talk*:

Wouldst like the bagman Cobden, see all
Perfection in one beau ideal
The dis-United States – and plan
For John the fate of Jonathan
Manifest fate of Uncle Sam
Whom wiser men call 'Uncle Sham'.[68]

There were many fiercer critics of the United States than Burton in the nineteenth century, some of them Americans.[69] But it is typical of Burton that he should work his anti-Americanism into symmetrical form and thus come full circle from his critique of the United States to what he considered its *reductio ad absurdum* in Mormonism. 'When the vexed passage, "We hold these truths to be self-evident, that all men are created equal," written in 1776, is interpreted in 1860, it must be read, "all (free white) men" to be consistent and intelligible. Similarly "persons bound to labour" must be considered a euphemism for slaves. The "American Mirabeau" Jefferson, who framed the celebrated

68

Declaration, certainly did not consider, as the context of his life proves, slaves to be his equal. What he intended the Mormons have expressed.'[70]

II
BRAZIL

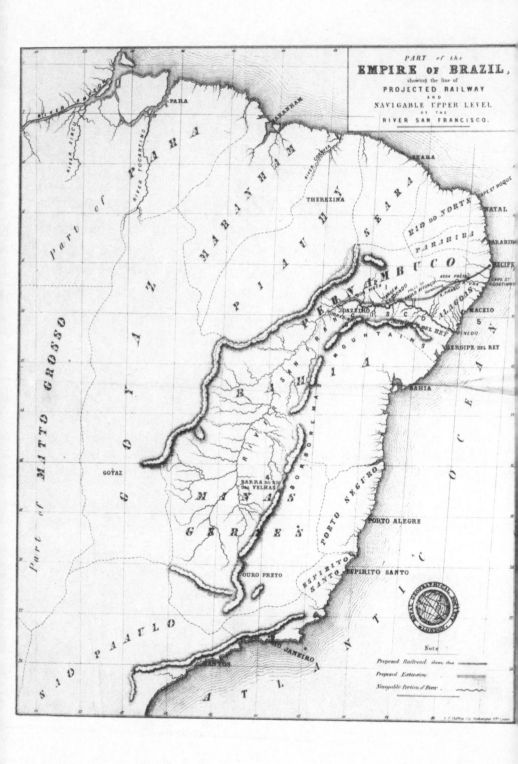

PART of the
EMPIRE OF BRAZIL,
showing the line of
PROJECTED RAILWAY
AND
NAVIGABLE UPPER LEVEL
OF THE
RIVER SAN FRANCISCO

Note
Proposed Railroad shewn thus
Proposed Extension
Navigable Portion of River

Part of MATTO GROSSO

Part of PARA

RIVER XINGU
RIVER TOCANTINS
PARA
MARANHAM
RIVER GURUPY
PIAUHY
THEREZINA
SEARA
RIO DO NORTE
CAPE ST ROQUE
NATAL
PARAHIBA
PARAHIBA
RECIFE
PERNAMBUCO
CAPE ST AGOSTINHO
AGOA PRETA
JOAZEIRO
S. FRANCISCO
ALAGOAS
MACHIO
SERGIPE DEL REY
PENEDO
DEL REY
BORBOREMA MOUNTAINS
BASIN
RIVER SAN FRANCISCO
BAHIA
GOYAZ
GOYAZ
BARRA DO RIO DAS VELHAS
MINAS GERAES
OURO PRETO
PORTO SEGURO
PORTO ALEGRE
ESPIRITO SANTO
ESPIRITO SANTO
SAO PAULO
SANTOS
RIO JANEIRO
ATLANTIC OCEAN

ROYAL GEOGRAPHICAL SOCIETY LONDON

Chapter Four

Imperial Brazil

Almost immediately on his return from North America, in January 1861, Burton married Isabel Arundell. This time she did not hesitate, but chose Richard over her mother, even though that matriarch was never reconciled to the match. But then came another crisis in Burton's life. He lobbied the Foreign Office for a consular post, and was granted the 'governmental crumb' of Fernando Po, a Spanish island in the Bight of Biafra, where he had jurisdiction over all British commercial interests in West Africa east of Lagos. Burton assumed that, like many other army officers, he could remain on the East India Company roll while enjoying his consular perquisites. He overlooked the fact that the Company had been casting about for years for an excuse to be rid of him, and that chill winds were blowing in the aftermath of the Indian Mutiny. The government in Bombay used the excuse of the West African consulate to strike Burton off the India list without giving him a penny in pension. As Isabel bitterly recorded: 'they swept out his whole nineteen years' service as if they had never been, without a vestige of pay or pension.'

Despite the fact that Richard had enjoyed, according to Isabel, seven months of sustained bliss in his newly married state during 1861, he did not take her with him to West Africa when he departed for post in August of that year. Until 1864 all she had of his company was a three-month leave. Meanwhile Burton soon proved as turbulent a subordinate in the Foreign Office as he had been in the East India Company. He was almost permanently absent from post on periods of 'sick leave' which enabled him to climb mountain peaks in the Cameroons, search for gorillas in Gabon and explore the reaches of the lower Congo river. Only the protection of powerful patrons in the Foreign Office shielded him from the collective wrath of the mandarins.

In July 1864 Burton was promoted to consul in Santos, Brazil. He was originally meant to have a mere two months' home leave before proceeding to post but, fortunately for him, the Parliamentary Select Committee on West Africa ordered him to testify before it, then postponed its deliberations until March 1865. The upshot was a two-month holiday in Ireland for the Burtons, followed by a further lotus-eating period in London. Isabel used the time to persuade her husband that this time she should be allowed to accompany him, be the mangrove swamps of Santos never so pestilential.

Lord Russell champed at the bit as Burton's leave stretched into almost a year's furlough. But until Burton had finished giving evidence to the Select Committee, there was little his Lordship could do to despatch the tardy consul to Santos.[1] Finally, the evidence to the Select Committee was completed, and there was no further excuse for delay. Burton's friends saw him off in style. The Anthropological Society of London, which Burton had founded four years earlier, gave him a grand farewell dinner. Burton gave a speech in which he expressed the hope that on his return from Brazil, the Society would have 1,500 members. Lord Derby, who was to become Prime Minister in 1866 and was the father of the Burtons' friend and protector, Edward, 15th Earl of Stanley, delivered a sparkling encomium on the talents of the departing explorer.[2]

At last, on 9 May 1865, Burton and Isabel embarked at Southampton. But they were not bound directly for Brazil. Their first port of call was Lisbon. A certain mystery attaches to this sojourn in Portugal, which the official records do nothing to clear up. If Russell was so keen to get Burton 'on the ground' at Santos, why did he not give him an unequivocal order to sail directly to post? It seems that Burton, the master Fabian, must again have been at work. Although he was fluent in Portuguese, dating from his convalescence in Goa in 1847, and was in any case one of the world's great linguists, perhaps he manipulated the Foreign Office into granting him 'language study leave'. Whatever the case, 16 May found him ensconced in Lisbon's Hotel Bragança, at the beginning of a two-month idyll of travel, rest and recuperation.[3]

But Isabel's mood was sombre in Lisbon. She had experienced her usual bad luck with sea voyages: it had taken them four days to get to the mouth of the Tagus in the teeth of ferocious gales; then, on arrival, despatches from London made it imperative that she return there to sort out Richard's tangled financial affairs (see below pp. 114-8) while he went on to Brazil alone. This was a bitter disappointment, and conditions in the Hotel Bragança did little to lift her spirits. Their room was infested by three-inch cockroaches. The fastidious Isabel got on a chair and screamed at the sight of the insects. Richard had no time for such feminine squeamishness. He rounded on her and pointed out that cockroaches were nothing compared with what was to come in South America. 'A nice sort of traveller and companion you are going to make. I suppose you think you look very pretty, and interesting, standing on that chair and howling at those innocent creatures.' This was exactly the sort of talk to use on Isabel. Besotted with Richard yet fearful that she would not measure up as his mate, she made her determination to be the 'perfect wife' prevail over her visceral repugnance. She got down from the chair, filled a basin with water, and went in search of the cockroaches with water and slipper. After bagging ninety-seven of the creatures, she had, according to her own testimony, cured herself for ever of fear of insects and reptiles.[4]

As a further 'toughening-up' exercise, Richard insisted she attend a bullfight. Secretly appalled at the idea, she gritted her teeth and endured the spectacle; luckily she found the art of the Portuguese toreador less cruel than that of his Spanish counterpart. There followed two months of detailed exploration of Portugal: Sintra, Mafra, Corregado, Sercal, Caldas, Alcobaça, Batalha, Pombal, Leiria, Coimbra, Oporto, Braga, Douro. Then Richard embarked for Brazil. His last glimpse of Europe for four years was El Pichel light.[5] Isabel set sail for England the same day but endured an even worse battering from storms than on the way down. Storm-tossed in the Bay of Biscay, then becalmed and befogged in the English Channel, she did not make landfall until the eighth day out from Lisbon. Burton himself fared better and was in Pernambuco (Recife) on 13 July, after following a track that took him past Madeira, the Cape Verde Islands and Fernando de Noronha.[6]

At Pernambuco Burton had a common experience of European travellers in South America – what might be termed the *senhor doctor* syndrome. Wishing to establish his identity, the men of Recife plied him with questions. Was he a merchant, an engineer, a naturalist? When the answer to this was no, they concluded he must be a *doctor* – the inevitable Latin appellation for anyone of indeterminate middle-class status.[7]

In Recife Burton played another machiavellian card in his perennial duel of wits with the Foreign Office. He requested permission to wait for Isabel either in Pernambuco or Bahia (Salvador), meanwhile visiting Pará (Belém) and the northern provinces of Brazil at his own expense. But he reckoned without Isabel's avidity to be at his side. The request arrived in London on 3 August, by which time Isabel had already concluded her business and was on the point of setting out for Brazil. The Foreign Office deemed that no reply was necessary.[8] Irritated and frustrated that his wife's speed had deprived him of the excuse for a leisurely exploration of northern Brazil, Burton proceeded to Rio.

Even in the 1860s Rio de Janeiro was a spectacular and populous city. The population was more than a quarter of a million or 400,000 including the suburbs. In the ten years before Burton's arrival, an impressive programme of urban renewal had been completed. The city streets were now paved and gaslit, there had been a huge increase in wheeled traffic of all kinds – omnibuses, carriages and other conveyances – while the municipal authorities had set in motion an ambitious programme of railroads and tramways. Landscaped public gardens with ornamental fountains augmented the impression of a thoroughly modern city. The Botanical Gardens, Corvocado mountain and the Sugarloaf were already world-famous landmarks and the desire to enter the amazing natural beauty of Rio harbour at dawn was every traveller's dream. The 'downtown' itself in this era was less impressive. Near the bay the streets were narrow and gloomy and depressing in their geographical regularity: all except the main thoroughfare (the Rua Direita) were drawn in straight lines. As the Mulhalls reported in their *Handbook*: 'some of the streets off Rua Ouvidor are so narrow that when a Brazilian grandee comes along in his mule carriage you must step into a shop on either side to let him pass.'[9]

Burton was able to spend a thorough and leisurely exploration of Rio before departing to his consulate at Santos, where he 'signed in' officially on 8 September, took a room at the Hotel Milton, and reported local commerce in a flourishing state.[10] But he did not tarry there long. Isabel's imminent arrival provided an excuse for another trip to Rio. She meanwhile had sailed from Southampton in a Royal Mail vessel and arrived at Pernambuco on 27 September, to find all the letters she had written to Richard in the last month stacked up unread in the Post Office. She had her usual ill-luck with the elements (rough seas on the stretch to Bahia), then arose at dawn for the spectacular approach to Rio harbour. It was there, on an October morning at 8.30 a.m., that she and Richard were united.[11]

The Estrangeiros Hotel in Rio combined fresh air and beautiful scenery with Isabel's old enemies, cockroaches and mosquitoes. But her first contact with life as a consul's wife was exhilarating and misleading. There was much socializing on board visiting Royal Navy ships and with the British Minister, Mr (later Sir) Edward Thornton and his wife and the rest of the diplomatic corps. Isabel, acutely conscious of social nuances, claimed that her high birth made her immune to the petty snobberies of the divide between 'first-class' diplomats and 'second-class' consuls, and that her 'naturalness' made her far more popular in Rio than her difficult and prickly husband.[12] However, the lady protested too much. She was, in fact, hypersensitive to slights, real and imaginary, from persons who, though her hierarchical superiors, she considered socially beneath her. Such people, in turn, were resentful at this consul's wife who played the *grande dame* and jealous of the way in which Edward Thornton and his wife seemed to defer to her and accept her at her own evaluation.

Burton meanwhile enjoyed living up to his reputation as the reckless amoral man who had 'committed every sin in the Decalogue'. After one particularly bibulous dinner party he suggested to his adoring young male admirers a stroll in the Botanical Gardens. Finding the gates locked, the revellers scaled the walls, only to beat a hasty retreat when they realized that the Gardens formed a nocturnal haven for all the city's snakes.[13]

There was a further delay before Burton took up full consular duties. Isabel went down with fever and exhibited symptoms so alarming that Burton fell back on hypnotism to assuage the worst of her deliriums. As soon as she was over the worst, the couple embarked for Santos in HMS *Triton*. Predictably the elements took a hand. A violent storm blew up and the swells were so huge that the *Triton* had to take refuge at Ilha Grande, just fifty-eight miles out from Rio. They limped on a further seventy-eight miles to São Sebastião – described by Isabel as a carbon copy of the Straits of Messina.[14] Finally the storm-battered *Triton* landed them at Santos on 9 November.

What kind of a society was this empire of Brazil in which the Burtons lived for the next three years? Independent since 1821, Brazil had been ruled since 1830 by Pedro II, son of the first emperor, who abdicated after the decisive triumph of the native Brazilian oligarchy against the old Portuguese élite in the rebellion that year. Five years old at the time of his accession, Pedro was forty in 1865, a proud, stubborn and already rather anachronistic figure.[15] The empire he presided over was a plantation society, mainly confined to a thin coastal strip of port cities and hinterland. The interior of Brazil, to Burton's delight, was almost as much a great white space as the Dark Continent he had penetrated a decade earlier. Geographically divided between plantations and ports, Brazil was rigidly stratified as between masters (white plantation owners and merchants) and slaves (blacks and mulattos) and freedmen: the former possessed the actual power of wealth, military force and control of information; the latter had merely the potential power of numbers. Between masters and slaves was a very small urban-based 'middle sector': bureaucrats, liberal professionals, clerical workers, small shopkeepers, etc.

In the 1860s Brazil was at the crossroads. The plantation economy depended on slavery, yet by 1850 the British had forced Brazil to abandon the international slave trade.[16] Men like William Wilberforce and the humanitarians of Exeter Hall (exactly the kind of people Burton so detested) claimed credit for this, but the major impetus towards the full-blooded military and naval campaigns by Britain to suppress the slave trade was economic rather than sentimental. The British West Indies lived in permanent fear of overproduction of sugar. Abolition of the slave trade would prevent overproduction by reducing the available labour supply. The only question was how to achieve the said abolition. Since Brazil was the major target of the British effort, there seemed to be two main possibilities in the 1820s. Britain's statesmen could either opt for the complete abolition of the Portuguese slave trade, or they could apply trade sanctions through a complete embargo of commerce between Brazil and Great Britain. Since the latter policy conflicted with the desire for profits of London's mercantile classes, Britain plumped for the former.

In return for its assistance during the Napoleonic wars, Britain extracted from Portugal a series of treaties abolishing the slave trade. But after independence, Brazil announced it did not consider itself bound by agreements made by the 'colonial power'. Yet Pedro I was soon (1825) forced to agree to the abolition of the trade as the price for securing British recognition of Brazil's independence. When significant backsliding occurred in the 1840s, Britain announced a naval blockade and the intention to try slavers in her own courts and not through the joint commission at Rio set up in 1825. Brazil faced the threat of a war with the British Empire at the very time she was embroiled in hostilities with the Argentine dictator Juan Manuel de Rosas in the River Plate area.[17] When the British forced the issue by sending its enforcement squadrons openly into Brazilian ports, Pedro II backed down and agreed to the final cessation of the slave trade (1853).[18]

One of the reasons Burton was so popular with Pedro II and the 'old' aristocracy was that he made no secret of his contempt for his country's behaviour in this regard. His particular animus was reserved for the 'Aberdeen Bill [which abolished the Brazilian slave trade], one of the greatest insults which a strong ever offered to a weak people'. He frankly thought abolition and prevention a waste of money. Would it not be better to cut out the blockade of the slavers and use the money instead to pay for the passages to Brazil of the million paupers in England who were on Poor Relief? The presence of such free labourers in Brazil would bring about the spontaneous euthanasia of slavery. Instead 'we still devote fifteen vessels of war, 1,500 men, and nearly a million of money per annum, to support a coffin or sentimental squadron, which has ever proved itself powerless to prevent negro-export, whenever and wherever black hands were in due demand, and whose main effect upon West Africa has been to pamper Sierra Leone, that Hamitic Sodom and Gomorrah, to fill a few pockets, to act as political machine for throwing dust into the public eyes, and greatly to increase the miseries of the slave and the misfortunes of his continent.'[19]

Behind the contingent reasons for the ending of the Brazilian slave trade was a more profound factor relating to inchoate changes in socio-economic structure. In a word, the centre of economic and political gravity began to shift from the sugar plantations of north-eastern Brazil to the coffee-growing areas of the provinces of Rio de Janeiro, São Paulo and Minas Gerais. Until 1870 this was a geographical rather than a qualitative shift: Brazil remained a plantation economy producing primary crops for the international market. But the changing power base from sugar to coffee removed one of the pillars of pro-slavery sentiment; it was thus cause rather than consequence of abolition. Even more importantly, the coffee growers and miners of gold and diamonds of Minas Gerais needed the kind of investment in infrastructure which would come only with an injection of British capital. The British at all costs had to be humoured.

During the years of Burton's consulate Brazilian society was riven with the fundamental 'contradiction' between a backward-looking plantocracy and a more progressive capitalist class in the 'new' provinces of São Paulo and Minas Gerais. If the abolition of the slave trade represented, at least in incipient form, the triumph of the latter, the virtually simultaneous Land Law of 1850 ensured that the plantocracy retained the monopoly of access to the virgin lands of the interior. Their motive was to control the impact of Europe. European capital investment inevitably meant also European immigration. It was vital for the interests of the plantation aristocracy that they seal off the frontier from European immigrants, so that they could not own land. Only then could a continuing pool of cheap labour be guaranteed.

Overlaying this complex mosaic of latent social conflict in the 1860s was the convulsive war with Paraguay. Exactly what led Brazil to become embroiled in the politics of the River Plate in

1864, so that she ended by forming a Triple Alliance with Argentina and Uruguay against the dictator Francisco Solano López of Paraguay, remains mysterious. Part of the reason seems to have been a crude imperialism, in which the personality of Pedro II played a significant part.[20] Partly Brazil was motivated by fears that the cattle-rich province of Rio Grande do Sul would secede if Uruguay ceased to be independent; this consideration was a staple of Brazilian power politics. Whatever the reason, the Paraguayan War of 1864-70 had a profound and, ultimately, devastating impact on Brazilian society, though its effects were pent-up and not immediately discernible.

Superficially, as the novels of Machado de Assis make clear, for Brazil the Paraguayan war was a remote affair which scarcely impinged on the consciousness of élite society in Rio. In this respect the impact of the conflict may be compared with that of the Napoleonic wars on the universe of Jane Austen. But beneath the surface powerful currents were awash, some of them so strong that they would eventually inundate the Empire itself.

At the simplest level, the Paraguayan war drained Brazil of its blood and treasure. There were 100,000 Brazilian deaths from battle or disease. Expenditure on the war topped $300 million. High taxation and an uncontrollable credit explosion brought the economy close to collapse. The impetus towards complete abolition of slavery was quickened. It was not just that Brazil was the only free nation in the world that practised slavery – and had been so since Abraham Lincoln's Emancipation Proclamation of 1863 – and therefore courted the powerful enmity of the USA. Beyond this, the need for huge war loans from London bankers placed Brazil further in thrall to British policy on slavery. Although the sugar plantations of the north-east could manage for a while with the existing pool of slaves, the more important coffee nexus of the south/central areas was increasingly running short of labour. European immigration would mean further concessions by the plantocracy to European labour demands. Finally, many slaves actually won their freedom in return for fighting at the bloody theatre of war in Paraguay. Pressure for complete abolition was bound to increase when slaves and freedmen fought alongside abolitionist nations and *against* abolitionist Paraguay. The squeeze was being exerted on Brazilian slavery from all directions. In August 1866 following a petition by French abolitionists to Dom Pedro, the government announced 'the emancipation of the slaves, a necessary consequence of the abolition of the slave trade, is only a question of form and opportunity.'[21]

But the impact on slavery was not merely direct. All major wars convulse the social structure of participants; the Paraguayan war was no exception. Indirectly slaves were affected by the revolution of aspirations. The *caboclos* or poor whites drafted into the Army had their eyes opened to new worlds and new ideas, and refused to return to the old ways. The spread of new and 'dangerous' ideas had a 'knock-on' effect on the slaves themselves. They became more aggressive and less deferential towards their masters. Edward Thornton reported that in the town of Constitución in São Paulo province a slave owner was fired on by his 'property' as he dismounted at his front door. When another slave owner was murdered in the same province, no less than thirty slaves came forward, each eager to claim credit for the 'heroic' deed.[22]

The war also stimulated scientific, technological and geographical progress, as do all wars. Interest was aroused in the extreme western provinces of Mato Grosso. By the end of 1866 the Amazon was open to international navigation. New roads and railways were built, telegraphs constructed, navigation improved, and in general technological change accelerated. The naval arsenal at Rio produced ironclads, while the munitions works and textile factories of São Paulo had to work overtime to satisfy demand. The war marked the beginning of Brazilian industrialization and an incipient shift away from the primary products of sugar and coffee (though this was always an extremely relative tendency), and this was helped by the modern financial and banking methods introduced by Baron Mauá.[23]

Most obviously of all, the war catapulted the military to the forefront of Brazilian political life. Before the war the Army was a tool of the politicians and bureaucrats. By the end of the conflict it was already the 'sorcerer's apprentice'. The mounting casualty lists in Paraguay carved gaping holes in the officer class and led to the rise of a new career officer typified by men of lesser social status than the old aristocratic colonels and majors. The shared experience of war fostered a feeling of camaraderie and solidarity, which in turn forged bonds of professionalism and engendered a novel sense of purpose. New commanders arose who owed their position entirely to military skill, and were thus not the playthings of politicians. The Army, rather, became 'politicized' in a different sense: it perceived itself as having special interests distinct from those of the general ruling class. Its ideology owed little to the imperial ideas of Pedro II: it took its inspiration instead from the liberalism of Bartolomé Mitre and Domingo Sarmiento, the two Argentine presidents, and thus ultimately from the positivism of Europe.

The rise of the Army signalled the beginning of the end for the imperial dynasty and the rural latifundia class, though in the 1860s this was still only a latent tendency. Other factors were the settlement of veterans on homesteads and the coming end of slavery, most vividly signalled by the 1871 Rio Branco bill, which declared that all children born to slave mothers were thenceforth free. Most important of all was the changing perception of monarchy. The new infant élites in the cities began to form their own power bases, independently from the plantocracy, and taking their inspiration from northern Europe, thus destroying the final vestiges of Portuguese cultural influence. The monarchy was increasingly seen as serving the interests of the older power blocs in Rio and the north-east. São Paulo province became especially restless. Its local élite saw itself underrepresented in the national political arena even as it shouldered most of the country's financial burden through the tax revenues on its coffee.

Indeed 1868, Burton's last year in Brazil, saw a clear conflict between the irreconcilable interests of the old and the new. Forced to choose between his military commander, the marquess (later duke) of Caxias, a staunch Conservative, and the president of the current ministry, Pedro II opted for his favourite, with disastrous long-term results. In order to indulge Caxias, who refused to work with the majority liberals, Pedro broke with precedent and chose for him a political collaborator among the minority Conservatives. When the Chamber responded with a vote of no confidence, the emperor dissolved it and called for elections so as to deliver the government to the Conservatives. The liberal opposition considered this a *de facto coup d'état*. The various factions in the new urban élites drew together to present a united front against Pedro. By the end of the 1870s their party manifesto was calling for an end to the empire. With the Army and professional classes already alienated, Pedro managed in the 1880s to add the clergy to his list of enemies. The final abolition of slavery in 1888 alienated his old stalwarts in the landowning aristocracy. The manumission of three-quarters of a million slaves was followed the next year by the abdication of Pedro himself and the establishment of a republic.

Burton was not a close observer of politics or socio-economic structures, so that the latent conflicts in Brazilian society largely passed him by. In any case, as a close friend of the emperor and in general an ideologue of the Right, Burton was fully in sympathy with all the most reactionary elements in Brazilian society. The two most popular subjects for social conversation were slavery and the Paraguayan war. 'Where my personal experience failed, it was not difficult to turn to account that of others,' he recorded about the war, in typical Burtonian half-ironical style.[24] But sometimes the war came closer to home. On one occasion he was approached by two British sailors, who threatened to write to *The Times* if Consul Burton did not rescue them from the predicament they had cast themselves in. It seemed that they had been paid $200 for taking the place of two Brazilians who had been drafted to the Paraguayan front. They promptly spent the money, then appealed for consular protection against the draft as subjects of Her Majesty.[25] They chose the wrong man for their operation. The last thing in the world Richard Burton feared was a letter to *The Times*. As for his superiors at the Foreign Office, he had already lost count of the number of complaints sent to them by British subjects overseas whom he refused to humour.

On slavery Burton was more forthright. Whether in Brazil, Africa or the Southern states of the USA, he always claimed to be better informed on the subject than anyone else and reserved a full measure of venom and contempt for the *bien-pensant* philanthropists and 'bleeding hearts' of Exeter Hall and the Anti-Slavery Society. He claimed that all educated Brazilians wanted to see an end of slavery, but that it was an economic necessity until large-scale immigration took place. In any case, British sentiment against Brazilian slavery was largely cant and humbug; the slave had many of the legal rights of the free man and was not exposed to the chill winds of the free labour market.[26] The myth of the 'happy slave' was always one of Burton's favourite fantasies, and he was never more exhilarated than when castigating missionaries and their allies over the exaggerated evils of the 'peculiar institution'.

Chapter Five

Daily Life in Santos and São Paulo

'If she found herself in a coal hole, she would have set to work to arrange the coals to the best possible advantage,' Isabel's official biographer said of her.[1] She needed all her famous toughness at Santos, for the port was in 1865 little more than a glorified mangrove swamp, where the sand ran up into the jungle and the heavy seas threw whalebones into the consular garden. On the beach were some scattered houses, chiefly used by the sea-bathing residents. The strand was dominated by an antiquated fort, supposed to have guarded the entrance to the estuary in colonial days. On the eastern seaward approach were the Alcatrazes, a set of rocks which towered hundreds of feet from the sea and were a notorious navigational hazard. It was true that the scenery around Santos was breathtaking. On the coastal side was a picturesque range of hills while across the estuary folds of green-covered mountain ranges fell away into the distance. But the town itself was a dismal affair – no more than a collection of warehouses for storing coffee and cotton, clustered around a single 'Main Street' which contained some good shops and a single theatre for the delectation of the 10,000 inhabitants. There was no piped water, mains drainage or gas lighting in the town, and the rude streets were paved with roughish stones which shod Europeans found almost impossible to walk on.

Exposure to the rigours of the place brought on a recrudescence of Isabel's fever. Once recovered she wrote in despair to her mother:

I do hate Santos. The climate is beastly, the people fluffy. The stinks, the vermin, the food, the niggers are all of a piece. There are no walks; and if you go one way, you sink knee-deep in mangrove swamps; another you are covered with sandflies; and a third is crawling up a steep mountain by a mule path to get a glimpse of sea, beyond the lagoons which surround Santos.[2]

It was decided that Isabel should escape to a healthier climate as soon as possible. She took a 'diligence' – no more than an open van drawn by seven mules – up on to the Serra and thence to São Paulo, in Brazil's 'highlands'. Burton's consular duties required his presence both in Santos and São Paulo, so it was settled that the two of them would take turns commuting between the two centres; they rationalized the task by arguing that the hard riding would be good for their health. But Santos never agreed with Isabel. On her second visit there, she tried sea-bathing but once again caught fever. Once well enough to travel, she preferred twelve hours' riding 'post' in the saddle to São Paulo to another minute spent among the sandflies, mosquitoes and mangroves.

São Paulo was much more to her taste. She began by renting (for £15 a month) a large apartment in a house in the highest, and therefore driest and healthiest, part of the town. She had four rooms to herself and the use of three others plus kitchen and servants. The arrangement was that Richard would not come up to São Paulo until she had provided a comfortable home. She began by unpacking her fifty-nine pieces of luggage, washing and storing the trunks, then airing the contents. This took her and her Irish maid Maria twelve days, during which they worked from six in the morning until late at night. Next she installed the English iron bedstead with spring mattress she had brought from London. She then began to gather around her the nucleus of a household staff. First to be hired was a maid, Kier. Then came the appointment she regarded as a genuine *trouvaille*: Chico. Chico was a coal-black midget, thirty-five years old and four feet high; he quickly made himself indispensable to Isabel. Her letters home purred with his praises. 'There is something superior and refined in my dwarf, and I treat him with the same consideration as I would a white servant. I see that he has plenty of good food, a good bed and proper exercise and sleep.'[3] She was not averse to engaging slaves, but salved her conscience by telling the unfortunates that they had souls and would be her equal in heaven. She prided herself that she had a happy household and never had to dismiss a single servant.

The awesome megalopolis of the late twentieth century was in the 1860s a sleepy provincial town of 25,000 inhabitants (out of a total Brazilian population of some nine million). In some ways it was the microcosm of a model city, for it possessed a hospital, barracks, gasworks, four banks, four printing offices, three public libraries, four newspapers, steam sawmills, breweries, distilleries, cigar factories, foundries, a cotton factory, an orphanage, a prison and penitentiary, a lunatic asylum, as well as a casino, clubs, tramways and botanical gardens. In other ways the abiding impression on the newcomer was that of a South American Heidelberg. The academic and contemplative life was well represented. A cathedral, five convents and three Protestant chapels provided the sacred side; the various colleges and the library, with its 10,000 volumes, the secular. The *paulistas* were proud of their 500-seater theatre, which was almost as large as that at Covent Garden and got all the best plays from Rio. São Paulo was also the seat of a provincial legislature (with thirty-six members), in addition to sending four senators and nine deputies to the imperial chambers at Rio. Finally, it was the headquarters of the provincial military commander, who had two regiments of the line on garrison duty throughout the province, and could call on 60,000 National Guardsmen.[4]

São Paulo was in 1865 a pretty straggling town on a hill, which ran down to high tableland. From a distance the clearest impression was of the ubiquitous whiteness of the houses, picked out against the well-wooded and watered landscape, with views of mountains in all directions. It always reminded Isabel of Bergamo in Italy.[5] In some ways it was already ahead of Rio, for a material resembling tarmacadam had been brought down from the neighbouring hills and used to make first-class paved roads, with the quality of pavement superior to that in the national capital. São Paulo was noisy out of all proportion to its size: old-fashioned wagons or carts on two solid wheels, drawn by oxen or mules, plus a plethora of riders of mules and horses with tinkling bells, created an impression of metropolitan bustle. 'A number of carriages and tilburys are constantly in motion, conveying passengers about the city or the outskirts, causing a degree of activity one would otherwise hardly expect to find.'[6]

The suburbs, studded with elegant country houses and plantations, stretched away to the river Tiete and brought the total population of greater São Paulo to some 67,000. Isabel found the climate too hot from 9 a.m. to 4 p.m. during the summer, but agreeably cool at all other hours. After Santos it was a paradise. Mosquitoes and jiggers could be endured by mere reflection on the fact that at the foot of the Serra these pests were joined by a multitude of others: snakes, jaguars, wild cats, centipedes, spiders, fleas, cockroaches, bugs and sandflies.

Her main complaint about São Paulo – and one in which the money-obsessed Richard joined vociferously – was the expense of living there. Even drinking water had to be purchased, at 3d a gallon. It was impossible for a 'gentleman' with no means but his consular salary to live at the level expected of a full-time representative of Her Majesty's Government. Consular life soon impressed on the Burtons the sober truth that England was the cheapest country in the world and London the cheapest capital. Burton later estimated that his annual outlay, on a consular salary of £650 a year, was £1,800 at Fernando Po, £1,500 at Santos and £2,000 at Damascus.[7] He later told the Consular Committee in London that his salary had been woefully inadequate and that he had had to dip into his own savings; £700 in Brazil went only as far as £300 in England. The Committee asked him how his predecessor (a baronet) had managed. Burton's reply was scathing: 'By living in one room over a shop and washing his own stockings.'[8]

But expense was only one aspect of life in São Paulo that initially militated against Isabel's pleasure in the temperate climate. This was her first time outside the cosy aristocratic circles of Europe, and her early letters evince clear signs of culture shock:

It is a fast and immoral place without any chic or style. It is full of students, and no one is religious or honest in money matters and I should never be surprised if fire were rained down upon it, as in a city of the Old Testament, for want of a just Brazilian . . . The English here mislead one about expenses. I am obliged to buy my own experience, and I do not expect to shake down into my income for three or four months more. The English like to appear grand, saving all the while; and they like to show me off as their lady consul, and make me run into expenses, while I honestly want to live within £700 a year, and have as much comfort as that will allow me . . . Only fancy, the Brazilians are dreadfully shocked at me for working! *They* never do anything but live in rags, filth, and discomfort at the back of their houses, and have one show room, and one show dress for strangers. The eighth deadly sin here is to be poor, or worse, economical.[9]

No sooner had Isabel settled into her apartments in São Paulo than she became discontented at the amount of casual social calling by her French landlady. She determined to find a new abode, to be rented from an absentee landlord, so as not to be bothered in this tiresome way. Even as she began looking, Richard arrived in São Paulo (16 January 1866), fresh from his investigations into the province's gold and diamond mines. Ever on the lookout for 'get rich quick' schemes, and perennially smitten with 'gold fever', he had reluctantly concluded that Brazilian gold was too far-flung and 'broadcast' to be worth prospecting for. He quoted approvingly the South American proverb: 'A silver mine brings wretchedness; a gold mine, ruin.'[10]

As if to demonstrate that Richard was a disruptive influence even in the calm of the first married home the Burtons had had together, his first sojourn with Isabel in São Paulo was marked by elemental eruption. On the very day after his return, a freak force fourteen storm struck the town. Doors and windows of houses were stove in as if on a ship at sea. The tempest blacked out the infant city, ripping up trees in the suburbs in the 150 m.p.h. winds, and cutting a swathe through the central areas. Red lightning flashed overhead as floods cascaded through the streets. Miraculously, no more than five people were killed. Then Nature's destructive surge ceased as suddenly as it had begun. Next day was hot and sunny, as if the typhoon-like winds had been a dream.[11]

Such violent storms were a feature of life particularly to be dreaded in the summer months of December-January, when temperatures soared to 115°F. They would appear from nowhere, with the wind force of genuine hurricanes. Balls of red, blue and yellow fire would appear flickeringly in the sky, the thunder and lightning was deafening, all the windows in the house would invariably be broken. On one occasion a bolt of lightning shivered Richard's study window and set fire to a rolling atlas on canvas.

One of the features of the household Richard immediately took exception to was the way Isabel fussed over Chico and spoiled him. Burton, who detested blacks of all denomination, resented the privileged position the dwarf occupied in Isabel's affections. Whenever Richard was away, which was often, Chico took the second horse and rode out at Isabel's side. She explained that in spoiling the midget she was making reparation for the cruel way Brazilians treated blacks. But her husband was not the right person to address on this issue. A convinced negrophobe himself, he thoroughly approved of keeping the black man 'in his place'. He bided his time, waiting for Chico to make a false move. The occasion came sooner than he expected.

About six weeks after Isabel hired Chico, she found him roasting her favourite cat over the fire. In fury she knocked him to the ground. In rushed Burton, in high delight. 'Brava! brava! I knew it would happen, but I did not think it would be quite so soon.' He ordered severe punishment for the hapless Chico, who pleaded vainly in self-defence that all Brazilian negroes were brought up to be cruel to cats. Once 'rehabilitated' and in predictable awe of his master, Chico took to aping Burton exactly, not just in dress but in demeanour, body language and opinions. Isabel related with a certain amount of pride: 'Each of the best families had one of these intelligent negroes; they used to give supper parties, and then stand up and make speeches, just like us. Mr Aubertin's used to talk about the railway shares, and the value of cotton, and used to stand up and speak of the "benighted souls of the black man and the brother" but our Chico used to declaim on "the Negro's place in Nature", as he had heard Richard do in his lectures, and talk of the progress that they had made from the original ape (Darwinism) and how they might eventually hope to rise into a white man.'[12] When Chico got into further scrapes in Burton's absence, Isabel could not resist divulging this to her mother, absurdly coupling the information with a plea that Mrs Arundell refrain from telling

Richard, who would insist on Chico's dismissal. She had evidently forgotten that her mother hated Richard and refused even to acknowledge his existence.

This is not the place to rehearse the various ways in which the Richard-Isabel 'idyll' was a far from happy marriage. But one of the more obvious symptoms was the amount of time Burton chose to spend apart from his wife. He would disappear for months on end on his own private explorations, giving only the vaguest hints as to where he was going. It was a case of 'watch and wait, for thou knowest not the hour when the master cometh'. It became Isabel's principal task to mystify the Foreign Office as to her husband's exact whereabouts at any given time. She retaliated by making lightning, unannounced visits to Santos when she knew Richard was there. But the fevers and squalor of Santos always drove her back again very soon.

Since Isabel burned Richard's diaries, it is not possible to plot on a day-to-day basis exactly where he went on these mysterious rovings.But a number of asides and casual references in his *oeuvre* enable us to reconstruct part of his wanderings. In November 1865, after Isabel left Santos for the healthier upland climes, Burton set out on a sea voyage to the mouth of the Rio Grande via São Sebastião Island, the San Sebastião Channel and Ubatuba. He thrilled to the sight of the Brazilian forest rising above and behind the mangroves: 'the Rhine in summer can show nothing like the might and majesty of this "Flowery Forest".'[13] He was amazed to find that because of the screening effect of the Alcatrazes – a fringe of scattered islets lying low on the water shortly after the mouth of the Rio Bertioga and shaped like an elephant's back – in calm weather it was possible to travel the sea route from Santos to Rio de Janeiro by canoe. His genius for languages enabled him to relate to the local fishermen in their own terms and in their own dialect. Part of the reason for Brazil's dear food became clear after one conversation. 'As at Fernando Po, the fishermen can easily clear £5 by a single day's haul; yet with all this wealth at hand, the people, from the Amazons to the Plata, actually import *bacalhao* (salt cod) from Newfoundland, and, with the sea at their feet, they will not take the trouble, or rather it is not worth their while, to lay out *salinas*. One of the divers boasted that he could remain ten minutes under water, and I put him on the path of making a fabulous fortune in

England or in the United States.'[14]

From March to May 1866 Burton was travelling in the interior of São Paulo province. It was here that he came upon some survivors of the notorious millenarian sect, the *Sebastianas*, who were rumoured to sacrifice women and children to hasten the second coming.[15] He himself was suspected of clandestine purposes (to wit, spying) when he visited a commune of French scientists and was turned away ignominiously, only to be summoned back with an apology when the community realized that the man they had barred the door to was *le grand Capitaine Burton*. The wilds of inner Brazil were a haven for all manner of eccentric sects and deviant groups, from defeated Confederates from the Southern states to the ultramontane Mennonites. In this respect, the interior of Brazil was to 'civilized' South America what Brigham Young's Utah was to the United States. Sure enough, in time Burton lit on his favourite sept of outcasts, from whom he sometimes claimed descent: the gypsies. On 3 May 1866 while riding from Rio Claro to Piracicaba in the province of São Paulo, he spent the night in an encampment of gypsies who actually owned black slaves. 'The scene was familiar: the tilt-tent swarmed with dark children, the pot hung from the triangle, and horses and ponies for carriage, and perhaps for sale, were picketed about. The features and complexions were those of the foreign tinker; the women, besides trumpery ornaments of brass, coral and beads, wore scarlet leg-wraps; and some of the girls were pretty and well-dressed as the memorable Selina, of Bagley Wood, Oxford.'[16]

Burton returned to São Paulo to find that Isabel had effected the move into her dream house – an old refurbished convent at 72 Rua do Carmo. The whole was gleaming with new paint and represented at last what Isabel regarded as suitable accommodation for a consul and his wife. But if she expected privacy after the incursions of her first landlady, she was at first disabused. The 'absentee' landlord turned out not to be so absent after all. He asked for the loan of the newly decorated chapel for the christening of his grandchild. Thinking the ceremony would not last longer than an hour, Isable consented. Six hours later a riotous party was still in full swing. By this time she had recovered from her initial culture shock and could take this sort of thing more in her stride. Bit by bit she was coming to appreciate the dazzling beauty of the landscape and the exotic flora and fauna. 'Some of these South American scenes are very lovely and on a magnificent scale. The canoes paddling down the river, the sun setting on the mountains, the large foliage and big insects, the cool, sweet-scented atmosphere, and a sort of evening hum in the air, the angelus in the distance, the thrum of the guitars from the bucks going home from work – all add to the charm.'[17]

What Isabel missed most of all was social life. Sometimes they went to a local oligarch ball, which lasted until sunrise. More often she, either alone or less often with Richard, attended the local *paulista* dances and *festas*: 'the gentlemen and the ladies dance as furiously as the Hungarians do the *czardas*, and the negro girls come to *their* balls *décolletée* in blue and pink cotton.' Occasionally, too, there were picnics at the very spot which marked the Tropic of Capricorn. But most of all she longed for the company of other Europeans. One of her first contacts was a young Englishwoman who died suddenly of yellow fever; in alarm at possible contagion, Richard took her on a gruelling ten-hour horseback ride to 'sweat out' the fever traces.

Dr and Mrs Hood, who lived at the foot of the Serra, were close friends but too distant for Isabel's purpose. A better bet was the Aubertin family. J.J. Aubertin, Company Superintendent of the Santos and São Paulo Railway, was one of Richard's few close friends. Three years older than Burton but just as devoted an enthusiast of the Portuguese epic poet Camoens, Aubertin served eight years in Brazil and received the Order of the Rose from Pedro II for his work.[18] He and Burton would spend long hours in the forest, discussing abstruse points of Camoens exegesis. He later produced a translation of the *Lusiads* which many critics account superior to Burton's. So keen was Isabel for the Aubertins' company that in the rainy season she used to put her best gown, shoes and pearls in a bag, mount up barefoot in her waterproof, and ride through the floods to her hosts' home.

Inevitably, then, much of the Burtons' social life centred on the railway that was being laboriously constructed over the Serra between Santos and São Paulo. Occasionally there would be grand dinners, attended by the entire English colony of São Paulo province, usually when some railway 'swell' was going home. Isabel early displayed her fearlessness (or recklessness) as an adventurer. The Burtons attended a launch party at the head of the Serra to celebrate the completion of the railway to that point. Nearby was a huge chasm with a seemingly bottomless drop over which the future railway would have to pass. Planks had been laid across, and while the corks popped, Isabel set out to walk the 200 yards to the other side. Only when she reached the other side did she become aware that no one had followed her, and that her husband and the others were gaping at her with stupefaction. Appalled by the danger, Richard had turned white with shock. By sign language they gave her to understand that the return was too dangerous and that she should come back another way over solid ground.[19]

The railway was the great talking point of São Paulo province in more senses than one. The nearest indigenous Indians to the town were the Botocudos. Lured by stories of the 'iron horse' they came down to São Paulo to investigate but found the monster more of a malignant beetle. Tempted on board the tender, they jumped off precipitately and ran for their lives when the whistle blew.

Yet there were only so many attractions in São Paulo to hold the attention of the cosmopolitan Burtons. As early as April 1866, just six months into his tour, Burton petitioned the Foreign Office for leave to go to Rio on 'urgent business'. His masters were not pleased by the request. Lord Clarendon granted him leave but pointed out tersely that he had already been on leave for two years out of five since he first became a consul. 'Such continual absence from your duties renders your services very unsatisfactory.'[20]

The Burtons very soon made clear just what was this 'urgent business' that drew them to the fleshpots of Rio. Richard intended to lobby the Brazilian government for a mining concession, in flat contradiction of his consular position. While the lobbying went on, the Burtons intended to enjoy themselves. Isabel had already acquired a taste for diplomatic receptions, and for Richard there was the attraction of the Diplomatic Club. The Alcazar theatre also hosted performances of Offenbach's operas and ballets shortly after their Paris premières.

The Imperial Palace, the original seat of Dom Pedro I, was located at Petrópolis, and it was to this 'Simla' of Rio, at 2,800 feet on a mountain slope, thirty-six miles from Rio bay, that the diplomatic community gravitated. Pedro II, who was an amateur scientist and fancied himself imbued with progressive European ideas, was keen to meet Burton. The first meeting was a twenty-minute private audience, and was a great success. Burton liked to intimidate people with his sinister physical presence: six feet tall with broad shoulders, drooping Chinaman moustaches and a swarthy, scowling appearance set off with the hideous scar he had received from a lance thrust at Berbera in 1855. But at six foot two, the broad-shouldered, chestnut-haired, blue-eyed Pedro, virtually an absolute ruler, went in fear of no man. Each recognized the other's strength, and from this grew subtle bonds. The second time they met, Pedro kept Burton talking for two and a half hours on Brazilian problems. On the third occasion Pedro started to treat his guest as one of the family and introduced him to his two sons-in-law, the Duc de Saxe and the Comte d'Eu, later Allied commander-in-chief in Paraguay. The Empress for her part took to Isabel on the strength of their common devout Catholicism. It was made clear to the Burtons that they would be welcome at the palace any time they cared to visit.[21]

Diplomatic protocol and the carefully graded Foreign Office hierarchy were soon thrown into chaos by the imperial family's partiality for the Burtons. At one reception in the palace the consuls were put in one room and the Ministers in another. Pedro at once sent down word that the Burtons were to go into the Ministers' room, which caused much fluttering in the diplomatic dovecots. Feathers were further ruffled when the emperor's aide-de-camp appeared at the door of the ministerial room and beckoned to the Burtons. When the true Ministers surged forward, the aide stopped them in their tracks. 'No, no, not you, gentlemen, but Captain and Mrs Burton.' After this the ambassadorial corps was so furious that when Burton later gave a grand dinner for his 'superiors', few of them deigned to appear.[22]

One night at a ball for Princess Isabella, Pedro noticed that Burton was not dancing and asked him why. 'I never dance, Your Majesty,' came the reply, ' – that is, not often; but the last time I did so, it was with the king of Dahomey, to the music of cutting off heads – in pantomime of course.' Pedro smiled, and the conversation turned to Burton's mission to the barbarous king Gelele of Dahomey. So enthralled did the emperor become at the recital that he asked for a private lecture on Burton's travels for his family. Later that month in Rio, Burton obliged with an 'edited highlights' version of his 1853 pilgrimage to Mecca in disguise.[23]

It says a great deal for Edward Thornton that he did not take against Burton for so signally stealing the limelight, even as the consul barefacedly lobbied for commercial interest. Although Thornton was obliged to express his misgivings on the mining concessions score, he was shrewd enough to see that Burton's friendship with the emperor was a great public relations asset for Britain. Consequently he and Mrs Thornton treated the Burtons as equals rather than hierarchical juniors, which drew from Isabel the appreciative remark: 'I am very fond of our Minister and his wife, Mr and Mrs Thornton, and I am very proud of them; they are people we can look up to.'[24]

In Rio Isabel thought it safe to swim in the sea, for the surge and thunder of Santos beach was absent. One day she started to swim out to a log about one hundred yards off shore. Suddenly the 'log' moved and proved to be a large shark. She beat a terrified retreat to the beach, aware that Brazil boasted two notorious breeds of man-eater, the *turbarão* and *mero*.[25]

Burton continued to enthral the diplomatic community with his travel anecdotes and tall stories. Homosexuality was always one of his interests, and he liked to hold forth on his theory that pederasty was a common practice among the Tupi Indians of Brazil until moderated by European influence. Putting himself into the third person, as ever, Burton described one incident thus: 'One of HM Consuls used to tell a tale of hilarity provoked in a "fashionable" assembly by the open declaration of a young gentleman that his mulatto "patient" had suddenly turned upon him, insisting on becoming agent.'[26]

Burton had been granted just one month in which to transact his 'urgent business'. Apparent triumph was snatched from him when, having been granted the concession to the gold and lead mines of Iporanga, he learned that the Council of State had raised a last-minute objection. Isabel was obliged to stay on while Richard returned to São Paulo to demonstrate to Lord Clarendon that he had kept his promise meticulously.[27] He rationalized his enforced return with a later 'sour grapes' remark on Rio: 'the beauty can look "ugly" enough when she pleases.'[28]

Isabel's good spirits soon evaporated in the tussles with Brazilian bureaucracy. She was for ever being promised a final resolution, only to find some new hitch or delay supervening. Worst of all, the new friend she had made in Rio, Mrs Elliott (daughter of Sir John Plackett and married to Admiral Elliott, son of Lord Minto), left when her husband was promoted, and there was a tearful farewell at the dockside. The combination of loneliness and frustration brought her out in such a severe attack of boils that she could not sit down. Not until 11 August did she secure the assurances on Richard's behalf she required.

What of Richard betimes? On this occasion a more bizarre adventure than usual beckoned him, as Isabel explained to her mother: 'Richard is gone to look after the sea serpent (but I do not tell this, as it might get him into a row with the Foreign Office). I forgot to tell you there is said to be a sea serpent here one hundred and sixty feet long.'[29] Burton himself confirmed that he was on the trail of a monster said to be 216 feet long and to swim like a snake. 'On August 1st 1866, I entered the Rio de Una, which now divides the municipalities of Santos and São Sebastião. My visit was for the purpose of inspecting a "gigantic marine monster" which had found its way into the papers . . . it became, in fact, a regular dragon of Wantley, which, with a tail unreasonably long, devoured the shepherd as well as the sheep.'[30]

Here Burton revealed himself as a true Victorian. While modern science is not yet in a position to say *for certain* that a marine animal roughly fitting the description of a 'sea serpent' does not exist, the odds have seriously lengthened against the possibility since the nineteenth century. Then, the 'monster of the deep' was taken as seriously as spiritualism – another Victorian fetish and again one of Burton's abiding interests. For a decade from 1817 there were sightings off the East Coast of the USA, especially at Nahant and Lynn Bay. The authority on sea serpents, Bernard Heuvelmans, catalogued more than 500 sightings in 150 years. The Victorian *locus classicus* was the report of HMS *Daedalus*, Captain Peter M'Quhae, in 1848. While cruising off the East Indies, this nineteen-gun frigate reported an unidentified creature, sixty feet long with a large snake head of four feet, holding on a south-westerly course for a full twenty minutes at the astonishing speed of twelve knots.[31]

Alas for Burton, when he arrived at the bar of the Una what he found was the ninety-nine-foot skeleton of a blue whale. He had to settle for a few days' exploration of the lead diggings in the São Sebastião area, then proceeded to the town of São Sebastião by sea instead of road. This proved to be a mistake, as Burton recorded: 'We put off for the coast of São Sebastião, which appeared a dark cul-de-sac, hardly inviting even to a returning fisherman – it sadly wants a lighthouse. Hardly had the oars dipped a dozen times when a simoom-blast came ploughing the sea like a tornado, and a succession of three huge waves raised us from the water and tossed us ashore, as if the large boat had been a walnut shell. A few contusions were the only result. The people rushed down to our assistance, and we met with the usual kindly reception of shipwrecked mariners at the hospitable house of Mattheus de Montra.'[32]

On Burton's many visits to São Sebastião in 1865-8 he always lodged with a bachelor friend, Benedito Fernando Coelho, who was president of the municipal chambers. A friend was useful in this territory, for the *Sebastianos* did not take kindly to strangers. In 1863 a rambunctious and drunken Frenchman was later found 'drowned' after annoying the locals. Each time Burton found some fresh aspect of the locality to reconnoitre. On this occasion the target was the 'sugarloaf' mountain of São Sebastião Island, where he and Commander Napier had first landed in September on HMS *Triton*. On 5 August 1866 he stood on the summit and took in the panoramic view of the largest island between the River Plate and the mouth of the Amazon. Next he investigated the great source of antimony, on the coastland immediately facing the island. He rounded off his trip with another visit to Ubatuba.[33]

The return to São Paulo was as fraught as the outward journey. All Burton would ever divulge to Isabel was that he had tried to emulate the locals by canoeing back through the ocean from Ubatuba to Santos, that his canoe had capsized, and that he had spent two days clinging to the craft in a heavy swell before local fishermen picked him up. On 12 August he crawled in, depressed and crestfallen, to the Burton home on the Rua do Carmo, to find Isabel had returned from Rio just hours before. For a few days Richard was grateful for home comforts. He found himself in a risible position, given his dislike of clerics and clergymen, when he had to officiate at the marriage of an English couple. 'Fancy him doing parson,' chuckled Isabel, who rejoiced at the prospect of a wedding feast which began at 5 p.m. and continued boisterously into the night with eighty bibulous, dancing couples.[34]

Two days after his return, Burton learned that his defence of British nationals dismissed from their jobs on the railway (see p. 113) had put him in bad odour with the railway syndicate, Aubertin's championship notwithstanding. In a pointed snub, neither Isabel nor Richard were invited to the *festa* to celebrate the completion of the length of track permitting the first train journey between Santos and Jundiaí. Burton never took kindly to slights. He had to wait until November for the last laugh, when person or persons unknown sabotaged the new railway line. Meanwhile he took himself off in dudgeon to make a retreat with the Capuchins at their *chácara* or country house. Though normally not over-enamoured of contemplatives and recluses, Burton was fond of these monks, as they were by far the best educated men in the province. His particular friends were Fray João, with whom he studied astronomy, and Père Germain, with whom he jousted over physics, metaphysics and algebra; Burton's favourite vade-mecum after the Bible and Shakespeare was Euclid. Also, there was a martial spirit to these Capuchins that Burton admired. One of them was an ex-cavalry officer, whom, all unknowingly, the local bully was foolish enough to call out. After imbibing a few glasses of *aguardiente*, this braggart liked to saunter up to the gate of the monastery and shout out: 'Come out, you miserable, petticoated monks, come out and fight!' After a few days of saintly restraint, the ex-officer's tolerance snapped. He emerged from the cloisters, challenged the bully to a fist fight, quickly made mincemeat of him, and warned him of the consequences if he ever showed his face outside the monastery again.[35]

But in early September Richard had had enough of domesticity and was on the move again. He set off into the wilds with two companions, three horse boys and a long string of mules. The hapless Isabel was given the task of going up to Rio again to lobby for finalization of the Iporanga concession. She found an epidemic of cholera raging among the diplomats and, according to her own account, narrowly escaped death only by a strict diet, constant exercise and a non-stop round of purposeful activity. Even so, a mild dose of the cholera which assailed her at 3 a.m. one morning caused her to make a will and settle her affairs in the belief that she was dying.[36]

It is clear that for much of her time in São Paulo Isabel was putting on a brave face to mask the disappointment she felt at Richard's almost constant absence. It seemed he preferred almost any form of adventure or activity rather than being at her side. Her mother advised Isabel to cut her losses and return home rather than be a 'jungle widow' but Isabel felt this would simply play into Richard's hands. 'I have just domesticated and tamed Richard a little; and it would not do to give him an excuse for becoming a wandering vagabond again.' But she felt Richard's rejection keenly, and sometimes the stoical mask slipped, as in this communication with her mother, when Isabel suddenly seeems to realize she has given too much away: 'Nobody knows all the difficulties in a colonial or tropical home till she has tried them – the difficulty of giving and taking, of being charitable and sweet-tempered and yet being mistress with proper dignity . . . I often think a parvenue, or half-bred woman, would burst if she had to do as I do. But do not notice any of this writing back.'[37]

Isabel rationalized her position by a rigid daily routine. She rose at 5 a.m., went for an early morning walk, attended Mass, then to the market and home. If Richard was in residence she would have a fencing lesson followed by a turn at Indian clubs. A cold bath would be followed by a full breakfast at 11 a.m. Then it was time for household administration, unless Richard was there, in which case she helped him with his literary work. She tried hard to master Portuguese, but possessed little linguistic talent, let alone Richard's genius. Richard could move easily among the Romance languages, switching from Spanish to Italian to Portuguese and even Latin at will. Isabel, however, found that she made progress in Portuguese only at the expense of blotting out the smattering of Spanish she already possessed. The day ended early, with dinner at 6 p.m. preparatory to lights out at nine.[38]

When Richard was away – which was often – she loved to ride with Chico in the forests and woods of São Paulo's hinterland. She revelled in the dangers she encountered, as they suggested to her that she was toughening herself suitably to be a true 'mate' for Richard. Once she was charged by two wild bulls. On another occasion a 'cobra' reared up in her path, but wriggled away fearfully into the bush at the sight of the horse and rider. After identifying the species of snake with Chico's help, she had one caught and bottled. Poisonous spiders in aspic soon joined the collection of specimens. On another occasion she had a more serious encounter with a forest marauder. It happened that for once she was riding alone, without Chico. A brigand or high-wayman attempted to apprehend her, and a mounted chase commenced. During her flight, Isabel was thrown violently against the pommel of the saddle when her horse stumbled. The horse recovered its footing and she threw off her pursuer, but the bruise was a serious one. Much later, she traced the cancer that finally killed her in 1896 to this forest incident thirty years earlier.[39]

At home Isabel was reluctantly coming to the conclusion that the hardline Richard had a point, that good treatment of slaves really was self-defeating, as it made them 'uppity'. Her dream of Christian fellowship was shattered by the rigid caste system demanded by her own household staff. Mealtimes stretched out interminably, as each stratum in the pecking order refused to sit down with the one below it. Thus Isabel ate with her guests, then her Irish maid Maria and her brother, who came out to work on the railway. After this the German servants took a separate repast, since they would not sit down with blacks. The freedmen in turn refused to associate with the slaves, so that each meal dissolved into a fivefold relay. The absurdity was compounded by the simple fare that the last three relays ate: largely a mess of beans called *feijão* (sometimes embellished by a savoury sauce and coarse flour which converted the dish to *feijoada*) and scones of *milho* or Indian corn, with butter. Nor was Isabel's temper improved by the reflection that Maria's brother, an 'inferior' at the dinner table, had come out on a stipend of £200 p.a. but by the end of 1866 (before his early death from disease) was earning £600 p.a., almost as much as the 'master of the house' but without any of his expenses.[40]

To the daily difficulties of her life and the sadness caused by Richard's absence was added the normal complement of hazards experienced by anyone living in Brazil. In addition to cholera and yellow fever, leprosy was endemic in the province of São Paulo, though the Burtons never knew a single case where a European caught the disease.[41] Snakes were a constant menace outside the urban areas, and at night even within them. Brazil boasted some of the most venomous snakes in the world, including a single species of rattlesnake (*crotalus durissus*) – as opposed to the nine in North America – the coral snake, the bushmaster and the *fer-de-lance*. The menacing clatter of rattlesnakes could often be heard in long grass. At night the wary traveller took with him a lantern on the end of a stick for fear of the *jararaca-assu* (also known locally as the *labarri*) or *fer-de-lance*, which liked to lie curled up in the middle of the road like a heap of dust. Though not an aggressive snake on the scale of the African black mamba, the *fer-de-lance* (*trimeresurus atrox*) was highly venomous; a single bite could prove fatal. Fortunately the even more poisonous and larger (up to eleven feet) *surucucu* or bushmaster (*lachesis muta*) mainly preferred to lurk in open country or in deserted houses.[42]

In the tropical forests, soldier ants were more of a threat than snakes. There were two varieties, black and red, which had the tenacity of bulldogs and 'allow themselves to be cut in two rather than relax the stubborn hold of their pincers'. Burton reported that in Brazil as in Africa the same rule held good: the ant was king. So commonplace were insect bites that the Brazilians shrugged them off with a euphemism: *imundícias*.[43]

But in the town itself the gravest pest was the jigger (*pulex penetrans*). About the size of a large mosquito, the jigger specialized in burrowing into the human foot and causing lameness. Brazilian negresses had a trick of extracting them with an ordinary pin, after which the pain in the foot stopped at once. This singular pest was unknown in West Africa when Burton was consul there during 1861-4. To his horror, on revisiting the Gold Coast in 1882, he found that Brazil had exported the jigger to Africa, doubtless as a 'compensation' for the slaves it had sucked out of the Dark Continent.[44]

Large hairy spiders were ubiquitous and liked to nestle inside boots and discarded clothing. Yet another menace was the *carrapato* – a kind of cross between a tick and a crab, the size of a fingernail. Anyone riding through a coffee plantation emerged covered with them. Pulling at them merely produced a festering wound, so the only efficacious counterattack was to soak in a hot bath, to which was added two bottles of the powerful local spirit *cachaça*, whose high alcohol concentration did for most of the pests. The tougher veterans had to be dislodged with a lighted cigarette.[45]

In a word, life in Brazil was not easy for a woman of Isabel's cloistered background. All in all, she acquitted herself amazingly well, though sometimes depression and misery clouded her judgment. She found the Brazilians loud and noisy even by Latin standards ('the Brazilians are to the Portuguese what the Americans are to us') and reacted with wounded fastidiousness to the easiness and overfamiliarity of the local matrons: 'the lady's society here is awful; they have all risen out of unknown depths'.[46] The subtext of all this was surely an agonized and lonely *cri de coeur* for the absent Richard.

The object of her affections, meanwhile, by constant travel and assiduous study of all he perceived, built up an encyclopedic knowledge of things Brazilian. His fame as an anthropologist had preceded him, and it is not surprising to find his work full of sharp insights into South American ethnology. Less expected perhaps is the general sociological overview, redolent of Montesquieu, that increasingly informs his observations. As ever, Burton was both original and eclectic. He makes use of Humboldt, Darwin, Wallace and a host of previous South American observers: Bates, Waterton, Gardner, Agassiz and others. At times his insights anticipate those of Freud, Malinowski and Wegener.

Burton was a highly talented amateur geographer, who was fascinated by the real and alleged homologies between Africa and South America, by geological structures (doubtless also with half an eye to mining possibilities) and, above all, like his great source of influence Montesquieu, by the effects of climate. Much about Brazil irresistibly recalled East Africa, even the similarity of their wet seasons. He therefore speculated that in primeval times the mountains of Pernambuco, Rio and other parts of South America adjacent to the Atlantic were connected with the similar and opposite chains that traversed the plains of the lower Congo and Loange.[47] The 'foul Golgotha' of Santos and São Paulo found an echoing counterpart in the West African plateau. Some kind of ancient race-memory, he thought, would explain the odd coincidence that the coronal of feathers (*Aganga Tara*) usually associated with the Tupi-Guaraní Indians, and considered peculiarly 'New World' in character, was also found in West Africa, where it was known as *Kennitare*. The homology between Angola and Pernambuco he found particularly striking: same latitude, same mountains, even the same kind of herring fish, the *Tainha* in Brazil and the *Vela* in West Africa.[48]

Burton's taste for comparative geographical studies also produced a model whereby the difference between east and west coasts in Africa was assimilated to that between Atlantic and Pacific coasts of South America. He cast around for as many illustrations of the principle as he could find. 'The middle Brazil is emphatically a land of rains, whilst Peru and Chili [sic] require artificial irrigation supplied by melted snow.'[49] The theory extended even into geology, the Brazilian coast being granitic and the Chilean consisting of various porphyries. Sometimes Burton was even prepared to reach out for a general theory of geographical causality, as when he mentioned the simultaneity of a *Pacific* earthquake in 1867 with the unusual cyclonic storms that battered the *east* coast of South America.[50] Above all, Burton was passionately interested in meteorology and rainfall. He kept detailed records of Brazilian precipitation, noting regularities and periodicities and the wild variation in climatic experience in such a huge country. In some parts of the empire the rain would fall in torrents for a week; in others thunder was heard no more than three times a year.[51]

But it was as anthropologist that Burton had mainly won the plaudits of the scientific community, and it was in the sphere of ethnology that he gathered his most interesting data. Unfortunately in Brazil he did not have immediate access to a thriving primitive culture, as in Dahomey. The consequent frustration gave rise to some of Burton's later infamous remarks: he claimed that American Indians 'were savages that can interest only Fenimore Cooper'.[52] But his intense interest in the Tupi Indians belies the hyperbole. Particularly in *Hans Stade of Hesse* he reveals a close study of the Tupis utterly irreconcilable with his 'Fenimore Cooper' dismissal. The cannibalism and homosexuality of the Tupi especially intrigued him, and his aside on anthropophagy is twenty-four carat Burton: 'The Tupi-Guaranís of Brazil, a country abounding in game, fish, wild fruits and vegetables, ate one another with a surprising relish . . . old travellers attribute the cannibalism of the Brazilian races to "gulosity" rather than superstition.'[53] He argued that cannibalism is not necessarily the ultimate sign of savagery. Torture was a symptom even more revealing: for example, the Tupis, though cannibals, did not torture their victims, as did the North American Indian. He marvelled at the skill of the South American Indian with bow and arrow. Such was their accuracy that they could pick out and shoot down a man in a crowd.[54]

Burton also seemed more interested in animal life in the New World than he had ever been in Africa. Doubtless it was his long-lived fear of snakes that led to his learned disquisitions on rattlesnakes and boas; but only boundless intellectual and zoological curiosity could produce some of his closely-detailed observations, on the balls of hair found in the stomach of Brazilian cows, on the bald *remedio* dogs, or the tameness of the bulls at Santos. We learn that the piebald horse in Brazil is called a 'garden' (*jardim*), that the mules of São Paulo and Minas Gerais are so trusty that they can pick their way across the firm patches in plashy bogs, and that jaguars and pumas are rarely dangerous to man, preferring as they do the flesh of dogs and monkeys.[55] But it was always ornithology that most appealed to Burton about life in the wild. He marvelled at the profusion and variety of species in Brazil. While he regarded the omnipresent peewits as exasperating spoilsports, other birds amply compensated. His favourites were the 'bull-fairs' who clustered at Gizzard Island and other rocky islets off the Santos coast. Completely without fear of humans, the 'bull-fairs' would peck lazily at intruders' ankles but would not bother to rise from their eggs. When in more sportive mood, they would amuse themselves by 'flirting' with the unfeathered bipeds.[56]

The interest in bird-song, imitative calls and onomatopoeia fed into his general mania for new dialects and languages. Tireless in his compilation of Brazilian variants of Portuguese words and original dialect or slang forms, Burton noted that Pedro II's subjects were particularly talented at reproducing bird calls, which then onomatopoeically passed into the language. Thus *sto fraca, sto fraca, sto fraca* ('I'm weak'), the local imitation of the cry of the guinea fowl, passed into the language.[57] Burton's natural inclination was towards general theories of all kinds:

hence he correlated the East African onomatopoeia for Zanzibar (from *'Zayn za'l barr'* – *'fair is this land'*) with Brazilian Olinda (and later with examples drawn from Argentina). Yet Burton was too good a field observer to be tempted to force disparate material into the same matrix. He conceded that no general theory of onomatopoeia seemed possible when different cultures perceived the sounds of nature so differently. So, for example, the bird known onomatopoeically in the USA as the whippoor-will was, on the same sound basis, given the name in Brazil of *João corta pão* (John cut bread).[58]

It was Burton's meticulous eye for significant detail that made his consular reports such mines of information. Burton's writings provide a synoptic picture of the Brazilian economy, seen not merely through dry statistics but through the refracting lens of the seasoned traveller. There are in Burton's *oeuvre* fascinating asides on sarsaparilla, sweet manioc and Brazilian *bhang* or cannabis, which was well known to the slave population, though few of their owners had heard of it.[59] Burton tells us that Brazilian mutton is inferior to its beef, that the English timber-cutting industry in Brazil never paid its way (though a patent for the manufacture of peat taken out in the early 1860s led to its export from Bahia by the end of the decade), that Brazilian oranges are far superior to the East African variety. In fact, the theme of comparison between the Brazilian economy and that of Zanzibar is a constant with Burton.[60]

Naturally, though, it is Brazil's principal crop, coffee, which engages Burton's particular attention; indeed he later remarked that his two most characteristic mnemonic images from South America were the coffee plantations of Brazil and the orange groves of Paraguay. In Brazil the richest lands were given over to coffee, the next best to sugar, and the worst to cotton and cereals. Burton expertly balances the pros and cons of Brazilian coffee cultivation. On the one hand was the extraordinary fecundity of the land: 'I well remember, at Hyderabad in Sind, that during the inundation of the Indus we could perceive in the morning that the maize had lengthened during the night, and the same is the case with certain toadstools and fungi in Brazil.' On the other was the fact that coffee trees were so rarely thinned that degeneracy tended to set in. Here Burton cannot resist a dig at the literal *bête noire* in his demonology: 'The Brazilian planter, though well aware of his loss, cannot prune his coffee shrub: his hands are all negroes, and if allowed to use cutting instruments, they would hack even the stem.'[61]

It must not be thought, however, that as a traveller Burton was purely a mixture of Montesquieu and Humboldt. He was just as adept at providing the telling detail on which modern travel writers so pride themselves. As Alan Moorehead has remarked about Burton, he misses nothing and can bring to bear on each unique experience a vast range of comparative instances; no one is better at making the kind of original connection between X and Y that would not occur to the ordinary mind.[62] Whether dealing with the swinging suspension bridges over the mountain gorges, or dilating on the differences between the *raki* of Syria and the *cachaça* of Brazil, Burton is always interesting.

From the ragbag of impressions and anecdotes of travel in the Brazilian back country, a few items recommend themselves. There is the 'contradiction' between the primitive nature of transport and the insistence by the Brazilian *senhor doctor* that to travel anywhere on foot is *infra dig*. The contrast between the old-fashioned 'box' and mules used for long-distance travel and the idleness of the Brazilian bourgeoisie never ceased to amaze Burton. It was very easy to become extremely unfit physically in Brazil, for the man going to church or the opera would rather send ten miles for his horse than walk the same number of yards to his destination.[63]

Burton very quickly mastered the bewildering range of local customs, mores and folkways he encountered on his travels. He found the freedman superior in civility to the African slave. He discovered that in the lowlands to pass by a village without paying it a visit was a great insult. He learned that an invitation to drink a *copa d'agua* was the invariable prelude to a sumptuous banquet, but that when you helped your neighbour to a fresh bottle, etiquette demanded that you first pour some drops into your own glass. Every house was supposed to fly its own bunting. The left hand was traditionally used for ablution and so, as in Islam, was considered unclean; for this reason country people would never take snuff with the right hand. Most amusingly of all, he learned that in popular folklore the English were regarded as a race of drunkards – doubtless an extrapolation from the behaviour of matelots on the binge in the major seaports. A magistrate friend of his once, on receiving a constable's report about an *Inglês bêbado* (drunken Englishman), remarked mischievously, 'What a pleonasm!'[64]

The one thing absent from Burton's account of his Brazilian travels is any real clue as to his inner life. A cryptic remark that in Brazil the man interested in sex will always opt for the negress or the mulatta over the creole may or may not indicate that Burton had sampled the said wares.[65] The sole occasion when the man of masks showed his true face was when John Steinhaeuser died. For the superstitious Burton the event had a particular significance. This was his diary entry for 27 July 1866: 'Dream that a bad tooth fell out, followed by five or six drops of blood; noted the day and found that my poor friend Steinhaeuser had died of heart disease quite suddenly in Switzerland that day.'[66]

The truth is that in Brazil Burton felt, deep down, depressed and alienated. It cannot have helped Isabel, in her lonely fastness in São Paulo, to fear or suspect that the reason for her husband's depression and long absences was not so much discontent with the backwater posting of Santos as profound regret that he had ever married *her*.

Chapter Six

Consul Burton

As a Foreign Office functionary Burton left a great deal to be desired. In his first posting, at Fernando Po, he had been regularly accused of running a far from tight consular ship. The accusation continued to dog him in Brazil.

Burton's consular duties in Santos were nowhere near as onerous as those in West Africa, where he had had to oversee the vital palm-oil trade in the Bights of Benin and Biafra. In South America his task was confined more nearly to the official brief laid out in the 1856 *Consul's Manual*, which concentrated on shipping matters. A consul was supposed to be present 'if possible, at the shipwreck of any of his countrymen's vessels' and to see that 'the abuses and plunder on wrecked ships, which generally occur, are not permitted'. Beyond that, consular duties embraced all matters relating to commerce, navigation and manufactures. 'Our Man in Santos' was supposed to remit regular statistical abstracts on the proper forms and through the established channels.

In fact Burton's geographical reports on São Paulo province and its cotton growing were models of lucidity.[1] As he later demonstrated in Damascus, Burton by no means limited his economic analysis to the province where he was consul, but extended it to give an overall picture of Brazil. We learn, for instance, that in 1864-5, out of total exports to Brazil of £13,160,000, Great Britain supplied £6,309,700. In 1865-6 the sums were respectively £13,809,500 and £7,375,100. Then Burton points out that because of the impact of the Paraguayan war, and the resulting depreciated currency and deficient industry, the figures fell; even so Britain exported £6,528,342. To offset this lesser trading performance, Brazil incurred war debts of some £14,000,000 to British financial institutions.[2] Part of Burton's efficiency in the compiling of official statistics can be attributed to the work-horse qualities of his wife. A letter from Isabel in São Paulo on 15 September 1866 lifts a corner on the way Burton habitually devolved the boring parts of his work on his wife. 'I am at present engaged with the Foreign Office reports: I have to copy 1) 32 pages on Cotton reports; 2) 125 pages Geographical Report; 3) 80 pages General Trade Report. This for Lord Stanley, so I do it cheerfully.'[3]

But Burton's superiors at the Foreign Office concentrated on his imperfect office administration rather than his statistical and analytical skills. The consular files for Santos contain frequent rebukes and reproaches at Burton's unwillingness or inability to operate 'by the book'. Irregularity of returns and failure to remit consular fees or to use the proper forms in correspondence form a staple item in the letters between Burton and the Foreign Office: 'what does this mean? pray let dockets be properly written,' is a typical example of exasperation wrung from irritated officialdom.[4]

Burton's defence was that when he arrived he found the Santos consular archive to consist of two baskets full of torn and stained official documents. Clearly he was not the only South American consul who found routine paperwork irksome! One immediate result was that it was not clear who was actually on the unpaid Vice-Consular roll. One José Verqueiro was still shown as Vice-Consul even though London's records indicated that he had resigned in 1858. It took a 160-mile ride to Verqueiro's estate at Yucabá before Burton could sort out the confusion. It transpired that Verqueiro had resigned *twice* in the past but was at present in post with no plans to retire. Burton eventually uncovered a plot to obfuscate the situation and discredit Verqueiro by his enemies in Santos.[5]

But Burton needed a Vice-Consul in Santos itself, who could take over the office while he disappeared on his own extended jaunts. He found such a man in Charles Archibald Glennie, an unambitious romantic drifter, who regarded the post as Santos consul, which Burton so despised, as the acme of achievement. Glennie was a Scot who had come to São Paulo province some forty years before and married a local girl. Never so happy as when attired in kilt, sporran and skean-dhu for a Caledonian occasion, Glennie with his lazy deferential ways made a great appeal to Burton. The consul was happy to leave Glennie in charge for long periods, and actually minuted London that the genial Scot should succeed him at the end of his tour. It seems that there was even some prospect of this, but shortly after Burton's departure from Santos in 1868 Glennie fell ill and died.[6]

Routine apart, there were three main matters which exercised Burton during the consulship of 1865-8: exiles from the Confederacy, the Santos-São Paulo railway, and mining concessions. When Lee surrendered to Grant at Appomatox on Palm Sunday 1865, Brazil became the sole significant and official slave state in the world. As such it was a magnet for die-hard refugees from the Southern states who were adamant that they would never settle down under 'Yankee tyranny'. Almost simultaneously with Burton's advent at post there arrived a General Wood, who commanded a division in the Southern armies. He proposed the settlement in São Paulo province of 60,000 families from the 'Deep South'. A year later one of the Southern preachers, 'Reverend' Mr Dunn, tried to institute a settlement in the metal-rich area of the Iguaçú river. From the British point of view it was imperative that all Her Majesty's Government's efforts to throttle Brazilian slavery by abolishing the transatlantic slave trade should not be thwarted by a back-door reintroduction of the 'peculiar institution' by exiled 'crackers' and 'white trash' from the defeated Confederacy. Burton's warnings were immediately relayed by Edward Thornton to London, and the appropriate diplomatic representations made in Rio.[7]

Altogether some 2,700 persons from the defeated South settled in São Paulo by 1868. In Rio province in 1867, out of a total immigration of just over 10,000 (half of them Portuguese), 1,500 came from the USA, as against 647 English, 220 Irish and 357 Germans. But the principal magnet for Southerners was the province of Paraná, with its capital at Curitiba. This was a favourite place for the wealthier type of Missourian, who brought in much-needed capital.[8] Burton had enjoyed his time in the South in 1860 and had supported the Confederacy during the American Civil War. But he was extremely critical of the men and women from south of the Mason-Dixon line who tried to make a new life in Brazil after 1865. They were *par excellence* 'economic refugees', attracted to Brazil because slavery was legal there. Burton found them prickly, combative, with an eye to the main chance and with all the arrogance and over-weening self-confidence of the uneducated. Instead of the geniality and hospitality he had experienced in the South in 1860, he found hostility and intense suspicion of strangers. 'Nothing appears to satisfy them; whatever is done for them might have been done "a heap deal better". As the phrase goes, they expect roast pig to run before them, and even then they would grumble because the "critter" was not properly fixed for them.'[9]

Burton was also less than enamoured with the attitudes of the entrepreneurs responsible for the breathtaking attempt to build a railway link between Santos and São Paulo, over some of the most formidable mountain terrain in Brazil. English labourers and artisans who had been hired by one of the original British railway speculators found themselves high and dry when the said entrepreneur went into liquidation. The original conditions of service, in the contract with the liquidated company, stipulated the right to paid passage home in the event of dismissal. But the other railway investors announced that henceforth they would refuse to pay the passage home of any Briton who resigned or was dismissed. On the other hand, as Burton pointed out, Consular Standing Orders made it clear that such 'surplus to requirements' individuals could expect no financial help from the Foreign Office. But, Burton protested, surely correctly, the Foreign Office had a *moral* obligation to its citizens.

Meanwhile he had to take executive action to prevent one of the dismissed men, a coppersmith named William Tompkins, from starving. Burton jumped the gun and paid his passage home as a 'distressed British subject'. To avoid the predictable countercharges when Edward Thornton put pressure on the authorities in Rio, Burton explained what 'gross misconduct' as a pretext for dismissal on the Santos-São Paulo railway actually meant. 'Perhaps the man is late at the office or returns an impudent answer to some young mechanical engineer.'[10]

So far Burton's consular interests had resulted in some judicious and exemplary reporting. The same could not be said for his third area of activity. It was an abiding dream with Burton – alas, never realized – to make a fortune from mining, preferably of gold. This 'gold fever' led him to form a mining company in partnership with the Brazilian A.J. Coimbra and then obtain a concession from the Brazilian government. Thoroughly alarmed by this blatant flouting of Burton's consular position, Thornton appealed to London for advice. The Foreign Office minute on the subject contained a severe implicit rebuke for Burton. First, amazement was expressed that Burton should have sought to set himself up as an entrepreneur without permission from London and without the knowledge of his local superiors in Rio. Burton was obviously seeking personal gain and advantage against the explicit instructions issued to every consul, who was told he must not 'recommend his private friends, abroad or at home, for employments of trust or profit under the government of the country in which he resides; and he will not ask or accept favours of that government for himself.' The only cases where consuls were permitted to trade were those when it was in the National Interest. (For example, it would be all right to promote Brazilian railways, subject to the usual permissions. But it could not be said that the opening of mines was justifiable under this rubric.) The upshot was that Lord Russell wrote to Thornton to advise him that Burton's mining concession *was* inconsistent with his official duties and to admonish him accordingly.[11]

But now Isabel lent a hand. Learning that her friend Lord Stanley was about to succeed Russell as Foreign Secretary, she wrote a private letter to him, enclosing the correspondence to date, and asking that he countermand Russell's directive. It is an amazing tribute to Stanley's partiality for Burton that he did exactly what was asked. In March 1867 the Foreign Office forwarded to Thornton Lord Stanley's private letter to Isabel. This made it clear that while he did not officially sanction Burton's acting as a director of the mining company, he was not prepared to prohibit him from this activity, provided he did not get into any financial scrapes.[12] There cannot have been many (any?) other lowly consular officials in the 1860s who could secure the favourable intervention of the Foreign Secretary on their behalf, overturning his successor's decision into the bargain.

The axis Isabel/Lord Stanley was also instrumental in rescuing Burton from the egregious financial mess in which he had embroiled himself in West Africa. There were three main elements in this, in ascending order of importance: a wrangle over expenses while exploring in West Africa; a dispute over expenses in refurbishing the consular house in Fernando Po; and a *cause célèbre* concerning alleged defalcation on the sale of the brig *Harriet*. Much of the consular correspondence in Brazil between Burton and the Foreign Office concerned the after effects of his controversial stewardship in the Bights, and it was still dragging on in 1867 when the explorer left for his journey in the Brazilian interior.

The wrangle over expenses in West Africa was essentially a storm in a teacup, but it underlines Burton's uneasy, Skimpole-like relationship with money. At heart Burton bitterly resented ever having to pay for *anything*. The aetiology for this particular species of unrealism must be sought in his childhood, when his mother 'defrauded' him out of his birthright by persuading Burton's grandfather to leave his money to her half-brother instead of her own son. Whatever the case, Burton's fraught relationship with money involved him in many a joust with officialdom during his consular career. On this occasion the bone of contention was travel and subsistence expenses incurred during July-September 1863 while on a trip to the lower Congo river. Out of boredom Burton had left his post at Fernando Po and taken passage on three separate Royal Navy vessels as far as the mouth of the Congo. His excuse for leaving his post without official permission was 'broken health', though it was an open secret that the true reason was his lust to explore new lands.

Burton claimed that his expenses while on his Congo trip should be defrayed from the public purse; the Foreign Office replied that since Burton was absent without leave at the time, his claim was the merest impertinence. Burton managed to stall by claiming that, irrespective of the disputed question as to whether he had been engaged in personal or official business in July-September 1863, Captain Perry of the *Griffon* told him that he was a guest and would not be charged for anything while on board. The Foreign Office then had to secure Perry's version. Predictably he denied having told Burton he was a guest, but by the time Perry's letter arrived in London (July 1865), Burton was *en route* to Brazil. The reiterated Foreign Office demand for payment, together with a copy of Perry's rebuttal, caught up with Burton in Santos in October 1865.[13]

After much more wrangling, which ended with his salary's being attached by the Foreign Office, Burton grudgingly accepted defeat but struck back by claiming a refund for some £400 he had spent refurbishing the consular dwelling in Fernando Po. The final solution to Burton's expenses was subsumed in the general resolution of the affair of the brig *Harriet*, which threatened for a while to end Burton's consular career in a miasma of charges of peculation and defalcation. Once again, much of Burton's consular correspondence in Brazil was consumed in an affair that took place during the Fernando Po consulate.

The case of the brig *Harriet* had unspectacular origins. The ship had belonged to one William Johnson, but on his death was found to be in urgent need of caulking, careening and other repairs. On 13 August 1863 Johnson's executors authorized Burton to sell the brig at auction. On 21 November a consortium of 'dummy buyers' bought it for £280. The real buyer was Vice-Consul John Edward Laughland, trader in his own right, who used proxies to avoid a charge of 'conflict of interest' between his private affairs and his vice-consular duties. On the day of the auction Laughland was absent on business, but since he and Burton were friends and 'thick as thieves' (to use a not inapposite expression), Burton himself signed the bill of sale in Laughland's absence. From this single Leda's egg was hatched a host of difficulties for the consul.[14]

Burton's consular career was a constant quest for leave, whether authorized or unauthorized. He had left Fernando Po on leave on 7 May 1864. His furlough entitlement expired on 17 September 1864, but then the Foreign Office had played into his hands by asking him to hold himself in readiness to appear before the Select Committee on West African affairs. As it happened, the Select Committee did not convene until the spring of 1865. By the time the Foreign Office notified Burton of the decision to stop his salary, he was in Portugal, on his leisurely way to Brazil, having already enjoyed twelve months' *de facto* leave. At once he saw in the *Harriet* imbroglio a chance to extend his leave still further. He offered to return to England to confer with Laughland and clear up the mess. But the Foreign Office refused to take the bait. Burton was ordered to proceed to post and sort things out from there. This was the real reason for Isabel's depature to London from Lisbon in May 1865.[15]

Since Isabel's and Laughland's story contradicted at all points that of the *Harriet*'s executors, the Foreign Office commissioned Commander Robinson, RN, who was on the spot with the Gold Coast station, to look into the matter and produce an official report. Robinson's report, dated 12 November 1866, was a devastating indictment of Burton, man and consul, and of his stewardship in the Bights during 1861-4. He first pointed up the close personal relationship of Burton and Laughland, then proceeded to detail the Vice-Consul's chicanery.[16]

At the end of 1866 the despondent Burtons' hopes lifted with the appointment of their friend Lord Stanley as Foreign Secretary. But Stanley's bid to rehabilitate Burton was torpedoed by the official inquiry instituted by his predecessor. Robinson's swingeing and damning attack on his favourite placed Stanley in a dilemma. His solution was twofold. In the first place he censored and annotated the worst passages of criticism. Even so, what remained was a fearful indictment. He therefore put pressure on Robinson to withdraw some of the more extreme criticisms of Burton. Robinson would have none of it. He replied that he stood by every word.[17] There was nothing for it, then, but to send out to Brazil a toned-down version of the report. Burton was held fully liable for the £280 owing to the executors. But Stanley sugared the pill by accepting in full the vouchers Burton had forwarded in support of the repair of the consular residence at Fernando Po. These amounted to £401-10-4. After deduction of the £280 owed to Johnson's executors, this left a balance of £121-10-4.[18]

Not until he was on the point of departing from Rio for the interior, and thus could not be recalled for 'impertinent' behaviour, did Burton reveal the depths of his anger on the way he had been treated.[19] He little realized that Lord Stanley had done all he could for him, in the teeth of hostility from his own officials and the Admiralty, and had actually excised Robinson's most biting criticisms. But the philippic he then despatched to London failed to sway the Law Lords of the Crown, to whom Stanley referred Burton's letter. They replied that there were insufficient grounds for altering the judgment of Her Majesty's Government. They added the hardly consoling thought that

Burton could always take legal action as a private individual, either against Laughland or against the plaintiff's solicitors.[20]

So ended the *Harriet* affair, which occupied the greater part of the consular file for Santos in the years 1865-7. Burton's official duties in São Paulo province were light, almost negligible. He received his £650 a year for a near sinecure; Isabel's posturing about a 'small, well-earned salary' betrays her habitual economy with the truth. The irony was that far more of his time than he could have wished was taken up with the backlog from his West African years. Controversy always dogged him whenever he was given an important posting. In that respect his years in Damascus in 1869-71 were to be Fernando Po writ large. Burton often complained about the boredom and inanity of his Santos consulate but, given his propensity for getting into hot water, the Brazilian interlude was an only half-disguised blessing.

Chapter Seven

Liberation

Isabel had to travel up to Rio again in December 1866 to iron out further difficulties over the Iporanga concession. Just before Christmas a weary Burton joined her there. He brought word of a noteworthy find. Around a remote shanty far up the Tiete river was a source of rubies. Moreover, the unsuspecting woman who lived in the shanty was willing to surrender her title deeds to the land round about for a mere £50. Isabel urged Richard to go back and strike the deal; would this not be the fortune they had always dreamed of? Richard demurred: he was unwilling to defraud the woman and anyway after three days they would almost certainly catch fever and end up like the dog in the fable, looking at the shadows in the water.[1]

With a mental shrug of her shoulders, Isabel grudgingly concurred. They proceeded to Petrópolis for Christmas but, chary of Thornton's beady eye, Richard did not tarry there long. He found time, however, to compare the Rio-Petrópolis journey with that from central London to Richmond. Edward Burt, the eighteenth-century traveller, claimed to prefer the view from Richmond Hill to all the grandeur of the Highlands. Burton felt much the same way about Petrópolis as compared with the back country. 'It is no small matter to find within five hours of Rio de Janeiro a spot where appetite is European, where exercise may be taken freely, and where you enjoy the luxury of sitting in a dry skin.'[2]

Once returned to São Paulo, Burton penned a few reports to

London to make it appear that he was at his desk before again heading into the wilderness. He waited just long enough to make an ostentatious appearance at the second inauguration of the Jundiaí railway on 14 February 1867 – this was the line that had been sabotaged the previous November. Through Aubertin, Burton had been restored to favour with the railway company; the seal of the Burtons' 'rehabilitation' was impressed when Isabel was allowed to drive one of the engines part of the way from Robeio to Ubá.[3] Immediately after this Richard departed for the trackless interior with his usual complement of mules.

While he was away, Isabel had to deal with a drunken English sailor, who got into the consular house and refused to leave until his passport and papers were made out. To cover up for Richard's absence, Isabel had to bribe the man with food and money to be rid of him. She implored her mother not to reveal the high price she had to pay to mask Richard's absenteeism, and defended herself against a presumptive charge of being 'soft' by shifting the issue on to general eleemosynary ground. 'Brazilians never give charity; and how can poor people judge between a true Catholic, and a Brazilian one, if some of us do not act up to our religion in the only way that speaks home to them?'[4]

This time illness forced Richard back home after just six weeks. He staggered into São Paulo with fever, only to learn that his eyrie was an eyrie no longer. The municipal authorities of São Paulo were building a new road, and in the process had fenced off a stretch of marshland. The marsh no longer discharged into the Tiete, and the resulting miasmata meant that the whole city was at risk from malaria. It must be remembered that in the 1860s nobody made the connection between malaria and the anopheles mosquito; it was therefore assumed that the source of the disease was 'noxious vapours'. There seemed to Isabel nothing for it but to brave the rigours of the detested consulate at Santos.

She planned a regime of ocean bathing and convalescence, while based in Santos's best hotel. But the 'hotel' proved to be a Swiss-shaped shed, rather like a pauper's cottage in England, with food to match. Here they were plagued by twenty different species of vermin: mosquitoes, sandflies, beetles, *borrachudos*, and others. A woman found a snake winding round her leg while she used the latrine. Other guests were so maniacal about the threat from jiggers and boils that they went to bed swathed in towels. Additionally, the wind was so ferocious that it nearly blew the shanty away. Behind the 'hotel' and all the way to the foothills of the Serra stretched a vast mangrove swamp. Out of fear of leprosy Isabel refused to sleep in the beds provided but slung her own hammock. The only positive memory she retained of Santos was the similarity of the riverine 'bar' at Santos to Cazalem in Goa.[5]

It was not long before the Burtons decided to beat a retreat to São Paulo and rather take the putative risk of malaria than the certain nightmare of Santos. While recovering his strength, Richard wrote a short report on Brazil for the Royal Geographical Society and gave further proofs of his presence to the Foreign Office.[6] With the approach of elections, fighting in the streets of São Paulo between rival factions was an everyday affair, and it was dangerous for foreigners to stir from their houses. This increased Burton's sense of isolation and anomie. He became increasingly depressed and disconsolate, so it was an unexpected pleasure to receive a long letter from his great friend and fellow-hellraiser, the poet Swinburne.

Burton and Swinburne had first met at one of Richard Monkton Milnes's stag breakfasts in 1861. There was an instant rapport, and Burton took the young poet under his wing for an extended course in drunken carousal and other debauchery. As Swinburne lamented when news of Burton's transfer to Santos was made public in 1865: 'My tempter and favourite audience has gone to Santos.' Burton was also one of the first recipients of the highly successful *Poems and Ballads*.[7] His letter to Burton evinces the free and easy spirit of their camaraderie:

Holmwood,
Henley on Thames,
January 11th 1867

My dear Burton,

I was within an ace of losing your letter altogether, and only recovered it from the Dead Letter Office by accident – or rather by the intervention of that all-wise and beneficent Providence which regulates all sublunary things. You may know perhaps that Messrs Moxon and Co., to whom it was addressed, tried to swamp my book by withdrawing it from circulation when the storm of warm water began to seethe and rage in the British tea-kettle, trusting that in British eyes their fraudulent breach of contract would be justified by the plea of virtuous abhorrence. Of course I withdrew all my books from their hands, and declined any further dealings with such a den of thieves. Consequently these denizens of the Cities of the Plain, whose fathers somehow escaped with Lot and his respectable family, pretended ignorance of my address and dismissed a whole heap of letters, papers, and books to the Dead Letter Office. But for this you would have heard from me long ago . . .

I am still the centre of such a moral chaos that our excellent Houghton maintains a discreet and consistent neutrality, except that he wrote me a letter thoroughly approving and applauding the move taken; but I have not set eyes on his revered form for months. Your impending opulence [presumably from the Brazilian mines], and my immediate infamy, will too evidently cut us from the shelter of his bosom. I wish you had been at hand or within reach this year, to see the missives I got from nameless quarters. One anonymous letter from Dublin threatened me, if I did not suppress my book within six weeks from that date, with castration. The writer 'when I least expected, would waylay me, slip my head in a bag, and remove the obnoxious organs; he had seen his gamekeeper do it with cats.' This is verbatim, though quoted from memory, as I bestowed the document on a friend who collects curiosities. I beg to add that my unoffending person is as yet no worse than it was . . .

I hope we shall have you back before '69, not only for the cellar's sake, sublime as that 'realized ideal' is certain to be. I have in mind a scheme of mixed verse and prose – a sort of *étude* à la Balzac *plus* the poetry – which I flatter myself will be more offensive and objectionable to Britannia than anything I have yet done. You see I have now a character to keep up, and by the grace of Cotytto, I will endeavour not to come short of it – at least in my writings. Tell me, if you have time, what you think of *Dolores* and *Anactoria* in full print.

I hope you will prevail on Mrs Burton to forgive the use

made in the former poem of the BVU, whose son I saw the other day mentioned in a tract by a Rabbinical Atheist as 'Joshua ben Joseph'. I wish I could run over to '5 o'clock tea', but can only send remembrances to you both, and hope you will not have forgotten me when you return to this *plaisant pays*.

Toujours à vous
A.C. Swinburne.[8]

Burton replied in good heart, developing some themes on Balzac and Tennyson and with some critical appreciation of *Poems and Ballads* and *Lesbia Brandon*. But his letter was strangely lacklustre, as if he could barely keep depression at bay.[9] Swinburne kept Monkton Milnes in touch with developments: 'I have heard from Brazil. HM Consul at Santos (whom I ought to answer today) writes me renewed congratulations on my success in bruising the head of British virtue. I *hope* Mrs Burton did *not* read Richard's remarks on "Faustine" – *et pour cause!*'[10]

At last, in May 1867, salvation loomed for the depressed Burton. It was his abiding dream to re-establish himself as an explorer; his career in this regard had been in the doldrums since his return from East Africa in 1859. During his month-long sojourn in Rio and Petrópolis in June 1866 Burton discussed with Edward Thornton a possible trip to Cuiabá in Mato Grosso. Thornton at once contacted London for guidance on the handling of this cuckoo in his diplomatic nest. It was perhaps fortunate for Burton that Lord Stanley took over the Foreign Office from Clarendon at this precise juncture. Stanley wrote back enthusiastically about the prospect of Burton's launching into the Brazilian unknown, and gave permission, subject to certain conditions: the Brazilian government should raise no objections, Burton should find a competent substitute in his absence, defray his expenses and make over the local allowances (but not salary) payable at post; most importantly, Burton was to provide Thornton with a detailed itinerary, so that the Minister could recall him at any time or curtail his movements if it was deemed necessary. Here Stanley was surely being disingenuous: nobody with any knowledge of the Brazilian interior seriously imagined it would be possible to 'recall' a traveller once he was beyond the ken of the coastal strip.[11]

Thornton passed on the good news to Burton, but advised that a trip to Cuiabá would entail a traveller's beginning the journey with at least thirty mules. During the Paraguayan war mules in Brazil were as gold dust; this meant his original project was financially impracticable. And even if by some miracle he *did* lay hands on such a team of mules, an overland journey to Cuiabá would take at least two and a half months.[12] Nothing daunted, Burton wrote back with a counter-suggestion. This involved a lengthy ride through the mining areas of Minas Gerais, with a trip down the river São Francisco as a grand finale. But since the rainy season was approaching, Burton suggested a postponement until May 1867. To Thornton's credit he laid aside his reservations on the wilder aspect of Burton's personality and backed his request to the hilt. He pointed out to Stanley that, although the interior of Brazil was little known, it was likely to have considerable commercial possibilities. Burton was just the man to come back with a sheaf of statistics on cotton, slavery and the rest – the kind of intelligence which all European diplomats so signally lacked.[13]

So it was that on 21 May 1867 Richard and Isabel quit São Paulo, leaving the trusty Charles Archibald Glennie in charge of the Santos consulate.[14] The Burtons spent three weeks in Rio, sampling the delights of the 'tropical *belle époque*', mindful of the Spartan conditions to come. Richard was, perhaps, already a little bored with *carioca* society. Certainly the interlude in Rio produced one of his most concentrated working periods. He began by obtaining from Emperor Pedro a *portaria* or licence to travel in the interior. He corresponded with the RGS on the subject of Dr Livingstone, then on his last African journey and lately (though falsely) reported dead. He wrote a report for the Anthropological Society on the prospects for the extinction of slavery. And he threw himself anew into the study of Camoens. When one of Burton's admirers, a certain Mr Cox, threw a grand dinner party in the famous traveller's honour, Burton arrived early but promptly disappeared. When the other guests arrived, there was no sign of 'the Captain'. Someone happened to look up at the highest tree in the compound, and there was the guest of honour, high among the branches, squatting like a monkey. He said he had gone up there to get some peace and collect his thoughts on the beloved *Lusiads*.[15]

At last, on 12 June 1867, the Burtons crossed Rio bay to Petró-polis in a steam launch. Brazil's 'Simla' seemed to Isabel this time 'a German town with Swiss valleys' – what she meant was that there was an Alpine feel to the town, bifurcated as it was by two main streets with a river running between, over which crossed many small bridges, the whole studded with Swiss-style chalets inhabited mostly by Germans.[16]

After a six-day stay they began the journey proper at daybreak in a large charabanc, holding eight people, in two and two, all facing the animals. Fourteen mules sped along a first-rate dirt road that wound around the mountains. Burton's choice of season for travelling was shrewd. The hard and cakey surface that enabled the mules to make such good time would by December be a muddy chaos, churned up by the droves of market cattle. After forty miles driving downhill, they changed mules. Then it was fifteen to twenty miles on the flat in the valley, before a gruelling uphill climb of thirty-nine miles, past the hill stations of Pedro do Rio, Posse and Entre Rios, alternating coffee plantations and virgin forests. At Serraria station they espied the province of Minas Gerais on the far side of the Paraibuna, then came to the overnight halt at Juiz de Fora, having covered one hundred miles in just over twelve hours. Juiz de Fora was memorable to Isabel for its nine different species of oranges: 'I have never tasted oranges equal, before or since.'[17] Richard's associations were very different. He remembered the splendid reception Juiz de Fora had given the Swiss naturalist Jean Louis Agassiz a couple of years earlier. Burton's tribute to Agassiz took the form of some lines from Spenser:

O what an endless task has he in hand
Who'd count the seas' abundant progeny,
Whose fruitful seed far surpasseth that on land.[18]

After spending the night in an agreeable French chalet as the only guests, Richard took a shine to Juiz de Fora and decided to spend another day there. There was a château atop a hill which had been constructed by a Brazilian planter at a cost of £40,000, complete with miniature lake, islands, bridges, swans and boats and even botanical and zoological gardens tricked out with copious chinoiserie. Richard was in such raptures over this 'folly' that he tore himself away at dawn next day only with great reluctance.

At 6 a.m. the Burtons said goodbye to their erstwhile travelling companions, who had come to Juiz de Fora purely for the 'folly'. Isabel reflected dolefully that by noon she and her short-lived friends would be a hundred miles apart. But there was little time for tristesse. 'The horn sounded; there was the usual fling of the mules' heads and legs in the air, and we made the start as if we had been shot out of a gun.' They ran sixty-six miles in the next twelve hours. From the bottom of the Serra da Mantiqueira there was a painful ten-mile ascent through Scotch mist and rain. As ever, Isabel's thoughts were with the animals: 'my heart ached for the mules.'[19]

They spent the night at a decent but not luxurious hotel at Barbacena, 3,800 feet above sea level, the terminus for travellers by coach. They stowed their heavy trunks at the inn and made up their effects into packs for the onward journey by horseback, taking no more than a change of linen, toothbrush, soapcake and comb. Next day James Fitzpatrick of the Morro Velho Company arrived, together with two blacks and ten horses Fitzpatrick had ordered from the Company to make straight the ways of such a distinguished traveller. That night there was good company: an Austrian lieutenant and some voluble Brazilians joined Fitzpatrick and the Burtons for dinner so that 'our table d'hôte was a motely and amusing group'. But when the subject of conversation turned to mesmerism, a particular interest of Richard's, but a bone of contention between him and Isabel, she retired early.

On 19 June Burton's party set off across country on horseback. Apart from Richard, Isabel and Fitzpatrick, the knot of riders comprised Chico, the two slaves and another Englishman, plus two spare horses and three cargo mules. They rode for twenty miles through rolling country as far as Barroso, a depressing hole, where, after a frugal dinner of rice, chicken and beans, the Burtons slept inside a shed-like 'cottage' while the others slung hammocks on the veranda. The al fresco sleepers were lucky, for next day they found the tell-tale incisor points of the dreaded vampire bat on the flanks of their horses. At 4 a.m. they mounted up, for another hard ride of twenty-four miles. Even veteran equestrians such as Isabel and Richard were sorely taxed physically by eight hours' jolting in hard saddles on semi-broken animals. They arrived in São João del Rei on 21 June, done in.[20] Their spirits rose after a chance meeting in the street with two Englishmen. One was Charles Copsey, who had been at Cambridge with Burton's brother Edward. The other, a Dr Lee from Kent, had lived in Brazil for thirty-five years. Lee took the travellers under his wing, entertained them, and showed them the local 'sights'. When Burton commented on the seeming paucity of local peasantry, Lee explained that many of them had fled into the bush to avoid being conscripted into the Paraguayan war.[21]

When they set out next day, Copsey came with them, intending to ride at their side for two days. The next night's stopover, at São José, exposed the travellers to the full rigours of travel in the primitive interior. The accommodation offered them was so rudimentary that Richard chose to stay up all night drinking with Copsey while Isabel snatched some fitful sleep. She awoke tired and grumpy, ready to recriminate with her bibulous husband, though significantly Isabel could never bring herself to level the accusation direct at her beloved Richard. 'We intended to leave São José at one o'clock a.m., but those who foolishly sat up had all kinds of mishaps. There had been a little too much conviviality; the animals had strayed; so, though we started before light, it was much later than we intended.' Nor did Isabel's prim censoriousness rest there. As they struggled on next day, making execrable progress, Iabel allowed herself another moan. 'The valiant people who would dance and drink all night dropped asleep upon the road.'[22]

It was long after sunset when they straggled into Alagoa Dourada, where English engineers were laying the foundations of a new railway track into the mountains, designed as an extension of the Dom Pedro Segundo line. They requested Isabel to do the inauguration honours; she obliged by cracking open a bottle of wine on the first sleeper. The coming of the strangers was the excuse for a great dinner given at the richest ranch in the neighbourhood. Isabel sat at the bottom of a long wood table, directly facing the local padre at the top. Seated on the benches on either side were eight Englishmen and seventeen Brazilian oligarchs. The laden board groaned with every variety of meat and fowl, rice, bread, cheese, *feijão, farinha*, beer, port and a variety of liqueurs. An animated discussion arose among the revellers as to whether married or single men were happier. To avenge Isabel's sullenness on the ride, Richard took Copsey's side in arguing for the superior felicity of the bachelor. Isabel affected a womanly disdain for the proceedings. 'If it had been in France, there would have been half a dozen duels, and I fully expected to see some kniving; but with them it was only hilarity and good spirits, and they embraced across the table at the very moment I thought they were going to hit one another.' Richard, though, was in his element. 'I have spent many a less merry Christmas in Merry England, and we shall not readily forget Midsummer's Day at Alagoa Dourada, in the year of grace 1867.'[23]

The swing from positive to negative fortunes came with alarming abruptness. It was almost as though in losing Copsey, who bade farewell to them at Alagoa Dourada, they had lost their talisman. After making dreadfully slow progress – just fifteen miles in five hours – they felt ready to collapse in a heap at the miserable village of Camapuã. The only room to rent – a hovel beside which a Highland bothy would have appeared to advantage – was in the gift of one José Antonio Azevedo, the most boorish, cross-grained and cantankerous individual the Burtons had yet encountered, 'original in rudeness, independence and suspicion'. After much haggling Azevedo reluctantly allowed Isabel to sling her hammock in the hovel. Richard slept on the table and the rest of the party huddled outside around a fire in the teeth of a bitterly cold night. In the night, through a thin partition wall, Isabel heard a hoarse whisper from Azevedo as he disputed with his wife. 'Don't bother me any more; it will be quite easy to kill them both, and I mean to do it.' Thoroughly alarmed, Isabel awoke Richard and told him what she had heard. They tiptoed out, fetched their guns from the stable and took turns to watch the door all night. Next morning their hosts served up a pair of roast chickens. Azevedo explained that the quarrel last night was about killing both *chickens*, which his wife had opposed. In relief that the curmudgeon had no homicidal intent, Richard paid him four times the going rate for 'bed' and board.[24]

It was hard going next day as well, since the road was potted with *atoleiros* – patches of quicksand, which were very hard to negotiate. They struggled on as far as the village of Congonhas do Campo where, following their usual custom, they enlisted the help of the local priest, who invariably knew all the 'wrinkles' in the life of his flock. But the final stretch of the long journey to Morro Velho proved the most trying of all. At Teixeras they were turned away from five houses before a cobbler took pity on them and took them in; Isabel at least slept in a bed of straw. The ordeal continued. 'Next day was a very hard day. We started at half past three in the morning; at half past ten we breakfasted under a tree by the river. We crossed different rivers about twelve times, wading our horses through. We passed through virgin forests, and up and down scarped rocky mountains till dark, and arrived at Corche d'Agua, a miserable place, where there were no beds or food. We started again before dawn, rode about twelve miles in the dark, passed two villages and about 9 a.m. arrived at Morro Velho.'[25]

But at Morro Velho they came to a secure haven, for here was a settlement of twenty-five Britons, headed by Mr Gordon, superintendent of the São João del Rei mining company, in charge of 3,000 black slaves. Mr and Mrs Gordon fêted and petted the Burtons to such good effect that it was almost six weeks before they moved on from Morro Velho. The two couples became firm friends and were still visiting each other socially twenty years later.[26]

Burton needed to gather extensive material on the mining in Minas Gerais to justify his 'study leave' to the Foreign Office. He therefore planned to swing round the province in a gigantic arc. The territory in which he now found himself was the *sertão* – the Brazilian equivalent of the pampa. This vast inland range had originally been used by the *vaqueiros* to graze their herds. In the early seventeenth century they had pressed on inland, up the São Francisco river to the mighty Paulo Afonso falls. The process accelerated the following century when herds were forbidden to graze within forty miles of the coast. But the cattle economy of the *sertão* came to a grinding halt after the drought of 1791-3, when seven-eighths of the herds perished. Rio Grande do Sul was thenceforth *the* ranching area of Brazil; the *sertão* meanwhile became an economic cul-de-sac. The best hope of inland São Paulo and Minas Gerais thereafter lay with the mines.

Burton began his tour of inspection with a visit to the Cuiabá mine on 4-5 July 1867, where Isabel thought the bearded Scots superintendent resembled God the Father. Gold-mining in

BRAZIL

South America, unlike the Rand in South Africa later in the
century but in common with the North American experience in
California and the Yukon, was alluvial. The gold was found in
mountain streams and obtained by panning. Silver, on the other
hand, was embedded in rock, and required the sinking of deep
shafts, plus tunnelling and a complex refining process, before it
could be separated from the ore.

They returned to the Gordons' hacienda to be regaled by slave
musters and Indian historical pageants; Isabel later gave Morro
Velho her vote as the most interesting place in Brazil. Then,
after a five-day rest, the Burtons set out on an eleven-day tour of
the province (Gordon accompanied them for the first two days),
involving some of the hardest riding yet. Nine and a quarter
hours in the saddle took them thirty-two miles, through the villages of São José de Morra Grande, Barro, Brumado and Santa
Bárbara, where they witnessed iron smelting by the Catalan
method. Next day it took five hours to cover the twenty miles to
Catas Altas, where they employed their old trick of wheedling
round the local priest.[27]

Here Gordon turned back to Morro Velho, but not before
giving the Burtons a 'strong tip' for the next night's stopover.
They proceeded through Agua Quente, Fonseca, Morreia to
Affeixonada, where Gordon's advice paid off in the form of a
pleasant ranch by a wimpling brook. All now seemed set fair, for
they had only to ride through Benito Rodriguez and Comargo
next day to reach Santa Ana, where the English supervisor of the
Passagem gold mine, Captain Treloar, would receive them, they
thought, like another Gordon. But the unexpected happened.
They got to Santa Ana only to find that Treloar's wife was on the
point of death. His household was in confusion and he was
unable to take in guests. Advised to divert to the pretty cathedral
town of Mariana, they found their English contact there also up
to his eyes in the Treloar business. They were obliged to spend
yet another miserable night in a wretched hovel, before Treloar's
son-in-law came to their rescue and put them up for the remaining three nights of their stay. To his irritation, Burton as consul
had to perform the funeral service. His misogynistic side was
assuaged by the absence of all women from the funeral: 'women
do not attend funerals, nor sales, nor shops, nor post offices in
Brazil'. But the Anglican service bored him rigid. 'We cannot

130

but think of the dictum of Dr Newman, the Oratorian, namely that Protestantism is the dreariest of all religions, and that the thought of the Anglican service makes men shudder. Surely it might be altered for the better, but is there any middle term between the God-like gift of reason or the un-reason of Rome.'[28]

Just before the service there was low drama. A dreadful scuffling noise arose in the kitchen. Isabel entered to investigate and found two blacks engaged in a knife fight to the death over the picayune tip the Burtons had left. Imperiously she faced down the combatants. Then, after a descent of the Passagem gold mine, the Burtons made haste to depart for Ouro Prêto. Wearily and thankfully they arrived, after a 133-mile journey which Richard clocked precisely at forty-one hours and fifty minutes of travelling spread over eight days.[29]

Ouro Prêto, 300 miles from Rio, set among rugged mountains in a cold and foggy ambience, was then the capital of Minas Gerais and as such a boom town, basking in the new prosperity that came from a fivefold increase in provincial trade (mainly cotton and coffee) between 1864-74. A small masterpiece of baroque splendour in its heyday, Ouro Prêto contrasted strikingly as 'gold strike' town with the ramshackle mining settlements of the North American gold-rushes. It contained two thousand houses, twelve churches, a government palace, town hall, penitentiary, two printing offices, a public library and the inevitable botanical gardens.[30] Here the Burtons sipped their first champagne since Petrópolis and were comfortably lodged with an English watchmaker and his family. Richard ascended the nearby Itacalumi summit, while Isabel preferred the gentler pleasures of a visit to the local 'tomb of the martyrs'. Neither of them took to Ouro Prêto, with its steep gradients and philistine ethos. This was Isabel's reaction: 'walking up and down the streets is quite as difficult as ascending and descending ladders, and there is an equal danger of falling. I think one could throw a stone from the top of a street to the bottom without its touching anything en route.' Richard was even more censorious in his assessment of the town:

Amongst its many disadvantages we may observe that carriages cannot be used, and that even riding is not safe in the city; there is no ground for extension, the streets are too narrow for rails, and the country is unfit for the iron horse. Hence we have the sights and sounds of a capital, the fair sex dressed in French toilettes –

'Beaux corps, jolis, parés très richement'

officers and men in uniform, civil and military, orderlies riding about, bells, guard-mounting, bugle sounds, and music ecclesiastical and military, whilst perhaps listening to the bandstands some old negress habited in male cloak, with rusty chimney pot hat proudly perched upon a dingy kerchief. Literature can hardly be said to flourish when the Ouro-Prêtanos cannot keep up a single bookseller's shop.[31]

But the enforced leisure gave Burton time to pen some reflections on Brazil in general. 1867 was an election year, and he noticed that party feeling ran as high in Ouro Prêto as in São Paulo – 'as it did amongst us when unbreeched boys were asked – "Are you for Pitt or Fox?"' Burton thought this a good thing – a natural and healthy aspect of a young society reaching towards political maturity. It prompted in him a further thought:

I find in Brazil another symptom of strong and healthy vitality. Men wage irreconcilable war with the present; they have no idea of the 'Rest and Be Thankful' state. They balance 'whatever is, is good' by the equation, 'Whatever is, is bad,' yet they are neither optimists nor pessimists. They have as little idea of finality as have New Yorkers. They will move and remove things quiet, and they will not leave well or ill alone. They are not yet, happily,

    Men of long enduring hopes
    And careless what the hour may bring.

Were infanticide disgracefully prevalent amongst them – it is as rare as in Ireland – they would find some means of checking it. They are determined to educate their children, unlike the lands where the political physicians allow the patient to perish whilst they wrangle over how to save him – what physic is to be or is not to be given. They will emancipate their women and convert them into 'persons'. They will provide against pauperism, and they study to bring the masses up to the high standards of Prussia and Belgium. They would assimilate their army to that of France, not preserve a 'sham army' or an 'army of deserters'. They would model their navy on that of the USA – not 'Monitors' – and so forth.

Since this is Burton, however, it is not long before we have a touch of negrophobia and misogyny. In a lengthy discussion of crime and punishment we encounter the following: 'In almost all cases of premeditated murder throughout Brazil, two of the active actors are a woman and a negro.'[32]

After two days of Ouro Prêto, the Burtons headed back to Morro Velho by the direct route. On the first leg, via Casa Branca and São Vicente, they overtook a party of North American immigrants on the road just half an hour before nightfall. They got in to the night's stopover at Rio das Pedras before they realized their luck. The sole accommodation in the village was a couple of rough beds and the most basic food. The Americans had to camp out for the night. Having thus pipped them to the post, Burton was disposed to be generous to his rivals. He spent the evening with this extended family from the Deep South, and found them shrewd, courteous and intelligent. There was an old patriarch with a mature daughter, two young married couples, a single man, a single young woman, a grey beard and a plethora of children, all searching for land on which they could be dirt farmers.

Next day Richard and Isabel got up early to avoid having to spend a second night on the road. They rode on through São Antonio and Santa Rita, and arrived in Morro Velho in the early evening to hear the church bells ringing. Isabel wanted to attend Mass, but Richard would not brook any further delay. Isabel solved the problem by paying two old women to hear Mass 'for her'. They galloped on to the Gordons, splashing through mud and rain as they went. They arrived looking like wet dogs but a bath and an excellent homecoming dinner wrought a miraculous transformation.[33]

They spent another two weeks with the Gordons. The highlight of this period came on 24 July when they descended the famous *Cachoeira* gold mine at Morro Velho, the largest and deepest in all Brazil. Few male visitors had descended into this maelstrom, and no women. Isabel prepared to chalk up a 'first' by attiring herself in brown Holland trousers, belt and cap, with a candle stuck to her head with a dab of clay, and a flask of brandy in case she felt faint. There were just two ways down into this Tartarus. One, invariably used by the black slave miners, was to descend by a 3,000-foot ladder. For a tyro this carried with it the danger of getting one's clothes caught between the rungs and the wall of the mine; additionally it was not recommended for anyone with the least scintilla of vertigo or acrophobia in their make-up, and was in any case beyond the physical strength of normal women: it took the miners, in peak health, half an hour to descend and three-quarters of an hour to climb back up. Isabel volunteered for the other way, which meant being lowered in a kibble or bucket, suspended by chains and wound down by hydraulic machinery where pre-stressed ropes and iron chains took the strain, much as in the London lifts of the time. This method took the occupant of the kibble to the bottom in twenty minutes, but was normally used only for hauling up stones or wounded men. The miners themselves feared that the links in the chain would break and pitch the bucket into the abyss.[34] This was no idle fear. The chain had broken a few weeks before, and did so the very next day but, as Isabel noted: 'our time was not yet come.'

Burton and Gordon got into the kibble, ready for the three-quarter-mile descent into the Stygian depths. As they disappeared from sight, Chico and the Gordons' black maid wailed antiphonally with terror. When Isabel and Mrs Gordon stepped into the kibble, Chico fled, exclaiming that nothing could prevail upon him to descend into such an inferno. The journey down was for Isabel an alternation between exhilaration and terror. 'It was wonderful when halfway down to see the lights, like fireflies in the forest, moving about.' But sometimes the kibble grazed against a jutting projection, and began to tilt over slightly, as if it would tip its occupants out. Thinking her last hour had come, Isabel began praying.

But soon the bucket touched terra firma. In fact, Isabel was later to find the ascent even more hair-raising. The reunited couples inspected the labyrinth of dark, slippery tunnels, with large and vaulted caverns, pit-propped with beams, the light provided by flambeaus set in niches in the walls. 'I think Dante must have seen a similar place wherewith to make his Inferno,' was Isabel's comment. Richard also used Dantesque imagery in

Isabel and Richard Burton, *c* 1869

An early portrait of Brigham Young, his second wife, Mary Ann Angell, and their children

Mormon pioneer company crossing the plains to Utah

Main Street, Salt Lake City in 1864

The baptismal font in the Temple at Salt Lake City supported by twelve life-sized cast-iron oxen

The Paulo Afonso Falls

THE

HIGHLANDS OF THE BRAZIL.

By CAPTAIN RICHARD F. BURTON,

F.R.G.S., ETC.

Brazil is usually represented by a Tupy Woman.

VOL II.

LONDON:

TINSLEY BROTHERS, 18, CATHERINE STREET, STRAND.
1869.

Title page of *The Highlands of Brazil*, Volume II

Burton shooting the rapids on the Rio das Velhas

General Bartolomé Mitre, commander of
allied forces of Brazil, Argentina and Uruguay
in the Paraguayan war

Marshal Francisco Solano López, President
of Paraguay and leader of the Paraguayan
troops

The Argentine Infantry charge at Lomas Valentinas

Paraguay's Via Dolorosa: the Army's retreat in August, 1869

his description. 'The heavy gloom, the fitful glare, and the savage chant, with the wall hanging like the stone of Sisyphus, like the sword of Damocles, suggesting a kind of Swedenborgian hell.' He asked Gordon what would happen if the mine caught fire. Gordon replied that this was impossible because of the damp wood and dripping water. Yet six months later the impossible happened, and the mine was gutted and all but destroyed.

Isabel noticed children working in these fuliginous depths and questioned Gordon sharply on the practice. Patiently Gordon explained that the mining company and the state government had collaborated to stop child labour, but that the children's families protested that they could not survive without the income from their mining offspring. Isabel's natural sense of compassion for the underdog found expression in a paean to the slaves, suitably toned down to avoid offending Victorian sensibilities. 'I cannot describe how kind and thoughtful all the rough workmen were. Everything was done to show us how much they were pleased and flattered by our visit, to allay fear, amuse us, and show us everything of interest. It would have been a good lesson in manners to many London drawing rooms.'[35]

Three days later, on 27 July, Richard lectured on his travels in Arabia and Africa as a prelude to a concert at an open-air theatre. It was dark before the amateur theatricals got under way. Isabel sang a song but on stepping off the stage in the dark, misjudged the distance to the ground and badly sprained her ankle. They were due to set off for Sabará next day for the start of their 1,500-mile canoeing adventure on the São Francisco river system. Richard postponed departure for ten days, but physicians warned Isabel that she was in no fit state to brave the wilds. She was in bed for five days, then walked on crutches for a further twenty. With heavy heart and agonized reluctance, Isabel bowed to the inevitable. Since she felt unable to ask Richard to abandon the trip he had lived for during the last two years, he would have to go on alone.

On 7 August she went down to nearby Sabará on the Rio das Velhas to see Richard off. Here he found himself at the mercy of an extortionate Portuguese storekeeper, who spoke English and fleeced in the manner of London cab drivers. He angered Burton by writing 'My labour gratis' at the end of a particularly steep bill. 'This reminded me of the "Nothing charged for grief" in the Irish wake.' Not for the first time he was embittered by the easy assumption that an expedition must either be government-financed or paid for from the coffers of a supremely wealthy individual. Either way, all explorations were regarded as fair game by plundering and leeching provisioners. He was even more angry later when he discovered that the raft he had bought for the river journey had attached to it a leaky starboard canoe, ineptly patched up with Sabará clay.

The next shock was the condition of the *ajojo* or raft itself. This was basically three canoes lashed together, with a central platform of balsa-wood. The canoes (thirty-three feet long and six feet broad) provided a solid foundation for the standing awning, which was made fast by five wooden stanchions. The tent itself was of rough Minas cotton. Inside was a writing desk and a bunk. In the stern was a galley, equipped with strips of dried beef. Burton hoped they could pick up rice and beans on the way. He intended to dole out a dram of rum each every evening to the men he hired; he himself had a personal supply of tea, sugar, salt beef and tongue, which the Gordons had supplied. But the first glimpse of the *ajojo* was dispiriting. 'I never saw such an old Noah's Ark, with its standing awning, a floating gypsy "pal", some seven feet high and twenty-two long, and pitched like a tent upon two hollowed logs. The river must indeed be safe, if this article can get down without accident.'[36]

Burton allowed himself no time for second thoughts. Isabel broke a bottle of wine on the raft and christened it the *Eliza*. Richard made his farewells to the Gordons and the other non-voyagers and quickly cast off. Yet even the iron man was not without emotion at parting. 'I confess to having felt an unusual sense of loneliness as the kindly faces faded in the distance.' Sadness was not the only emotion. When his crew of fifteen men came on board, the raft sank alarmingly in the water. The upper platform was deluged by the resultant wake, and the pilot reacted nervously.

They floated down the Rio das Velhas that afternoon as far as the village of Santo Antonio da Roca Grande, where Chico was waiting with the animals to take Isabel home. She went ashore and made her farewells even as the sun began to set behind the mountains. Then the *Eliza* cast off again on its riverine odyssey.

Isabel watched and waved until she could do so no more. 'From a bank I watched the barque with dim eyes round a winding of the river, which hid it from my sight. The sun was sinking as I turned away.'[37]

Isabel stayed on with the Gordons a further eighteen days. Once she had jettisoned her crutches, the Gordons thought up a scheme to keep her busy. They suggested she accompany the local parish priest on his rounds. Isabel set out to do the Morro Velho circuit with the cleric, who was evidently something of a dandy, got up 'in the height of Minas elegance and fashion, wearing jackboots, white corduroys, embroidered Roman collar and enormous silver spurs'. Her initial suspicions that this was not really the right sort of personality to minister to the poor and dispossessed hardened into certainty when Gordon asked her to look into the wants of black Catholics in the church and hospital. In the ward for incurables Isabel quickly discovered that the priest had never set foot in the place, let alone administer the sacraments. The discovery uncorked the full zealous fury of this 'old English Catholic'. She burst in on the priest and demanded an explanation. Nervously he blurted out a lame excuse that he had no pyx or vessel in which to carry the sacraments. The riposte was pure outraged Isabel. '*Well*, Father, I have been commissioned by the Superintendent to look into these things, and to report to him what *is* done and what *ought* to be done, and he is going to see it carried out; so you will oblige me by going to hear all those confessions, *now at once*, and taking the holy ingredients in a wineglass!'[38]

We may conjecture that there was at least one citizen of Morro Velho who was glad to see the back of her when she finally departed for Rio on 25 August. Gordon supplied horses and camping equipment for her and Chico. She set out with a muleteer, seven animals and two other slaves, but with no weapons of any description. They met no dangers along the way and little to distress them, unless it was the copious evidence of the way Brazilian women would accept the most ferocious beatings from their men. But the Morro Velho priest was not the only individual on this trip to feel the force of Isabel's tongue. When her caravan trooped into Rio on the fifteenth day after leaving Morro Velho, she was disconcerted to find her favourite hotel, the Estrangeiros (where she was well known), full. She proceeded to the second best, but since she was dirty and dishevelled from the long journey, the manager failed to peg her into the right social class. Disdainfully he pointed to a hostelry for sailors' wives on the other side of the street. 'I think that will be about your place, my good woman, not here.' Isabel faced him down with a basilisk stare. 'Well, I think I am coming in here all the same.' She then insisted on taking the best rooms in the hotel and sent for Maria, who had her boxes at the Estrangeiros. Her maid, 'who was a great swell', arrived. Meanwhile Isabel had bathed and changed and ordered some supper. When the manager came up with the meal, he was surprised to see the 'great swell' dancing attendance on a strange woman. Thinking that the first tatterdemalion female was the first in a hierarchy of servants, he addressed Isabel. 'Did that woman come to take apartments for you, madam? I do beg your pardon; I am afraid I was rather rude to her.' Isabel was gracious. 'Well, I am that woman myself; but you need not apologize, because I saw myself in the glass and I don't wonder at it.' Needless to say, the flustered manager was all grovelling apologies and sycophancy thereafter.[39]

Isabel returned to Santos and tried to calculate exactly when Richard would arrive back in Rio, since he made it a point of principle that she should be there to meet him whenever he returned from a long journey. It continued to irritate her that the accident of a sprained ankle had prevented her from going with Richard on what promised to be high adventure. Rivers had always fascinated him, from his early days on the Indus to his consulate on the delta of the Niger. He had already claimed to have discovered the source of the Nile and had penetrated farther up the Congo than any man since Tuckey. Perhaps his work on the São Francisco would restore him to a front rank among explorers. Perhaps this particular river god would bestow on him the laurels that lesser men such as Speke had so treacherously garnered.

Chapter Eight

Down the Rio São Francisco

For the first stretch of the river journey Burton had two pass-
sengers. One was a rocketmaker called Antonio Pinto. The other
was a refugee named Hock from the defeated Condeferate states.
He was the sole survivor of a party of twenty Southerners carried
off by fever at Sabará. Dazed by this disaster, he was wandering
around Brazil aimlessly, with some thought that he might be
able to help in the building of railways. Hock approved of the
equipment Burton had laid in: a boathook, anchor and strong
English ropes for 'cordelling' when swinging around in the
rapids, and most of all the two large jars of porous earth which
contained the water supply, which the travellers intended to top
up each night. But he agreed with Burton on the poor quality of
the pilot, one Manoel Vieira, who had brought his two sons with
him. They stood mournfully in the bow with long poles but, as
Burton soon noticed:

> The men were mere landlubbers; they felt, or affected to
> feel, nervous at every obstacle. They had been rowing all
> their lives, and yet they knew not how to back water . . .
> they pulled with all their might for a few minutes when the
> river was rapid, so as to incur possible risks, and when the
> water was almost dead, they lay upon their oars and lazily
> allowed themselves to be floated down.[1]

Burton soon became frustrated at the lack of system of Vieiras

139

and his brood. They made little headway, despite being on the river all day between 7 a.m. and 5 p.m. The only thing they seemed to like doing was blowing noisily on conches and cowhorns, thus waking up sleepy settlements on the bank. Between Sabará and Santa Luísa the raft grounded regularly in the shallows where the river bed broadened. Along this stretch there was a minimum of water and a maximum of contrary wind. The one hopeful sign was that the *ajojo* behaved impressively on the water.[2]

Burton settled into a routine. At night he anchored the *Eliza* and tried to find billets in the villages they passed. By day he attempted to work in his 'study', though subject to constant interruptions from his two loans from the Gordons: a Morro Velho boy called Agostinho, who acted as his personal attendant, and a savage mastiff called 'Negra'. Soon they came in sight of Santa Luísa, capped with two double-towered churches, divided by fine large whitewashed houses. Alas for Burton, he was not destined to spend his night in one of these but in a ramshackle hovel. But he was in good spirits. 'The next morning was delicious, and the face of nature was as calm as if it could show no other expression. The sword-like rays of the sun, radiating from the unseen centre before it arose in its splendour, soon dispersed the thin mists that slept tranquilly upon the cool river bed.'[3] This was a rare disquisition on the sun. Burton usually preferred to concentrate on the moon ('sublunary' was one of his favourite words), as in the following well-known lines in his poem the *Kasidah*:

That gentle moon, the lesser light, the Lover's lamp, the swains's delight,
A ruined world, a globe burnt out, a corpse upon the road of night.

On the Rio São Francisco his lunar predilection found expression in the following: 'The moon, that traveller's friend, a companion to the solitary man, like the blazing hearth of Northern climates, rose behind the filmy tree tops and made us hail the gentle light. We have not the same feeling for the stars, or even the planets, though Jupiter and Venus give more light than does the Crescent in England; they are too distant, too far above us, whilst the Moon is of the earth, earthy, a member of our body physical, the complement of our atom.'

Two miles below Santa Luísa the landscape changed and they saw their first cotton plantations; the hills were covered with thin brown-grey grass as if hoary with frost. At the next landfall, Burton identified a nunnery and decided to target it for his night's billet, knowing that the religious in Brazil always chose congenial spots for their retreats. But the mother superior proved the double of the ogress in *The Comedy of Errors* and refused the visitors so much as a cup of coffee. Burton trumped her ace by sending in his card to the parish priest – the trick he and Isabel had perfected on the way to Morro Velho. The ploy worked. The 'reverend vicar' invited him for dinner and gave a guided tour of the infirmary run by the sisters, much to the friaress's fury. She was, however, able to confine Burton to the raft for the night by exclaiming loudly about the virginal status of her sisters. But after a good dinner Burton was again in fine fettle: 'I spent the night at this place on the raft; the moon and stars were unusually bright, and the night was delightfully clear and cool.'[4]

Once at Jaguarano, Burton dismissed the Vieiras and set about engaging another crew for the run to Diamantina. The five days soon stretched into a week for, as Burton noted: 'hospitality is the greatest delay in Brazilian travel. It is the old style of Colonial greeting; you may do what you like, you may stay for a month, but not for a day.'[5] He spent the time making notes on the local fauna. Jaguarano, as the name implied, was a well-known centre for the jaguar and the puma. Burton took careful measurements of the pug marks left by recent prowlers. Even more interesting was the dreaded piranha, whose ferocity was, however, exaggerated by the Amazon travellers of the late nineteenth and early twentieth centuries. It is significant that the early naturalists mention the piranha not at all or merely in passing. Waterton, Edwards, Wallace and Spruce had nothing to say on the matter, while Humboldt recorded its existence dispassionately. Only in the work of Schomburgk is there any warrant for the sensationalism with which Theodore Roosevelt bludgeoned the popular imagination. It was Roosevelt's *Through the Brazilian Wilderness* (1914) which pegged the piranha as the stuff of modern nightmares, though most of his horror stories were taken at second hand from General da Silva Rondon, and from third hand through him. Burton's encounter with the 'killer fish' was limited to eating one. He found the flesh dry, of poor flavour and full of spines. [6]

The people at Jaguarano jeered that the *Eliza* would not even get as far as the confluence of the São Francisco and das Velhas at Pirapora. Brooding on this when he finally got under way after a week, Burton was pleased to come upon a party of nine US immigrants at Casa Branca, the first halt after Jaguarano. He took a liking to a certain Mr Davidson from Tennessee and engaged him as 'adjutant general' for the passage to the great falls of Paulo Afonso, his intended journey's end. On the debit side, Burton again suffered delay from the exigencies of Brazilian hospitality. He arrived on Friday but his host would not permit him to leave until after breakfast on Monday.[7]

The first encounter with white water and portaging came at the Maquine and Ounce rapids. He was not entirely satisfied with the way his crew shaped up during their passage, and it was probably deep-gnawing anxiety that produced the stark picture of inland Brazil, ostensibly triggered by some women selling chickens on the bank. 'I felt saddened by this contact with my kind. It was the Present in its baldest, most prosaic form; the bright kaleidoscope of cultivated life here becomes the dullest affair of unvarying shape and changeless colour. There is no poverty, much less want; nor is there competency, much less wealth. There is no purpose; no progress where progress might so easily be; no collision of opinion amongst a people who are yet abundant in intelligence. Existence is, in fact, a sort of *Nihil Album*, of which the black variety is Death. I prefer real hearty barbarism to such torpid semi-civilization.'[8]

Ahead loomed the rapids of *Cachoeira Grande*, by common consent far more ferocious than anything ridden out so far. Quite by chance, on 24 August Burton saw a band of armed desperadoes on the shore. Appealing to their *machismo* he challenged them to shoot the rapids with him. The irregulars accepted. There followed a hair-raising sixteen-minute zigzag descent through the boiling waters. The experienced aplomb with which these veterans of the waterways negotiated the switchback course of the river made a deep impression on Burton. When his helpers, having been as good as their word, made as though to depart, Burton persuaded them to stay by uncorking a keg of his best *restilo*. The upshot was that they agreed to shoot the next cataract with him. They shot through the seething eddies of the *Cachoeira das Gallinhas* in nine minutes. The 'pilots' then departed with nine dollars (one per minute of rapid) and a further bottle of *restilo* (a Brazilian brew, similar to *aguardiente*) for their pains. Burton was under no illusion about them. They were cut-throats, but they had saved him a lot of trouble.[9]

The next landfall was Bom Sucesso, where they stayed until 11 September. Using the town as a base, Burton set off for an extensive reconnaissance of the Diamantina mining area. He travelled first the ninety-three miles to Diamantina city, on muleback for a day and a night. Here he stayed for three days as guest of the diamond merchant João Ribeiro. The fantastically carved overhanging roofs and brackets and the colonial churches of this centre of the diamond industry, 3,670 feet up in the interior of Minas Gerais, appealed mightily to Burton, and it was here he recorded his warmest impressions of Brazil. 'The men were the frankest, and the women the prettiest and most amiable, of any it had been my fortune to meet in Brazil.'[10] Burton was interested to see that, the Aberdeen Bill abolishing the slave trade notwithstanding, Brazilians admired and respected the British.

It always irritated him that the return for Brazilian friendliness and hospitality was that most foreigners maligned Brazil and anyone who spoke well of her was accused of having been bought. This curiosity had been confirmed by other travellers, most recently by Agassiz.[11] To spite the critics Burton decided to go right out on a limb and turn the criticism back on Europe. 'It may be said with truth, and greatly to the credit of Brazil, that no man feels degraded by honest industry, however humble. Consequently society ignores the *mauvaise honte* about professions which distinguishes the old world, where I have seen a man blush to own that his father was a "doctor", and where Faraday was lauded because he dared to confess in public that his brother was a gas-fitter.'[12] Even more annoying was the fact that Anglo-Brazilian cordiality was impaired by certain Europeans who masked their misdemeanours by claiming they were Englishmen, thus bringing Albion into disrepute; Burton instanced a Skimpole-like freemasonic Prussian ne'er-do-well scrounger in

Diamantina as a prime example.

The lighter side of all this was provided by Brazilian naïveté. There were Englishmen enough in Minas Gerais; for the latter pat of his stay Burton lodged with John Rose, a Cornishman who had worked in Brazil as diamond-digger, carpenter and mason before accumulating enough to retire on. But the expatriates had, it seemed, been unable to impress their hosts with the populousness of England or even with its variety of accent. At one of the mines Burton met another Cornishman, Thomas Piddington, who had come out to Brazil thirty years earlier and had not seen his wife and children since. It was so long since Piddington had heard an upper-class drawl that on hearing Burton's familiar 'Yaas' he became convinced he was an American. A Brazilian family at a ranch where he stopped for coffee went one better. 'They openly told me that I was the Chief of Police from Ouro Prêto, and they were most anxious to know my business. They laughed to scorn the idea of my being an Englishman. "If this be true," they asked, "how is it that you do not know 'Nicholas', your countryman, who is living within musket shot of us?"'[13]

Burton thoroughly enjoyed himself at Diamantina and, distaste for dancing aside, even put in an appearance at a ball thrown by a wealthy widow. He was less impressed with Brazilian mining methods. 'As the Brazil borrowed her gold-mining through Portugal from the Romans, so she has taken her system of diamond-mining from Hindostan.'[14] But it was with deep regret that, on his eleventh day out, he finally turned back towards Bom Sucesso and the *Eliza*.

The *ajojo* continued down river towards Coroa do Gallo. It was in this area that Burton saw most signs of the animals dangerous to man for which Brazil is famous. There were plenty of alligators or *jacaré (crocodilus sclerops)* in the river, though none of them exceeded five feet in length. Swimming dogs took little notice of the alligators, and local lore deemed them harmless, in contrast to a feared lake variety in Mato Grosso, though Burton noted a recent case of a woman who was taken at the water's edge. The South American alligator receives its worse press in the pages of Humboldt and Bates, who recount many gory stories of death and narrow escape at the jaws of the saurians. Spruce, by contrast, is more sober and sceptical and relates that spearfishermen would often jump into the river alongside alligators to retrieve their stricken catch, even when it was pumping blood. But there seem too many well-authenticated stories of attacks on humans to discount the potential threat from alligators entirely. Burton's caution appears entirely justified.[15]

The *jacaré* was not the only reptile to cause a frisson on this expedition. They encountered the *fer-de-lance*, fortunately at a distance, and frequently saw rattlesnakes of a length between four and eight feet. Although the locals claimed poisonous snakes sometimes attacked cattle, he could find no authentic story of a spontaneous attack on man by venomous reptile. Most snakebites occurred when humans accidentally trod on them. For this reason Burton concurred with the other famous South American travellers in holding that the fear of snakes soon diminished in Brazil, for the facts belied the legendary dangers.[16] Burton took pleasure in exposing one local snake superstition. He killed a whip snake in a tree, even though the bystanders swore up and down that the serpent would fly through the air like an arrow at its assailant.

In any case, the aboriginal Brazilians had devised a number of remedies for snakebite wounds. One was a ligature above the wound for delaying the flow of infected blood to the heart. Another was a potion of alcohol and gunpowder, which saved the patient as soon as he became intoxicated. As a result of these efficacious cures, comparatively few indigenous Brazilians died after being bitten by venomous reptiles, especially considering the vast numbers of snakes that infested the rainforests of the interior.[17]

Even more gruesome were the traces Burton's party found of the dreaded *sucuriu* (variants *sucuriuba* or *sucruyu*) or anaconda. The giant snakes of South America invariably elicited a peculiar horror in travellers, who did not always take the trouble to distinguish the anaconda (Waterton's *camondi*) proper from the more common water boa. The boa constrictor or *coulanacara* (variant *giboia* and properly *constrictor constrictor*) was arguably the more dangerous from the human point of view. Waterton had a famous encounter with a fourteen-foot boa which he first pinned down with a lance, then kept in a sack all night before slitting its throat. It was this incident that provoked Sydney Smith's well-known remark in his review of Waterton:

'the boa constrictor swallows him [the tortoise], shell and all,
and consumes him slowly in the interior, as the Court of Chan-
cery does a great estate.'[18] But Waterton confused the boa with
the anaconda when he referred to a Dutch friend of his who had
shot a huge snake with a stag's antlers still in its mouth. The
snake had swallowed the stag but could not get the horn down,
so had to wait in patience until the stomach digested the body,
leaving the horns to drop off. This was clearly an anaconda; Burton tells us that in parts of Brazil the snake was named *Cobra de
Veado* after its supposed fondness for venison. [19]

Burton believed that, when not disturbed by man or prairie
fire and allowed to loll in remote, stagnant waters, the anaconda
could attain a length of thirty feet. Bates confirmed that this serpent was a reliable menace. One eighteen-foot specimen made
for his flotilla of canoes and carried off two of his hens while his
men were sleeping. On another occasion a twenty-one-foot anaconda attacked a ten-year-old boy before being killed by the lad's
father, armed with a machete.[20]

Stimulated by the yarns told with gusto around Brazilian
camp fires, Burton was even prepared to believe in the existence
of huge anacondas or unknown varieties of snake more than sixty
feet long, capable of attacking a man on horseback or swallowing
an ox. Burton credited a report from a man in Maranhão who
appeared to verify the explorer George Gardner's tale of a huge
reptile swimming across the river with a pair of horns protruding
from its mouth. To some extent this was a case of the 'will to
believe' for Burton had a vested interest, as his quest for the 'sea
serpent' in 1866 had shown, in stories of monstrous snakes. Here
he could certainly find support in local lore, for the inhabitants
of Brazil's river systems almost universally believed in the existence of giant water serpents. Bates and Waterton confirmed the
proposition before Burton, and Weeks, who sailed the São Francisco in Burton's wake in 1874, endorsed it also.[21]

Whether there really were (or are) gigantic serpents in the
depths of the Brazilian river systems has never been completely
cleared up even to this day. There is evidently something about
the anaconda that stimulates the wildest fantasies. The
American explorer Commander George Dyott hit the nail on the
head when he reported an encounter with an anaconda by moon-
light. The snake looked 'every inch of forty feet, which meant

that he must have been nearer twenty'.[22] Much the most in-
fluential promoter of the anaconda legend was the ill-starred
Colonel Percy Fawcett, who claimed to have shot one sixty-two
feet long. [23] Nobody has ever returned to civilization with the
pelt of any such monster. Supporters of the 'giant snake' theory,
like Burton, object that to demand such proof is to ask for the
impossible in a context where it was difficult enough for an explorer to drag himself out of the jungle, let alone haul some
weighty pelt which would probably shrink on the way. Burton
based his belief firmly on the evidence of Gardner and other
early travellers of impeccable credentials. He was particularly
fond of citing in this regard the eighteenth-century explorer
Lacerda, who journeyed up the Tiete to Cuiabá and Mato
Grosso. Lacerda relates that one of his slaves mistook a huge
snake for an old canoe, and began to burn it before he realized
his mistake. [24]

It has to be conceded that there is much circumstantial evidence on Burton's side. The missionary Father Victor Heinz
claimed to have witnessed clearly, in 1922, a snake with a body as
thick as an oil drum and about eighty feet long. In 1948 the *Dia-
rio* of Pernambuco published a photograph purporting to be an
anaconda weighing five tons, caught in Manaus. In the same
year a 115- foot monster was said to have emerged from the River
Oyapock and terrified the locals until the state militia slaughtered it with a machine gun. But the fact remains that no hard
evidence for the existence of such ophidic leviathans has ever
been produced. Theodore Roosevelt did much to bring sanity
into this area by putting up a reward of $5,000 in 1914 for anyone
who could produce unimpeachable evidence of a snake greater
than thirty feet long. In the aftermath of the slump in Amazo-
nian rubber, the reward was as the wealth of Croesus. Yet no one
claimed the prize, nor has anyone since, even when the Bronx
Zoo raised the standing offer to $15,000. The most liberal expert
is not prepared to go beyond thirty-seven feet as the maximum
possible length, though it is not clear how even those dimensions
have been arrived at. [25]

On 14 September Burton spent his last night on the Rio das
Velhas. The morrow would bring the confluence of the São
Francisco itself at Guaicuí (Pirapora). Burton did not relish the
thought of entering Guaicuí. By now he was thoroughly en-

amoured of the trusty *Eliza*, which he had underestimated at first.[26] And there were two further considerations. In the first place he would have to break up and disband the successful crew who had signed up only to this point. In the second, he would have to face 'civilization' again – not a prospect he relished. 'After a few days of traveller's life and liberty, of existence in the open air, of sleep under the soft blue skies, of days without neck-ties, the sensation of returning to "society" is by no means plea-sant; all have felt, although perhaps all will not own the un-amiable effort which it has cost them. The idea of entering a town after a spell on the Prairie or on the River is distasteful to me as to any Bedouin of the purer breed, who must stuff his nos-trils with cotton to exclude the noxious atmosphere.'[27]

Burton anchored the *Eliza* at Guaicuí for three days, while he took a side trip to the famous rapids of Pirapora. After a nine-hour overland slog through a gale to the accompaniment of heavy forked lightning, Burton and comrades came to the turbu-lent cataracts, which marked the southern limits of the São Fran-cisco's navigability. Above the Pirapora rapids, and all the way to the *Casca d'Anta* at the river's source, the São Francisco was a mass of cataracts, where the fading echoes of one set of falls are immediately counterpointed by the fresh sounds of a new cat-aract. Burton was bowled over. 'I have seen nothing like it since my visit to the African Congo,' he confessed. 'It was . . . a true fall, divided into two sections, and we tremble to think what the Paulo Afonso might be.'[28]

Guaicuí marked the end of the first act on the river. Burton was by now a seasoned river traveller. Already the Brazilian all-leather travelling suit was second nature to him. This was an outfit softer, more durable and in every way far superior to the product supplied in the 1860s by London tailors. Made from deerskin, the full suit consisted of the *chapéu*, a billycock hat, sometimes flapped behind like a sou'wester, and the *gibão*, or jerkin, a short jacket opening in front and with pockets extend-ing outside the *guardapeito* – an oblong piece of skin extending from the throat to the stomach, with a hole through which the head is passed. This garment acted as a waistcoat. Meanwhile the *perneiras* or tights reached down to the ankles. Over these, boots were drawn on to the feet and protected by closely-fitting soleless shoes, like the master slippers of Egypt. The durability

of this leather outfit had to be set against its drawbacks: hot in
hot weather, cold in cold, wet in wet.[29]

Reluctantly Burton paid off his crew and hired a fresh one.
Because of supply and demand, he discovered that crewmen's
rates of pay were much lower on the São Francisco than on the
Rio das Velhas; even so, the daily cost of travel on the great river
was four times that of a luxury stateroom on a Royal Mail
oceanic steamer.[30] As pilots for the next stretch of waterway he
hired two coal-black cousins, both six foot three tall: 'they were
well acquainted with the water, civil and obliging, but they
lacked the pluck and bottom of the Highland crew.' On the São
Francisco itself, Burton found the culture of the *barqueiro* rampant (complete with belief in a river serpent 120 feet long) – in
many ways very much like that of the bargee of Old England except in one regard: little foul language was used, and in this respect the Brazilians most resembled the backwoodsmen of the
USA. The unique, and to Burton, puzzling aspect about travel
on the São Francisco was that the 'horseboat' – common to both
Europe and the USA – was utterly unknown. Burton reasoned
that a horse on a treadmill linked to an 'idler' axle and working
the paddles could effect a daily journey on the São Francisco of
thirty miles, with a tithe of the current trouble.[31]

As the *Eliza* glided out on to the main São Francisco, bound
for its final destination at the Paulo Afonso falls 1,000 miles to
the north, Burton mentally put the river in perspective, employing his favourite Montesquieu-like 'sociology of homology'. At
the most obvious level, at nearly 2,000 miles long the São Francisco was either the fourth or fifth largest (the point is disputed)
river in South America and around the twentieth longest in the
world (again there are rival claimants).[32] More interesting to
Burton than mere length was the river's functionality in terms of
national economy, infrastructure and ecosystem. In his typol-
ogy, the true homology between North and South America river
systems was that between the Amazon and the St Lawrence;
South America's Mississippi was the Rio de la Plata, with the
Paraguay in the role of the Missouri and the Paraná that of the
Ohio, while the Pilcomayo, Bermejo and Salado were, respectively, the Platte, Arkansas and Red rivers. Burton declared that
the São Francisco had no real equivalent in North America; its
nearest analogue was the Niger.[33]

Burton was on firm ground in maintaining that the São Francisco was an exception to the general rule that in nineteenth-century South America rivers did little to ease transport problems. Even the gold diggings of distant Cuiabá in Mato Grosso could be reached from São Paulo by an intricate network of rivers, of which the São Francisco was the most important. Although the Amazon led to the heart of South America, it did not play a role comparable to that of the Mississippi or St Lawrence in North America. But as early as the first decade of the seventeenth century cattle ranchers and *vaqueiros* moved inland up the São Francisco as far as Paulo Afonso falls, an internal exodus that was intensified after 1701 when the agricultural lobby won the battle with the ranching interests and cattle were forbidden to graze within forty miles of the coast. The *sertão* of the north-east, with its satellite cattle economy, was linked to the coast by the São Francisco, which in turn linked the mines of Minas Gerais with São Paulo and Santos, thus making the São Francisco waterway vital for the inter-provincial slave trade of the middle nineteenth century. In many ways the river Burton was now exploring was *the* fulcrum on which the nineteenth-century Brazilian economy turned before the coming of the railways. The only conceivable rival to the São Francisco in terms of South American infrastructure was the Magdalena of Colombia.

Another reason why Burton searched for the analogy for the São Francisco in Africa was that, like the Nile and the Congo, it flooded during the dry season. Moreover, it was in many respects irresistibly reminiscent of the Congo on which Burton had travelled in 1863. There was the same sudden dramatic broadening, often from 1,200 to 1,600 yards in a matter of minutes, and the same limpid green colour. The profusion of caymans and otters recalled the crocodile-infested lower Congo, and there was the same mass of shoals, sandbanks and sandbars to negotiate. But one salient difference impressed itself at once. It was thickly populated; the traveller could hardly travel a league without seeing a fresh cluster of huts. In a word, the São Francisco was tamer, more civilized and less picturesque than the lower Rio das Velhas. There was little chance of running across giant anacondas now. Even the insistent whippoorwill, which had given Burton sleepless nights on the tributary, was now listened to with nostalgia for the great days on the das Velhas.[34]

Making good progress downstream, the *Eliza*, with its new crew, soon reached the town of São Romão. This proved so inhospitable that Burton returned on board the *ajojo* for the night, disgruntled but determined not to make the mistake made by a certain Dr Douville, who through contumacious behaviour and exorbitant medical fees got himself murdered by the locals.[35] But he was secretly angry with the people of São Romão: 'It was not easy to sleep for the babel of sounds, for the Romanenses were decidedly ill-behaved and uncivilized, and made night hideous with their orgies.'[36]

Next morning they set out in driving rain for Januária. It seemed that the rainy season would soon be upon them, for these were clearly premonitory squalls. The São Francisco rose in October at the onset of the monsoons and continued to do so until March. Burton had chosen well his season for travelling, unlike certain other travellers on this river, but from now on the voyage seemed likely to be a close-run thing.[37] There was a continual downpour until 30 September, when the travellers at last enjoyed their first fine day on the great river. The ceaseless drenching rain also increased their problems with the swift-flowing current, which began to show signs of incipient flooding.

Januária found Burton in sour mood. His first problem was that the crew hired at Guaicuí refused to proceed farther, while it was impossible for him to employ fresh *barqueiros*. The Paraguayan war had begun to bite along the São Francisco. Brazil's appalling battle casualties at Curupaití, Tuyutí, Humaitá and elsewhere led to a nationwide draft. Many of the watermen had been pressed into service in Paraguay, while others had fled into the jungle to avoid recruitment. Those who remained at large in Januária feared that if they ventured into a strange town, they too would be drafted. Additional complicating factors were that it was the local harvesting season *and* that there was no real poverty to compel the locals to work for a stranger. There were no less than six *ajojos* tied up at the quayside, all in need of a crew. In the end it was only by offering the top daily rate he had paid on the Rio das Velhas that Burton secured a complement.

Burton's second headache was that he was by now ill-used to the sheer din of populated areas. He made a bad mistake by turning down the offer of a house from a well-known liberal politician who entertained the famous traveller on his first night in

Januária. Stupidly, Burton chose to spend his nights on the *Eliza*. He soon regretted it when lashed by the incessant rains. He explained his decision: 'For liberty's sake I preferred the raft, also to escape from the screams of children, which, throughout Brazil, form the terribly persistent music of the home. The mothers, I presume, physically enjoy being noisy by proxy, and the fathers do not object to losing a night's rest by a performance which could be settled in a second.'[38]

On 27 September, the *Eliza* and the new crew started for Carunhanha. They immediately ran into violent cyclonic storms which churned up waves alarmingly. Burton's new men pleased him by proving themselves true watermen. Next day they passed the confluence of the Rio Verde. Near here, at São João dos Indios, Burton had his only contact with aboriginal Indians in the whole trip.[39] At Carunhanha Burton was entertained by the Rio-educated Dr João Lopez Rodriguez.[40]

But still the wind and rain continued to assail them. On shoving off from Carunhanha 'we reached the raft in time to prepare for a night of devilry let loose.' A north wind was blowing and a ferocious gale at once sprang up. Then the wind veered and came howling in from the east. Thunder roared and lightning flashed. The stream rose in wavelets which washed over the *Eliza*'s gunwales. It took until dawn to reach the crisis of the storm. Then 'we snatched a few minutes of such sleep as hot heads and cold feet, and dogs persistently baying at the weather would permit.'[41]

When the sun finally came out on 30 September, they took the right channel through sandbags and snags, the very spot where the earlier nineteenth-century Brazilian traveller Henrique Halfeld had encountered a veritable plague of alligators.[42] The saurians seemed to have been shot out in the intervening decade, for though the area teemed with bird life – storks, crane, *jaburu*, ibis and spoonbill, there was no sign of the *jacaré*. But there needed no tussle with wild beasts to fill Burton's cup to overflowing. On the last day of September he and his men camped on an island, only to find themselves nearly marooned next morning. The water level had fallen so dramatically in the night that the *Eliza* was all but beached. They made a short provision stop at Senhor Bom Jesus da Lapa shortly afterwards, but once in open water were again assailed by storms. The roaring gale forced them to anchor on the windward side. They proceeded to 'bush' the *ajojo*: that is, they prevented waves from washing over the shallow raft by cutting off the heads of young trees and leafy branches which then, fastened alongside or to the bows, acted as screens. It was at this juncture that Burton comforted himself by remembering the lines from Camoens:

> Amid such scenes with danger fraught and pain
> Serving the fiery spirit more to flame
> Who woos bright honour, he shall ever win
> A true nobility, a deathless fame:
> Not they who love to lean, unjustly vain,
> Upon the ancestral trunk's departed claim;
> Nor they reclining on gilded beds
> Where Moscow's rebeline dowry softness spreads.[43]

The travail continued. On 2 October the travellers passed a night of scant comfort. It was not just that guinea fowl clucked all night; more seriously, for the first time on the river, they were prey to noxious insects, particularly an almost minute variety of mosquito, whose bite was like a needle-prick. The one consolation was a successful fishing expedition next day, which added freshness to the monotonous diet of *bacalhao* or dried cod. When Burton was given coffee by a local judge at Urubu, he accounted it a great luxury.

They reached Bom Jardim, at the frontier of the provinces of Minas Gerais and Bahia, a key nodal point connected with the Atlantic by two roads and also by land and water with 'that Brazilian Mediterranean, the Amazon'. The temperature was now in the eighties Fahrenheit, with hot sultry nights. A few days later they came to Barra, at the confluence of the São Francisco and the Rio Grande. There was a wooden quality about the people that did not appeal to Burton. 'I found them civil and courteous, as indeed is the rule for Brazil, but the Bahiano did not shine after the Paulista or the Mineiro.'[44]

Mid-October found the voyagers floundering. In his journal for the 15th Burton recorded that they sheltered all day from the north-east winds, while he read pocket classics of Horace, Martial, Camoens and Hafiz. Next day they made just two hours' progress against the headwind; the same pattern was repeated on the 17th, 18th and 19th, when they anchored exhausted in the evening at Villa de Sento Se. Burton's depressed state emerges clearly in his animadversions on the people of Sento Se:

> The life of these country places has a barbarous uniformity. The people say of the country *'e muito atrasado'* and they show in their proper persons all the reasons of the *atraso*. It is every man's object to do as little as he can and he limits his utmost industry to the labours of the smallest *fazenda*.

Burton painted a disapproving lotus-land picture of the lives of the locals, which pre-echoes much European disdain for 'lazy' Latin Americans. The country people rose late, breakfasted at once (a habit Burton detested), dropped in on their neighbours, then spent the hot hours in hammocks, swinging, dozing, smoking, eating melons. Dinner at 2 p.m. would consist of fish, meat, manioc, vegetables and the inevitable pepper sauce. Coffee and tobacco shortened the tedious hours until evening, which was given over to strolling or sitting in a shady spot and receiving callers. Supper followed, then songs, drumming, dancing and drinking, which went on till daybreak. 'Thus they lose energy, they lose memory, they cannot persuade themselves to undertake anything, and all exertion seems absolutely impossible to them. At Sento Se the citizens languidly talk of a canal which is to be brought down from the Rio de São Francisco at an expense of £1,680. But no one dreams of doing anything beyond talking. 'Government' must do everything for them, they will do nothing for themselves. After a day or two's halt in these hotbeds of indolence, I begin to feel like one of those who are raised here.'[45]

Burton's sour and dyspeptic mood was not abated as the wind continued against the *Eliza* and they made little headway. They were forced to land and scout for provisions which were becoming scarce. The boatmen, regarding all Nature's elements as feminine in their capriciousness, 'avenged' themselves on the wind and rain by singing songs about the fickleness and treachery of women and denounced *'mulher que engana tropeiro'*.[46]

At Santa Ana Burton engaged a new pilot for the fearsome stretch of rapids ahead. On 22 October they started battle with the *Cachoeira do Sobradinho*. With the wind against them, it took two hours and forty-five minutes to get through the stretch of seething white water. It was 4.25 p.m. before the pilot sounded the all clear. The passage was notable for divulging to Burton another quaint item of Brazilian folklore. The necessity of baring the leg or tucking up skirts was widely considered a serious calamity. But the cataracts cared nothing for the cult of *senhor doctor*. In revenge, the locals dubbed one of the rapids on this stretch *Tira-Calcoens* – the 'take off your trousers rapids'.[47]

Burton had hoped for compensation in the town of Joareiro (reached 24 October), which had been spoken of as an outpost of civilization on the São Francisco and even, somewhat hyperbolically, as 'a little Paris'. But he was very impressed with the landscape between Joareiro and Boa Vista: 'the lower gardens of the São Francisco, perhaps a finer tract than that about the Pirapora.'

His spirits lifted. He reflected that in four months in the wilds (three of them on the river) he had not known an hour of sickness. He and his men avoided alcohol during the day and took the precaution of thoroughly washing their drinking gourds and jars every night. On a typical day he would rise before dawn and take coffee and biscuits. At daybreak the *Eliza* got under way. Bacon and beans would be served at 7 a.m., after which he would work until 11 a.m. A cold bath in the back of one of the canoes would be followed by smoking and reading. At sunset Burton and his men would eat rice and any fish or meat they could lay hands on. When the night birds started their nocturnal chorus, they chose an insect-free spot and turned in. Burton was always warmly clothed when sleeping – a trick he had learned from the Arabs of East Africa. If he was feeling particularly depressed, he liked to take two grains of quinine, and made it a rule never to dwell on the *spes finis*.[48]

After Joareiro both river and landscape combined to make the 'black dog' a rarity. The stream became swift, with the current averaging four miles per hour. The swirling and boiling of the water showed it had depth, and the *Eliza* began to make rapid progress. They were now in a valley studded with pyramidal hills and they sped past densely cultivated fields on either bank, complete with scarecrows. Manioc, maize and beans were the main crops. The rapidity with which landscape changed on this river never ceased to amaze him. [49]

But at Capim Grosso Burton's mood swung towards the negative again when he encountered a real-life exemplification of his most profound secret fear: that all women were at heart lustful volcanoes ready to erupt. On 27 October they reached Capim Grosso 'which deserves to be called Villa Grosseira . . . the wildest place we have yet seen . . . it did not show a trace of hospitality or even of civility . . . the women greatly outnumbered the men. We had inadvertently made fast near their bathing ground; after dark they disported themselves in the water all around us, and debated, giggling, about the advisability of doffing the innermost garment.'[50]

At Boa Vista next day Burton handed his letter of introduction from Emperor Pedro to the military commander, who at once found him a new pilot and paddleman. In desultory conversation with the officers at the Army post here, Burton was surprised to discover that none of them had bothered to visit the great Paulo Afonso falls even when riding within a few miles of it on their way to the coast.

The new pilot was a sixty-five-year-old named Manoel Cipriano. 'He has a queer dry humour, he delights in chaffing the people upon the banks, he twangs the guitar, he takes snuff as most boatmen do, but requires a snuff pocket like our grandfathers, and he has a private bottle of country rum wrapped up carefully as if it were a baby. He never works except when half seas over, and I should fear to trust him when dead sober . . . yet he is the only real pilot that I saw upon the river, he knows it thoroughly, he *will* be master on board . . . we soon learned to confide in his nerve, force and precision. There was something more interesting even than beauty in his danger-look, when, working his paddle like the tail fin of a monstrous fish and firmly planted in the stern canoe of the rocking and tossing craft, he bent slightly forwards, steadily eying with straining glance the grim wall upon which we were dashing at the rate of twenty knots an hour, and, by a few ingenious strokes of the helm at the exact moment, brought round the bows and almost grazed the reef.' Burton's only mistake with Cipriano was to let him choose his own crew; he chose sluggards. The crew turned out so lazy that Cipriano was forced to hire a local *barqueiro* three days later. This man, fortunately, justified all the good things said about the river people below Joareiro. [51]

Below Boa Vista stretched thirty leagues of rapids. Luckily the river bed was usually (though not always) too winding for the wind to form high waves, and the cataracts were more dangerous for those *ascending* the river. On the sixth day out they encountered nine rapids, two whirlpools and two shallows within a five-league stretch – obstructions more serious than the total encountered on the Rio das Velhas. The first day of November saw them running through dangerous rapids while lashed by a gale. Through the scudding mists they caught a momentary glimpse of an old Jesuit mission abandoned in 1759 when the Society of Jesus was suppressed in Brazil. The second day of November, however, saw Burton penning the following: ' It was a delicious morning; the air was sweet and rain-washed and the temperature that of Cairo in the cold season. How much would be paid for such a day at such a season upon the banks of the Thames! All creation looked at its best, and the birds, unusually numerous, sang gaily in the bush.'[52]

The third day of November found the *Eliza* beginning the passage of another cruel stretch of rapids. The cruelty was contagious. The *barqueiros* reproached Burton for not killing a harmless water snake and amused themselves with bullying an unfortunate frog of large size, which they credited with being able to swallow sparks of fire. But Burton's mind was elsewhere. The journey down the São Francisco was taking longer than he expected, and this raised the spectre of further passages of arms with the Foreign Office. How much behind schedule Burton was can be gauged from the diary entries of another British traveller, F.J. Stevenson, who had on this very day given up waiting for him at the Paulo Afonso falls. 'I would very gladly have spent a day or two longer at the Falls, especially as I wanted very much to meet Captain Richard Burton – who is now about due to arrive from the interior – to deliver to him the dispatches entrusted to me by Senhor Campos of Penedo, and also to have an opportunity of making the acquaintance of such a very interesting and celebrated traveller. But the date of his arrival was very uncertain, and as I was anxious to catch the steamer that leaves Penedo for Bahia on the 8th, and the French boat from there on to Rio on the 14th, I could not afford to spend any more time at the Falls.'[53]

4 November 1867 was a critical day: in a seven-league stretch the *Eliza* passed nine swirling patches of raging water. The ex-

perience elicited some Melvillian prose from the traveller: 'There is something majestic in the aspect of the São Francisco, whose turbid waters, here building up, there lying low, now flowing in silent grandeur, fanned by the gentle breeze, and reflecting the gold and azure of the sky, assume an angry, sullen and relentless aspect when some obstacle of exceptional importance would bar its mighty path.' Yet the reality of shooting the rapids was less serene. The *Eliza* rolled in mid-stream, through the boiling, glassy water, fringed by an insistent, noisily-flowing surge. Soon cross waves from the north-west indicated the approach of the maelstrom. The raft was struck full on the beam by a current, more flying than flowing, and was nearly swamped. At 3.15 that afternoon they passed directly into the eye of the worst whirlpool of all. 'I confess to having felt cold hands at the sight of the infamous turnings, the whirlpools which the *Relatorio* calls the terror of navigation, and the potholes some fifteen inches deep in the water.'

Head on the *ajojo* dashed for the rocks. The boatmen braced themselves for the shock. Suddenly the pilot gave the craft a broad sheer with the sweep of his heavy and powerful paddle, carrying them safely through places where they could touch death at either side. The *Eliza* pitched, rolled and yawed, swaying and surging like a shivering whale, as she coursed down the roaring, raging waters. 'Shout, boys, shout!' yelled Cipriano. The men taunted the rocks and the whirlpool. After fifteen exhilarating minutes they shot clear of the 'gouge-eye' of the maelstrom.

It was now 4.40 p.m. Dusk was not far off as they came in earshot of the ninth rapid, so Cipriano proposed postponing the assault. But Burton insisted they shoot it at once. After the joust with the eighth whirlpool, the ninth was an anticlimax. By 5.15 they were through the entire stretch, having covered twenty-seven miles that day, as against the daily average of fourteen since leaving Boa Vista. Burton greeted the calm light-blue of the São Francisco, now stained with the gorgeous red of the setting sun. He was elated at the thought that all the *cachoeiras* were now behind him. [54]

At Varzea Redonda, on 7 November, Burton came to the end of his river voyage. He had floated down the river over 1,000 nautical miles, nearly three times the length of England. [55]

Offered accommodation by a local judge, Burton accepted with the proviso that he spent his last night aboard the *ajojo* for sentimental reasons, before paying off his men. He came to regret this decision, for a storm blew up which nearly battered the *Eliza* to pieces; the crew were no use, being by this time in the last stages of noisy, intoxicated celebration. Burton was relieved next morning when he paid them and they decamped. He dismantled the raft and gave the planks and anchor as souvenirs to his host the justice. Even better than the prospect of seeing the last of the *barqueiros* was getting rid of 'Negra' the mastiff. The dog had been worse than useless as a companion, having uniquely combined savagery and cowardice. It could not be trusted near children or small animals but would flee at the first sight of a porker.[56]

The hospitality of the local judge proved a mixed blessing. Nepotism dictated that Burton's guides for the overland journey to Paulo Afonso falls were all selected from his extended family, with the result that 'when the party was made up, it consisted of the worst men, the worst mules and the worst equipment I had ever seen in Brazil.'[57] But Burton could be as bloody-minded as the worst skrimshanker. In an uncanny replay of the incident that had brought him into public contumely in 1859 after the Lake Regions exploration of Central Africa, Burton retaliated by refusing to pay his porters at journey's end. He was flatly unrepentant about his actions. 'Mere calumny will never deter me from what I there and then did. Travellers will never be well treated as long as their predecessors act upon the principle – or rather non-principle – of forgive and forget at journey's end, because it is the journey's end.'[58]

Leaving Varzea Redonda on 10 November, after two days and nights, Burton arrived at the falls on the 12th. It was soon clear why the São Francisco was not navigable after Varzea Redonda. A mile above the falls the river was funnelled to a breadth of fifty-one feet. The rate of flow of the stream was retarded by the rapids ahead, and the waters backed up in the manner of a tidal wave, ready for the tremendous leap over the lip of the gorge.[59]

The Paulo Afonso cataracts (now the location of the giant Tres Marias dam and power station) are one of the great waterfalls of the world, rivalled in South America only by the Angel falls in Roraima, Brazil, and the Iguaçú falls on the triangular border of Brazil, Argentina and Paraguay.[60] There are seven cataracts, three in the middle of the river, separated by small rocky islands, and four towards the river bank. The falls and their associated rapids stretched on for sixty miles, and it was this fact, combined with the bar at the Atlantic estuary of the São Francisco, that made early travellers like George Gardner sceptical about the economic viability of the river.[61]

Both the approach to the falls and the sensation of sitting at the edge, gazing down into the cascading waters were unforgettable:

> The *quebrada* or gorge is here 260 feet deep; in the narrowest part it is choked to a minimum breadth of fifty-one feet. It is filled with what seems not water but froth and milk, a dashing and dazzling, whirling and churning surfaceless mass, which gives a wondrous study of fluid in motion. Here the luminous whiteness of the chaotic foam-crest, hurled in billows and breakers against the blackness of the rock, is burnt into flakes and spray that leap halfway up the immuring trough. Then the stream boils over and canopies the tremendous scene. In the stilly air of dull, warm grey, the mists surge up, deepening still more the dizzy fall that yawns under our feet . . . The general effect of the picture – and the same may be said of all great cataracts – is the 'realized idea' of power, of power tremendous, inexorable, irresistible. The eye is spellbound by the contrast of this impetuous motion, this wrathful maddened haste to escape, with the frail steadfastness of the bits of rainbow, hovering above . . . The fancy is electrified by the aspect of this Durga of Nature, this evil working good, this life-in-death, this creation and construction by destruction . . . Magic, I may observe, is of the atmosphere of Paulo Afonso; it is the natural expression of the glory and majesty, the splendour and the glamour of the scene, which Greece would have peopled with shapes of beauty, and in which Germany would be haunted by choirs of flying sylphs and dancing undines . . . I sat over the *quebrada* till convinced it was not possible to become 'one with the waters': what at first seemed grand and sublime at last had a feeling of awe too intense to be in any way enjoyable, and I left the place that the

confusion and emotion might pass away.[62]

Next day Burton explored the falls again thoroughly from three different stations and entered the ninety-foot-high Vampire's Grotto (*Furna do Morcêgo*), on the upper rapids, 300 feet above the curdling and creaming waters below. Then 'my task was done. I won its reward, and the strength passed from me.' Two days of tedious riding brought him to Pôrto das Piranhas, only to learn that the oceanic steamer for Rio had just departed. He made a more leisurely progress by tramp steamer to take him the 150 miles down river to the Atlantic, and visited President Barros of Alagoas province at his capital, Maceió. Thence he took ship for Aracaju and Bahia. Only there did he finally pick up a fast steamer for Rio. For the first time since Varzea Redonda his spirits drooped as he realized the days of roving were over and he was bound for his dispiriting berth in Santos, 'alias the Wapping of the Far West'.
[63]

Chapter Nine

Brazilian Finale

When Isabel thought the time for Richard's return was nigh, she went up to Rio to meet the incoming liners. Steamer after steamer docked, but still there was no sign of her husband. In a state of high anxiety, she even toyed with going up to Bahia to see if there was any news there. In some agitation she wrote to her mother. 'I fear Richard is ill, or taken prisoner, or has his money stolen. He always would carry gigantic sums in pocket, hanging half out; and he only has four slaves with him, and has to sleep among them. I am not afraid of anything except the wild Indians, fever, ague and a vicious fish [piranha] which can easily be avoided. There are no other dangers.'[1]

At this juncture Isabel met Wilfred Scawen Blunt, later a famous poet and traveller, but then a Foreign Office junior on his way to a posting in Buenos Aires. Perhaps it was the fact that Blunt was travelling with his sister Alice, or perhaps she already discerned signs of Blunt's sympathy for the underdog that was to make him famous (or notorious). In later years he supported Arabi Pasha against his own countrymen, regarded Omdurman as an unjustified massacre of the innocent, and everywhere supported the rights of the black man against his white oppressor. Whatever the case, Isabel broke down in the Blunts' presence and wept uncontrollably over Richard's four-month absence.[2]

In her grief, she failed to be meticulous about meeting *every* steamer. Needless to say, the one she did not meet turned out to be the one Richard was on. The final irony was that Isabel then had to endure a lecture on wifely duty from a husband irate at her 'insouciant behaviour'. That the incident was still rankling a few days later is clear from the diaries of F.J. Stevenson, the man who had just missed meeting Burton at Paulo Afonso. Stevenson's testimony is all the more worthwhile, since his diaries are a source no previous biographer of Burton has used.

Burton called to thank Stevenson for the Campos despatches. They chatted about the problems of travel in the Brazilian back country. Burton said his next trip would be up the river Paraná to its watershed or tributaries, and thence through the diamond country to the headwaters of the Xingu, then a virtually unknown satellite river of the Amazon. Stevenson knew little of the Xingu, but was able to pass on a few tips about canoeing on the Amazon. Rather taken with his rival traveller, Burton invited him to dinner a few nights later. Stevenson left the following impressions of both meetings:

> Burton is without doubt a very extraordinary character – a splended traveller and intrepid explorer – a wonderful linguist and, I think, the most resolute and determined-looking man I have ever met. He is certainly apt to be a little reckless in his conversation, often very greatly overstepping the bounds of propriety, but is always an exceedingly interesting raconteur, especially when he can be persuaded to talk about his experiences as an explorer and traveller in Africa and the East . . . One night when I was dining with him and Mrs – or as I ought perhaps to call her, Lady Burton – as she is the daughter of an Irish peer, and, I think, a lady in her own right – Burton was telling me about his nigger servant-boys at Santos, how good and honest they were 'until she (pointing to his wife) undertook to make them all Roman Catholics herself, and then they took to stealing my shirts and cigars!' He worked himself up into a most unseemly fury, threatening to throw the effigy of the Blessed Virgin Mary that his wife had in her oratory at Santos out of the window, if she continued to interfere with his 'damned little niggers'. She took it all very quietly, merely saying, 'Now Richard, behave yourself and don't make yourself ridiculous. Mr Stevenson must take you for a perfect brute.'[3]

It is quite clear that the anticlimax of returning to Rio and his quotidian consular life affected Burton badly and made him a cross-grained, cantankerous individual. One night an Englishman freshly arrived from the motherland sought the advice of the famous traveller about the diamonds of the São Francisco. He explained that he had been persuaded to part with £1,500 on the promise of a hundredfold return from the fabulous treasures on the river. Burton scornfully told him that the only diamonds in the São Francisco valley were the *pingua d'água* or 'fool's diamonds'. At this the fortune hunter became quite incensed and stormed out of the meeting.[4]

Reluctantly Burton departed for Santos, where he arrived on 7 January 1868. This time it was impossible for him to do his usual disappearing act into the wilderness for, despite Vice-Consul Glennie's best efforts, a mountain of paperwork requiring Burton's signature or official authorization had accumulated. The next three months were spent commuting between Santos and São Paulo while returns on consular fees, shipping figures, Brazilian exports and even pay for Glennie were laboriously written up by Isabel.[5] To assuage the boredom, Burton kept a weather book and meteorological register from 1 March (which he continued until 7 October). From this we can learn of the freak weather of São Paulo province, including the three days of snow from 2 to 4 April.[6] The Southern hemisphere was an ideal place for observing celestial phenomena such as meteors and ball lightning. 'At São Paulo I have often seen the electric fluid ascending in the south-eastern sky, and at the height of sixty degrees projecting a number of globes, like a monstrous Roman candle.'[7]

The highlight of the first three months of 1868 was the satisfaction of seeing the British-built Santos–São Paulo railway finally in full operation. It had cost £3 million and paid an 8% dividend. Burton's consulate coincided with the beginnings of the Brazilian railway-building boom, which in the 1870s saw São Paulo province crisscrossed with track. In 1867 Brazil had a total of just 427 miles of railway.[8] By the end of the 1870s there were 2,682 additional miles. But the pioneering Santos–São Paulo railroad was always unique. The section of track from Santos up Alto da Serra was already hailed as one of the railway wonders of the world. For seven miles the track ran parallel to the old São Paulo road. The track ran across a bridge at Cubatão (an arm of the sea), then cut through six and a half miles of dense jungle to the foot of the Serra. One of the Burtons' English guests, William Hadfield, who travelled the line with Richard in March 1868, reported: 'How they have hitherto been able to carry on the traffic between Santos and São Paulo is a mystery when we look at the country and the miles of wood passed through.'[9]

At the station at the foot of the Serra, the locomotive started to climb an incline of one in ten. An anfractuous bend in the foot-hills brought the traveller, after one and a quarter miles, to the first lift. Six carriages were then taken up in two lifts to the second leg of a four-stage elevator system, the last of which was hard by a spectacular viaduct across a mountain chasm. The viaduct rested on iron pillars, with a stone foundation driven down 200 feet deep. At the top of the Serra the six carriages were then linked to a fresh locomotive, ready for the forty-eight-mile run through thickly wooded country to the swampy, tufted-grass plain of São Paulo. The entire journey took three and a half hours, most of the time being accounted for by the ascent by lift. After São Paulo the railway line ran on forty-four miles to Jundiaí, a cotton centre – the first coffee plantations were a further thirty miles on. On 23 March 1868 Burton, Hadfield and Aubertin had a memorable day's excursion on this stretch. Hadfield commented: 'Formerly a voyage to Rio de Janeiro was quite an undertaking; now, by rail and steam, it is an affair of two days . . . the Paulistas ought to be proud of their railway, and the Englishmen of the skill and endurance of their countrymen in making it.'[10]

Hadfield was an honoured guest in the Burton household. Richard took him to the French seminary; allowing another man to penetrate his contemplative retreat was a rare mark of privilege. Isabel went riding with him to the Luz quarter, over the Tiete bridge, where there was a marvellous view of São Paulo. Hadfield's stay with the Burtons also enables us to test the oft-reiterated (by both Richard and Isabel) proposition that provisions were so scarce during the Paraguayan war that Isabel had to range far and wide to stock the larder. Hadfield, however, saw none of this. He found the province awash with food, especially fruit and vegetables. 'Indeed, a great many of the comforts and conveniences of life are to be found here which do not exist in other Brazilian towns, whilst the climate is infinitely superior.'[11]

The truth is probably that Richard, chafing at the perennial shortage of mules (which genuinely *were* hard to come by in the Brazil of the Paraguayan war period) for his inland journeys, asserted for his own purposes that *everything* was scarce. This would, after all, make 'good copy' for the Consular Committee in London.

But Hadfield does verify one of Isabel's odder stories. He accompanied her on a visit to Nossa Senhora de Penha, where she took a fancy to a flock of geese and bought them up at a knockdown price, with a view to a grand dinner with the Aubertins. Herding them back to the consulate in São Paulo was not easy, as the sale took place in the teeming rain. When this odd party of mounted drovers and gaggling geese reached the city, the people began to pelt them with wax water balls – for it was the time of the old festival of *Intrudo*, still celebrated in São Paulo, but considered old-fashioned by Rio standards. The geese became alarmed and began to honk furiously and dash in all directions. Scenes of near-chaos ensued before Isabel and her helpers got the flock safely deposited in the consular grounds. Hadfield queried why the geese should have been pelted in the first place. Isabel replied that there was a prejudice against them on the supposed grounds that they ate snakes. But there was nothing wrong with their meat, as Hadfield was able to testify.[12]

The carefree days at São Paulo came to an end on 17 April 1868. On this day Burton went down with a bad fever. Soon complications set in and the patient was in almost continual pain, often at screaming pitch. The local physician diagnosed congestion of the liver combined with inflammation of the lungs, where the two organs met – in other words, hepatitis *and* pneumonia. A variety of 'remedies' was attempted. The physician put twelve leaches on him, lanced him in thirty-eight places, dosed him with tartar emetic, had him rubbed with embrocation every half hour and brought up a powerful blister on his painful side. Nothing seemed to work. Isabel began to fear for his life. 'The agony was fearful, and poor Richard could not move hand or foot, not speak, swallow or breathe without a paroxysm of pain that made him scream for a quarter of an hour.'[13]

Isabel suggested that Richard receive the sacraments (especially Extreme Unction) according to the rites of the Catholic Church. In his agony, Richard was prepared to try anything, but stipulated that he would not be attended by anyone other than Fray João at the Capuchin monastery. Unfortunately he turned out to be absent, on an expedition upcountry. Isabel persuaded the always superstitious Burton to allow her to try Catholic panaceas. She prayed, put some holy water on his head and placed scapulars round his neck. She did not stray from the house for seventeen days, spending most of the time, day and night, at his bedside. The physician, meanwhile, pursued a parallel track with chlorodyne, ether pills and the application of mustard to calves and legs. Isabel always liked to think it was the scapulars that had done the trick but, at all events, by 3 May she was convinced her husband was past the crisis. He got out of bed and spent half an hour in his chair, and even tasted chicken broth, his first food in fifteen days.

Gradually he recovered. By mid-May he was in his study again and a week later he took his first drive. Isabel, too, found adjustment to normality difficult. The first time she went into the garden, after so many days in the sickroom, she almost fainted. Typically, she wrote to her mother: 'Don't mention my fatigue or health in writing back.' But Richard would never be the same man again, physically. He found difficulty in getting the infected lung back to normal, and suffered from wheezing and impaired breathing. 'He is awfully thin and grey and looks about sixty.' He admitted to Isabel that he had given up all hope of making his Mato Grosso expedition and was thinking instead of a quiet trip to the River Plate.[14]

Once fully recovered, he confided to Isabel that he intended to throw up his consulship. Brazil was tolerable to him only if he could continue to explore the great empty map of the interior. His health now prohibited that, so there was an end to it. The euphoria on the São Francisco about not having had a day's illness gave way to a feeling almost of grudge against Brazil which had, as he saw it, brought him to the threshold of death. 'It had given him his illness; it was far from the world; it was no advancement; it led to nothing.'[15] Concerned about the financial implications, Isabel agreed they should sell up in São Paulo and move down to Santos for immediate embarkation. But she persuaded Richard not to burn his boats at once; would it not be better to ask the Foreign Office for an extended period of sick leave, pending a final decision about the future? Richard agreed.

He wrote to request sick leave from 1 August 1868 to 31 May 1869 in order to visit the La Plata region; the consulate meanwhile would be left in Glennie's hands. As to why the River Plate was a good spot for a convalescent: 'Santos offers small chance of complete recovery after a severe attack of hepatitis and pneumonia, and São Paulo has become during this year exceptionally unhealthy.'[16]

The Foreign Office granted him his request. The letter of permission crossed with another one from Burton in which he clarified that the leave was to be on full pay (with Glennie receiving the local allowances). He also asked that if his health had not improved by the end of May 1869, he should, on production of the proper medical certificates, be allowed to return to England to recuperate.[17]

The Burtons stayed just long enought in Santos to witness a six-nation regatta. This was a great triumph for the Portuguese-speaking nations and a blow to the boastful, blustering Anglo-Saxons. Portugal and Brazil came in first and second, while Great Britain and the USA were respectively last and second last (with France and Germany in the middle berths). Isabel noted: 'Tremendous fighting and quarrelling ensued, red and angry faces and "bargee" language. I am very glad; it will produce a good feeling on the Brazilian side, a general emulation, and take our English snots down a peg or two, which they sadly want.'[18]

On 24 July 1868, without having received official word from London, the Burtons departed for Rio. They spent two weeks there, but on 6 August Richard boarded the *Arno* for the River Plate. He displayed his usual cavalier insouciance at parting from Isabel, but there is an unwonted trace of bitterness in Isabel's note of the parting: 'A voyage de luxe for him, for these places are all within writing latitudes and some little civilization.'[19] She was bound for London, to fulfil the usual chores at Richard's behest. The most important of these was to try to interest investors in the Iporanga mines and to find a publisher for the travel book *The Highlands of Brazil*, dedicated to Lord Stanley, which Richard had finished on his very last day in Santos.[20] Once in London, she performed with her usual efficiency. The book was published in the spring of 1869 while Richard was still in South America. But she used her power of attorney to astonishing effect by printing a disclaimer in the foreword to the book, dissociating herself from Richard's strictures on the Catholic Church and his advocacy of polygamy to populate Brazil's empty spaces. 'I point the finger of indignation particularly at what misrepresents our Holy Roman Catholic Church and at what upholds that unnatural and repulsive law, Polygamy, which the author is careful not to practise himself, but from a high moral pedestal he preaches to the ignorant as a means of population in young countries.'[21]

Isabel had her usual ill-luck with ocean voyages. There were high seas and biting trade winds all the way home during a bitterly cold August. She was exhausted when her family met her at Southampton on 1 September. But for all the foolishness of which Wilfred Blunt later complained, Isabel was a doer as well as a talker, as she proved during the homeward stopover at Bahia. She went to lunch there with a friend of Richard's called Charley Williams. Williams kept a small menagerie, including a cage of poisonous snakes. He insisted on showing Isabel his collection of reptiles and took one of the rattlesnakes by its head out of the cage. He was so used to doing this that he became careless; the snake slipped through his hands and bit him on the wrist. Since his friends had all bolted once the cage was open, it was as much as Williams could do to thrust the snake back into the cage and lock it, before staggering against a wall. Isabel, who had prepared herself mentally for just such an emergency, struck a series of lucifer matches and kept cramming them into the snakebite on the wrist until she had made a hole. Then she tied her handkerchief tightly round the wound and called to the servants for a bottle of whisky. She forced the whole bottle down Williams's throat, then, with the help of the servants, kept him on the move for three hours. Finally they got him to bed. Next morning he had made a complete recovery.[22]

Burton's departure from Brazil provides an opportunity to sum up on his three years there. Despite Foreign Office grumbling, he had performed his duties with reasonable efficiency and gained a deep understanding of Brazilian culture. This point was not lost on his superiors. After the débâcle of Burton's 1869-71 consulate in Damascus, they offered him the post at Pará (Belém) at the mouth of the Amazon, whence forays into the Xingu and upper Amazon would be eminently feasible. Burton declined on the grounds that the proposed posting was 'too small a berth for me after Damascus'.[23]

The most basic problem was that in Brazil Burton was bored, and soon ran out of self-made challenges. His explorations turned out disappointingly. Illness prevented him from getting to grips with the Xingu, which might genuinely have inspired him, and the trip down the São Francisco patently lacked the drama of his pilgrimage to Mecca, the journey to the forbidden city of Harar or the trek to the Lake Regions of Central Africa. There was a certain element of 'going through the motions' about Burton's Brazilian adventures which sometimes communicated itself to his writings, a point the critics of *The Highlands of Brazil* were not slow to pick up.[24] But Burton's travel writings have always had their champions. Theodore Roosevelt commented: 'Burton's writings on the interior of Brazil offer an excellent instance of the value of a sojourn or trip of this type, even without an especial scientific object.'[25]

As a linguist, Burton found little to challenge him in Brazil. His Portuguese was outstanding – indeed it was his second favourite language after the beloved Arabic – and he even found the Béarnais dialect he had mastered as a youth useful in certain parts of the Empire.[26] He also had little to get his teeth into in the anthropological sphere. His work in this area was solid but unexciting: an investigation of the primordial inhabitants of Minas Gerais, notes on the 'kitchen-middens' of São Paulo, an annotation of Waitz's *Anthropology of Primitive Peoples*.[27] It was a far cry from his absorbing studies of the 'customs' in Dahomey, and from his ethnologies of the Ethiopian Danakil, the Arabian Bedouin, the East African Gogo or the North American Sioux. Still, he acquired enough knowledge to be regarded as a scholarly expert on Brazil, and the Royal Geographical Society later used him as a referee in this capacity.[28]

Burton was always limited as a zoologist. Even so, except when momentarily excited by tales of giant snakes or sea monsters, he seems to have had even less interest than usual in wildlife. One can almost perceive the yawn when he remarks with lordly disdain: 'the labours of ichthyologists, especially upon the river Amazonas, have proved that the distribution of the genera and species is distinctly limited.'[29] But when Burton bothers to record zoological and geographical impressions, they are always remarkably accurate. Endorsements for his observations come thick and fast, whether from contemporaries like Stevenson on the spread through the continent of the Derby gamecock (and the consequent rise of cockfighting), from W.H. Hudson later in the nineteenth century on the ticks and jiggers, or from scholarly geographers in our own era on the soil erosion of São Paulo province.[30]

One of the reasons Burton was less than comfortable in Brazil was precisely the dominance of the Catholic Church he railed about in *Highlands*, much to Isabel's disgust. He hated especially the cult of virginity disingenuously extrapolated from the Church's mariolatry. American Indians, he thought, instancing the Chibchas and the Caribs, regarded female virginity as a reproach: it meant the woman had never inspired love.[31] And in general he detested the juggernaut manner in which the Catholic Church had 'rolled over' indigenous Indian culture. This was a subject always likely to work him up into a lather: 'The good missionaries, who saw the Devil, in every faith except their own, of course made their barbarous rival [the witchdoctor] a priest of the foul Fiend. They could not discern the soul of good in things evil, such as slavery and cannibalism. But the institution has its uses: it was and it is the first step towards emerging from the purely savage state. It gave method and direction to the vague fears which primeval man shared with the gorilla; it created a comparatively learned class, whose business in life was to study and to think; and it taught the art of governing as well as being governed. Of course the time came when it had done its work, and then, as is the course of things human, it was succeeded by something better, and was looked back upon, not with respect and gratitude, but with a childish and unreasonable horror.'[32]

But, at the root, there was a fundamental lack of rapport between Burton and Latin American culture. Partly this was a simple boredom and a feeling that the New World was 'bald and tame' compared with his beloved Arabia. Isabel was often told by her Brazilian friends that she suffered from a yearning for other places or persons connoted by the Brazilian word *saudades*. Richard felt this acutely. As he remarked in Damascus: 'the New World, which had been my latest scene of action, wearies with its want of history, of association, and consequently of romance.'[33]

But beyond this there was operating in Burton a further principle – one we can only term metaphysical. Many great writers have testified to the unnatural horror conjured in them by the colour white: we find this in D.H. Lawrence's 'white mental consciousness', Jack London's 'white logic', and, most famously, in Herman Melville's 'whiteness of the whale'. For Burton the 'unnatural' colour was green, the colour of the rainforests and the jungles. At a deep level he was always miserable in the damp heat of Brazil. He considered that the Wordsworthian dictum 'not melancholy, no, for it is green' should be reversed. He felt happy in the Arabian desert but not in the so-called forest Elysium.[34] In the forest, man's brain was confused with the sheer multiplicity of objects, and one's sensations were as though in a gorgeous jail. For this reason Burton always suffered from sustained melancholia in evergreen regions: whether western India, Central Africa or Brazil. It seemed to him that in forests Nature mastered Man, but in deserts Man mastered Nature. There are few more revealing statements than the one where Burton raises a hymn to the desert as a place of limitless possibilities, where man is a bare potential. Here Burton is wholly and fully the existentialist *avant la lettre*. 'It is the type of liberty, which is life, whilst the idea of Immensity, of Sublimity, of Infinity, is always present.'[35]

III
RIVER PLATE

Chapter Ten

To the Paraguayan Front

After a fortnight's convalescence in Rio, Burton departed for the River Plate on Thursday 6 August 1868 aboard the *Arno*. He tried to do his bit for the consular posting he had just left by proposing to the captain that Royal Mail Lines steamers should henceforth call at Santos on the way down to La Plata. The captain informed him that such a stopover did not yet make commercial sense. Burton prowled around the ship, finding fault with everything. This time it was the presence on board of Englishmen who were 'specimens of the £10 householder' that particularly excited his ire. Nor was his cross-grained, dyspeptic mood improved by a rough passage to the Plate estuary, as the *Arno* was buffeted by the *pampeiro* to the point of boxing the compass.

He arrived at Montevideo on 11 August and found a berth in an appallingly dingy hotel; not being one of the *cognoscenti*, he did not know that the only hotel in Uruguay acceptable to Europeans was the 'Oriental'.[1] In this epoch there were little signs in Montevideo of the sophistication that would win Uruguay the appellation (at least in the first half of the twentieth century) 'the Switzerland of Latin America'. 'One palazzo at Rome or Naples contains, I believe, far more of art than the combined treasures of South America,' was his waspish first impression. But he cheered up when he found that one of the street argots was the identical dialect of the Neapolitan *lazzaroni* he had mastered in his youth. As he recorded later: 'I found them all at Montevideo and Buenos Aires, dressed in *cacciatore* and swearing *"M'nnac-cia anima tua!"*; they were impressed with a conviction that I myself was a *lazzarone* in luck.'[2] But the pendulum swung back again when he witnessed the 'unacceptable face' of Catholicism. 'Here a scaffolding lately fell, with a mass of masonry, injuring sundry workmen. Mr Adams, the Protestant Minister, passing at the time, rushed with a British energy, regardless where he trod, to assist the hurt. Whereupon came forth the sturdy old genius loci, the Padre, and in peremptory accents warned his heretic brother against harming the bricks.'[3]

It was evident that Montevideo was not Richard Burton's kind of town. On 15 August he embarked in the *Yi* for a voyage that would take him by stages to the famous Paraguayan fortress of Humaitá, lately fallen to the Allies. The passage, costing £14, involved stopping at Buenos Aires to pick up further 'notable' passengers, and, after a few days getting to know the place, proceeding up 676 miles of the Paraná to Humaitá.

On the way upriver Burton pondered the causes and consequences of South America's bloodiest war. British diplomatic opinion (and especially that of Edward Thornton, who before becoming Minister in Rio had been HMG's representative in Buenos Aires) overwhelmingly favoured the idea that the war was caused by the mindless, paranoid overreactions of a crazed Paraguayan dictator, Francisco Solano López.[4] Burton, rightly, thought this view simplistic. How had it come about, he asked, that the traditional rivals for mastery in the Banda Oriental (Brazil and Argentina) had ended by allying themselves *with* the nation they normally fought over (Uruguay) and *against* one with whom they had no previous serious quarrels? Some said that Pedro II had been looking for foreign adventure to divert attention from economic problems at home, and it was true that once the war began, the emperor betrayed all the symptoms of crude imperialism.[5] Others thought that Brazil had intervened massively in Uruguay out of fear that unless there was a satellite government there, the cattle-rich southern province of Rio Grande do Sul might contemplate seceding from the empire and uniting itself with the precariously independent Oriental Republic.[6] This would explain Brazil's intervention on the *colorado* side against the *blancos* in the Uruguayan civil war of 1863-5. But hitherto Brazilian intervention in Uruguay had always led to war with Argentina. What was different this time?

Anticipating the line followed by revisionist historians more than a hundred years later, Burton favoured the 'Paraguay not guilty' thesis on the causes of the War of Triple Alliance. Shrewdly, he saw that the real villain of the piece was Argentina. The new factor in River Plate politics in the 1860s was an Argentina newly united (under Bartolomé Mitre) beneath the banner of liberal capitalism.[7] Mitre's Argentina was surrounded by many enemies: the *blancos* in Uruguay, ex-President Urquiza in the province of Entre Ríos and, more distantly, Paraguay, which represented an ideological and economic alternative to his programme: state control and hostility to foreign capital as against free trade and *laissez-faire*. When the *montoneros* in the interior of Argentina rebelled in 1863 and called for a return to the old regime under Urquiza, Mitre hit back by arming the exiled *colorados* and sending them across the River Plate to destabilize Uruguay. When Brazil inevitably became sucked into this maelstrom in 1864, Mitre, with masterly sleight of hand, managed to inveigle Brazil with Paraguay instead.[8] The timid and defensive Solano López of 1863 was converted into the sabre-rattling 'paranoiac' of 1864 by the very real fear that his own country would be swallowed up by the Brazilian military behemoth Mitre had summoned south to do his own dirty work. In a word, Mitre identified Paraguay as the true long-term enemy of his united Argentina and, in a masterpiece of diplomatic machiavellianism, managed to manipulate Brazil into bearing the brunt of a war that worked in his interests, not those of the empire. A profound reading of the Paraguayan war construes it as the most serious manifestation of a continuing civil war in Argentina, which began with the *montonero* uprising of 1863 and ended only with the defeat of the final López Jordán rebellion in 1873.[9]

It says much about Burton's percipience that he was not taken in for one minute by anti-Paraguayan propaganda. He realized that Solano López's 'tyranny' was in fact an alternative political model. At the ideological level the war was divine right of kings against liberalism, Jesuit *étatisme* against *laissez-faire* capitalism. Burton saw Paraguay as the inheritor of the Spanish tradition of the 'marvellous, Oriental, fatalistic patience under despotisms'. Such despotism was endogenous and seemed both natural and inevitable to Paraguayans. Whereas the rest of Latin

America took its inspiration from Bolívar and the French Revolution, 'Paraguay was ever a repertoire of Old World ideas.' With his perennial capacity to draw illuminating analogies, Burton compared isolationist Paraguay with Japan before 1853, and saw Francisco Solano's father, Carlos Antonio López, as Brigham Young to the Joseph Smith played by Dr Francia, the founder and first dictator of the country.[10]

By the time Burton was steaming up the Paraná in the Yi, Brazil and Paraguay had been at war for four years (Argentina joined in on a trumped-up pretext in April 1865). On paper the result was a foregone conclusion but Paraguayan resistance had been terrific. Paraguay's maximum manpower was 150,000 (counting all males between twelve and sixty) out of a total population of just 450,000. Brazil could draw on a population of 9,000,000, and her National Guard alone numbered some 200,000. Against this, at the onset of hostilities, Paraguay held a technical advantage in trains and telegraphs, river-mines, torpedoes and rocket-launchers. Asunción also boasted a newly-completed foundry, where guns were cast from bells contributed by the country's churches. López, however, could not obtain modern artillery and had no effective answer to the crushing vice of Brazilian naval power. The empire was able to put forty-five gunboats on the Paraná at the beginning of the war, and would later weigh in with the latest ironclads.

The Allies could draw on an almost limitless reservoir of manpower and were sustained by the bankers of Europe, who made them generous war loans. López received no such subventions and had not had time to build up his arsenal. Had the war broken out just one year later, things would have been very different. As Burton commented: 'The war . . . was altogether premature: had the cuirassed ships and the Whitworths ordered by the Marshal-President begun the campaign, he might now have supplied the place of Mexico with a third great Latin empire.' As it was, the war was 'waged by hundreds against thousands; a battle of Brown Bess and poor old flint muskets against Spencer and Enfield rifles; of honey-combed carronades, long and short, against Whitworths and Lahittes; of punts and canoes against ironclads.'[11]

The Yi passed the island of Martin García and came to the port of Rosario, ancient trading rival of Buenos Aires. Here Burton met his friend, Consul Thomas Hutchinson, who introduced him to the great railway entrepreneur William Wheelwright. Wheelwright had brought 'Yankee know-how' to the southern hemisphere and built Argentina's first railways. But the less pleasant aspect of Rosario was cholera, a by-product of the war. The disease had cut huge swathes through the Allied armies: 492 Argentine soldiers had died of it in April 1868 alone.[12]

The halt at Rosario was brief. Soon the *Yi* was at Goya, the most southerly point reached by the Paraguayan invaders. Brazil's military intervention in Uruguay in 1864 had led ultimately to a declaration of war by Solano López on the empire. But the great *blanco* stronghold of Paysandú in Uruguay had been blown apart by Brazilian cannon before Paraguayan troops could get into the fight. It was López's desire to rush his troops southwards that led to his worst miscalculation. By far the shortest route from Asunción to Uruguay was on to the river Uruguay across the uninhabited Misiones strip, in the extreme north of the Argentine province of Corrientes. López naïvely thought that officially neutral Argentina would give the same rights of transit to him as to Brazil. When Mitre peremptorily refused López's harmless request, the dictator sent his trooops across Misiones anyway. This was exactly what Mitre had hoped for. He was able to dragoon his unwilling citizens into a war on the side of the hated *macacos* ('monkeys' – the inevitable Argentine term for the Brazilians), citing López's 'aggression'. For most of 1865 the theatre of war was on the soil of Corrientes. The Paraguayans invaded down both the Paraná and Uruguay rivers, but were heavily defeated and forced to retire on to Paraguayan soil.

Ever northward pressed the steamer, past the agricultural colonies of Santa Fé province – designed as a buffer against the still unsubdued Indians of northern Argentina – and into the Chaco Austral, which Burton characterized as similar to west Texas. He noticed the likeness of the Paraná to Brazil's São Francisco – how, in the manner of the rivers of the southern hemisphere, it cut into the south bank. On 5 September the *Yi* docked at the city of Corrientes, the most northerly point of Argentina on the Paraná. This had long been virtually a garrison town, with all the unpleasant connotations of the term. Another British traveller, who also visited the town in 1868, left this impression: 'One was painfully struck on walking through the city with the evident signs of demoralization caused by the presence of such a large body of troops and their followers; debauchery of every kind was going on, often ending in murder.'[13]

Even worse, when Burton arrived, the province of Corrientes was in the grip of civil war, between supporters of President Mitre and ex-President Urquiza. Despite serious misgivings, Urquiza had remained loyal to Mitre during the early years of the Paraguayan war, even though his followers mutinied and re- fused to serve at the front. But by 1868 anti-war feeling and hatred of the Brazilians had combined with local feuding and factionalism in the littoral provinces (Entre Ríos, Santa Fé and Corrientes) to produce potentially the worst internal crisis of the war. It was Mitre's abiding nightmare that all his plans for a 'greater Argentina' would founder if Urquiza turned his flank. In September 1868 men under Urquiza's banner had rejected their leader's tentative approach and were in open rebellion against government forces.[14]

Burton learned of the crisis almost by accident. 'I found out that a revolution was going on only by asking about a picquet of cavalry stationed in the church porch.' But he was as cynical about Latin American 'revolutions' as most European travellers, then and since. 'Here a revolution usually begins by a dozen ruf- fians or so rushing into the chief magistrate's house and stabbing or shooting him. The principal then appears at the window and screams "Liberty". His friends clear him lustily, his enemies, after firing a few shots, make themselves scarce, and he and his turn their steps towards the National Treasury. Next morning a new Governor and a new Government appear in order, and that is all.'[15]

After Corrientes the *Yi* crossed into Paraguay proper. By now Burton was well accustomed to the leisurely daily life on the ship. A breakfast of coffee and biscuits was served at dawn, then at between 9 and 10 a.m. a huge dinner(!) was spread before them. Olives, ham and sausages as *hors-d'oeuvres* were followed by *puchero* – a heavy stew of potatoes, cabbage and meat re- miniscent of the Brazilian *feijoada*. Table wines were free, but a mediocre bottle of port cost thirty-two shillings. Coffee and 'cowslip tea' were the signal for smoking and a small bout of gambling. The siesta was universal from noon to 3 p.m. Then *maté* was served, and close on its heels a second dinner, identical to the first, at 4 p.m. Candles and cigars were then lit and the soirée started. Some watched the night upon the poop; others conversed, played music and sang or simply listened. By far the favourite pastime was gambling, which turned the fore saloon into a standing hell. The Brazilians were the keenest players, often going on well into the small hours. One passenger lost $8,000 (£2,000) during the trip from Buenos Aires to Humaitá. The only way Burton could snatch a few hours' sleep in the midst of the incessant babel was to open the skylight and let the inrush of cold air clear the gamblers away.

Not surprisingly, the querulous aspect of Burton's character, always in evidence on overcrowded ships, was well to the fore:

> The three stewards are expected to do the work of one man; they are exceedingly civil, and they do nothing. Of course, this is the fault of the *comisario*, or purser, a small Spanish bantam, or rather 'hen-harrier', who spends all his time in trifling with the feminine heart. The captain, Don Pedro Lorenzo Flores – do not forget the Don, and if you want anything say 'Señor Don' – was an ex-item of that infinitesimal body, the national navy of the Banda Oriental. He brought out *Yi* for its Company from the United States, and he avenges himself upon Northern and Anglo-American coarseness by calling all Yankees 'rascals'. His chief duty is to bale out the soup, to pass cigars, and to send round sherry after dinner. This must be done to everybody at the table, or the excluded will take offence and sulk like small boys . . . In Brazil the siesta is not the rule, but the Brazilians rarely begin the day at Bengal hours. On this parallel, the further we go westward, and the more backward becomes the land, the longer will last the siesta; the cause being simply that the population, having nothing to do, very wisely allows its arteries to contract.[16]

North of Corrientes was the scene of the bloodiest battles of the Paraguayan war. The hard-fought battle of Paso de la Patria (January 1866) brought home to the Allies the calibre of the foe. Mitre's boast, on declaring war in April 1865, that he would be in Asunción in three months already looked the hollowest bravado. Man for man the Paraguayans were far superior as warriors, Burton's sneering reference notwithstanding. 'The war brings before us an anthropological type which, like the England of a past generation, holds every Paraguayan boy-man equal, single-handed to at least any half dozen of his enemies.'[17]

On 25 April 1866 the long-delayed Allied invasion of Paraguay at last started. At the end of May was fought the battle of Tuyuti, in terms of numbers involved the greatest fought on South American soil until then. Commander-in-chief Mitre's pyrrhic victory solved nothing strategically, and the huge casualty lists hardened opposition to the war in Argentina. Argentines had entered the conflict reluctantly to vindicate national honour, but it was widely felt that the expulsion of López from Corrientes marked the limit of what was justifiable or desirable.[18]

In September Mitre met Solano López at Yataiti-Cora for an abortive attempt to hammer out peace terms. Burton considered that the conference was a stalling tactic by López to gain time for his depleted forces. Later historians consider that López's overtures were genuine, but that Mitre was intransigent and demanded impossible terms. Whatever the case, the conference was immediately followed by the Allies' darkest hour. At Curupaiti in September 1866 a frontal assault on the entrenched Paraguayan positions was repulsed with great slaughter: the attack cost 2,082 dead and 1,961 Brazilians.[19] But the great Paraguayan victory masked López's defects as strategist, which Burton summed up as follows: 'The great strategical error committed by the Paraguayans was that of the Confederate States – an attempt to fight along extended lines. Instead of holding along the stream of a succession of outposts, which were all lost by direct attack or by evacuation, they should have concentrated themselves at fewer places, and should have rendered them doubly and trebly strong.'[20]

After Curupaití the Paraguayans dug in at a seemingly impregnable position at Humaitá. It consisted of a series of trenches and strong points running along the crests of the few small slopes in the area, and covering all the openings and passes through the swamps of the Bellaco, which in effect sealed in the whole Paraguayan army. Owing to its shape on the maps, this defensive system was known to the Allies as the *cuadrilátero*. It hinged upon the fortress of Humaitá, which commanded a sharp, horse-shoe bend in the river Paraguay and was regarded with excessive respect by Allies and Paraguayans alike. The only way the Allies could take the *cuadrilátero*, other than by frontal assault as at Curupaití, was for the Brazilian fleet to force passage of the river, or for the land forces to attempt a dangerous and extensive flanking movement to the east, through the difficult terrain of the largely unknown Chaco. The Paraguayans strengthened the *cuadrilátero* by widening and deepening the great trench at Curupaití, and mounting more guns in the battery itself. They cut roads and tracks through the woods to facilitate communications; they deepened the channels in the marshland by building dams; they erected sluice gates so that large areas could be flooded at a moment's notice.

Once again there was a long delay before the Allies resumed the offensive. On 22 July 1867 they threw all their resources into the attempted encirclement of Humaitá. The Paraguayans contested every yard of ground yielded and López, in Burton's words, made 'every abandoned place a small Moscow'. It took until 2 November for the Brazilians to complete their flanking movement; now the only escape route was at Timbo, across the river from Humaitá.

On 3 November 1867 López counterattacked. At the second battle of Tuyutí the Paraguayans carried all before them but failed to take the citadel, as López stupidly allowed his men to disperse and plunder before they had finished the job. This allowed the Allies to counterattack. They regained the field of battle, while the Paraguayans staggered away with armfuls of booty. Allied propaganda converted military defeat into victory but even the notoriously pro-Allies Thornton was compelled to report to London: 'A curious incident connected with the recent engagement . . . is that the vanquished seized, and were able to carry off, several pieces of artillery belonging to the victors; a proceeding unusual, I believe, in modern military annals.'[21]

But the Allies did now hold most of the cards. After López's failure to seize an ironclad in March 1868, he retreated across the river Paraguay into the Chaco, leaving a skeleton force at Humaitá. His main army crossed the river Bermejo, recrossed the Paraguay, and took up new positions on the north bank of the river Tebicuarí. The Allies meanwhile tried to starve out the Humaitá garrison. The Paraguayan defender, Colonel Martinez, pretended to evacuate it. On 15 July 1868 ironclads bombarded the fortress. When there was no answering volley, they landed 12,000 men. The concealed Paraguayans rose from their hiding places and cut them down in a hail of bullets. It was said that 2,000 Allied troops died within an hour. But this was the Paraguayans' last hurrah. On the night of 23-24 July they finally did evacuate Humaitá. While crossing to the Chaco by Laguna Vera, Martinez's men took terrible punishment and part of his force was compelled to surrender. Allied jubilation at the capture of a weakly-defended fortress after thirteen months of assault was unbounded, even though, as a modern historian has pointed out, the fall of Humaitá 'proved to be no more indicative of the war's early end than had the final collapse of Vicksburg in the American Civil War'.[22]

Humaitá, then, had been in Allied hands barely two months when Burton came in sight of it in the *Yi*. But first Burton experienced the confluence of the Paraná and Paraguay rivers, which he thought easily dwarfed the similar meeting of the São Francisco and Rio das Velhas in Minas Gerais.

It prompted one of Burton's inevitable river homologies: the Paraná was to the Ohio as the Paraguay to the Missouri, with the Salado, Bermejo and Pilcomayo playing the roles, respectively, of the Red River, Arkansas and Platte.[23]

Once arrived at Humaitá itself, Burton confessed to a feeling of grievous disappointment. The fortress which had been hyperbolically compared with Kars, Sebastopol, Luxembourg, Richmond, Vicksburg and Gibraltar he found a paper tiger, a monstrous humbug. He expressed incredulity that such flimsy defences should have held 40,000 Allied veterans and the pride of the Brazilian navy at bay for so long. By an association of ideas he proceeded to attack the French geographer Elisée Reclus, 'that prince of humbugs' whose exaggerated descriptions of Humaitá had recently appeared in the *Revue des Deux Mondes*.[24] What most astonished Burton was the almost unbelievable antiquity of the guns abandoned by López. Two of the cannon had been cast in Seville in the 1670s. This was of a piece with general experience. Out of five guns captured by the Allies after the battle of Uruguaiana in September 1865, one had been manufactured at Douai in 1790, another at Barcelona in 1788 and a third was from Seville, vintage 1679.[25]

On 26 August Burton completed a five-hour inspection on horseback of the entire twenty-mile *cuadrilátero*. Next day he proceeded upriver to the front at Guardia Tacuara, at the confluence of the Rio Bermejo. The Brazilians refused to allow him near the actual fighting, so he contented himself with a foray into the Paraguayan jungle. The landscape ran the gamut from orange groves to swamps, taking in grassy plains and palm forests. Travellers were assailed by day by sandflies and at night by mosquitoes; in addition the blood-sucking *culex* insect, which could bite through the closest cloth, was a constant hazard. War zone or not, the forests teemed with birds: peewits, snipe, snippet, water hens, *jacuanas*, lily-trotters, carrion birds, fish-hawks, *caracará*, stork, *urubu*, turkey buzzard and spoonbill. 'Flights varying in number from seven to twenty formed long triangles, and their wings of the finest rose, merging into a dark pink, caught the reflection of the sun, who sank like a cloven king in his own blood. The pure light of heaven, absorbed by transparent vapour and by impurities of the lower atmospheric strata, glowed with

Flaming gold, till all below
Grew the colour of the crow

Then the weird grey shadow, simulating a cloud bank, rose in the west and the moon saw us safely home.'[26]

From Humaitá Burton returned to Corrientes, where he spent a fretful week from 5 to 12 September. At the Allied camp at nearby Paso de Patria he was able to make a sustained examination of the Brazilian and Argentine armies. What he saw shocked and depressed him. Many of the Allied soldiers were openly begging, since they took their pay in the form of rations. There were so many dogs sniffing round the camp that when the army resumed its offensive, and the dogs' food supply was cut off, their howling became so oppressive that the soldiers remaining in the rearguard were forced to slaughter thousands of the starving beasts. But Paso de Patria was a Babylon of billiard halls, dance salons, barbers' shops, vaudeville theatres, photographic studios and, above all, countless brothels. Burton could accept the use of 'Amazons' in the Paraguayan army, since López was desperately short of manpower. But he detested the 'unnatural' appearance of the Allied camp followers and was appalled at their numbers – 4,000 in all, 'mounted *en Amazone*, and made conspicuous by mushroom straw hats, with the usual profusion of beads and blossoms . . . My Brazilian friends declared them to be a necessary evil. I can see the evil, but not the necessity. Anything more hideous and revolting than such specimens of femininity it is hard to imagine.'[27]

Burton paid a visit to the Allied General Osorio, whom he rated far the best of their commanders. But since he was the only officer respected by both Brazilians and Argentines alike, this aroused the jealousy of his superiors and his talents were largely squandered. The Argentine and Brazilian soldiery were of poor quality, but at least they were there in large numbers. Of the Uruguayans, who had in a sense precipitated the conflict, there was scarcely a sign. This did not prevent the Uruguayans who had come upriver on the *Yi* from behaving in the most arrogant and high-handed manner. 'They were hardly civil to a courteous Brazilian officer of rank – it proved to be General Argolo – who, riding past with his staff, invited us, though perfect strangers, to drink beer at his quarters. They would not even inspect the lines of the *macacos*, as they called their Imperial Allies. Again and again they boasted the prowess of their own party, stating how five hundred of them had defended Paysandú against a host.'[28]

Militarily, the most interesting part of Burton's inspection was the information yielded on Allied experiments with balloons. These had begun in 1867. A Polish officer called Chodasiewicz, formerly a Russian army officer who had deserted in the Crimea in 1853, ascended to 270 feet in a balloon and took detailed notes on López's defences. After fourteen such aerial reconnaissances, López struck back. He threw up smokescreens in front of the balloon, then spread the rumour that the Allies were trying to dump poisonous gas on his men.[29] Chodasiewicz, incidentally, was just one of many foreign mercenaries employed on both sides in this conflict. In Corrientes Burton fell in with another, a Belgian of Scots descent named Edouard Peterkin, a contractor who supplied Enfields to the Allies.

Perhaps most astonishing of all aspects of the war was its astronomical cost. Great fortunes were made by Argentine provisioners and victuallers. The brunt of the cost was borne by Brazil, partly because Pedro II refused to stint on an enterprise that so redounded to the 'glory' of the empire. Every Brazilian soldier had a generous ration entitlement, including a bottle of rum a day between six men. It was this largesse, plus the promise of manumission, that had lured so many black slaves into the imperial army – a trend which Burton, a notorious negrophobe ('ignorant, bloodthirsty brutes') so deplored. But the cost of the war for Brazil was about $200,000 a day, or some £14,400,000 a year. An astonishing report from British sources in 1869 estimated that fully £2,000,000 of this went on feeding and maintaining horses for the imperial cavalry.[30]

Burton returned to Buenos Aires for a brief rest, then, on 6 October, set out on another journey north. This time he intended to visit the 1865 battlefields on the upper river Uruguay. He found the river 'masculine' as against the 'femininity' of the Paraná. He and his companions landed first at Concepción del Uruguay, where an invitation awaited them to visit the great *caudillo* Justo José de Urquiza at his palace in San José. The travellers set off overland on horseback. At San José they found extensive gardens and aviaries, where African lories brushed wings with turkeys and leadbeater cockatoos, and ounces and pumas prowled in enclosures. In a gesture reminiscent of his great adventure in Harar in 1855, Burton halted at the gate and sent in his name. The travellers were invited to enter the palace by the main gate. Burton was then summoned for interview at once – an unusual honour, since many foreign travellers were kept waiting on the *caudillo*'s pleasure for an entire week.[31]

Within minutes Burton was ushered into the presence of the man who was still arguably the most powerful individual in Argentina, and certainly the richest. At sixty-seven Urquiza was the veteran of four great battles: Vences, Caseros, Cepeda and Pavón. Overthrower of the dictator Rosas in 1852, he presided over the Argentine confederation until 1859 (with the province of Buenos Aires in secession). After the inconclusive hostilities with Buenos Aires that ended with the battle of Pavón in 1861, Urquiza threw in his lot with Mitre. He backed him, reluctantly, against Paraguay, even though the troops drawn from his province of Entre Ríos deserted *en masse*. When Burton met him, Urquiza was still smarting from humiliating defeat in the 1868 presidential election, when Domingo Sarmiento succeeded Mitre for a non-renewable six-year term.[32]

Burton was a shrewd reader of men, so decided to lay it on with a trowel. 'I made my compliments, expressing in all sincerity my pleasure at seeing a name so well-known throughout the civilized world: Don Justo received this little tribute with a bow and a smile, welcomed and shook hands with the whole party, and seated us near him upon the settee, opposite his full-length portrait, which painters persist in making too grim.[33]

Ever an investigator with a nose for money, Burton quickly knifed through to the nub of Urquiza's power: the teeming pastoral wealth of Entre Ríos, of which Urquiza was the main beneficiary. Burton did a quick calculation and worked out that the *caudillo* owned 3,600,000 acres, 200,000 sheep and 800,000 cattle, and that he had an income of £225,000 a year. However, 'he is not a good paymaster, his peons are often six months in arrears, his agents, like the publishers of M. de Balzac, court ruination.' Burton overestimated the real estate but severely underestimated the pastoral riches. In 1868-9 it was estimated that the province contained 2,000,000 cattle, 2,000,000 sheep and 500,000 horses. Urquiza himself owned 600,000 of the cattle, 500,000 sheep and 20,000 horses. In Entre Ríos alone he owned 1,650,000 acres of land, plus another 600,000 acres elsewhere in Argentina. He carried on a flourishing export trade both with advanced countries like Britain, the United States and Spain, to which he exported leather and wool, and with less advanced nations such as Brazil and Cuba, to which he exported jerked and salted beef. With the coming of the railways he had also diversified into tallow and axle grease. When to the value of his real estates, herds and pastoral exports is added that of the palace at San José, and its paintings and other treasures, Urquiza emerged in sterling terms as a millionaire.[34]

Urquiza had in any case made a second fortune out of supplying horses and provisions to the Brazilian army. He confided to Burton that if Solano López had not made the mistake of crossing the Misiones strip, he would have sent 15,000 men to aid him in the fight against the hated *macacos* – for the *caudillo* was quite willing to take the money of men he detested at a deep level of racial prejudice. He warned that if Brazil failed in the war against Paraguay, Rio Grande do Sul would certainly secede from the empire and advised that it was fear of the combined threat from himself and the province that had led Pedro II to avoid making Rio Grande the base for his operations against Paraguay. Much more political talk over billiards after dinner, and the gift of a personally signed safe conduct which would make every gaucho on the pampas doff his hat to the stranger, left Burton deeply convinced by the monarch of San José.[35]

Returning to Concepción del Uruguay, Burton crossed the river to the Uruguayan side to visit Paysandú, scene of the bloody siege by the Brazilians in January 1865. A storm delayed the passage of the next steamer upriver until the morning of 9 October. Eventually he got as far north as Salto and Concordia, but here it was discovered that heavy flooding had swollen streams and washed out roads. It would not, after all, be possible to inspect the battlefield of Uruguaiana, in a northern triangle of the upper river where Uruguay, Corrientes and the Brazilian province of Rio Grande do Sul all met. Disappointed, Burton returned to Buenos Aires to ponder his next step.

Chapter Eleven

Exploring Argentina

Buenos Aires, Burton's base for the best part of the twelve months he spent as a freelance adventurer in 1868-9, was still essentially a large village in Burton's day. On the waterfront activity was brisk, but the rest of the city basked somnolently behind the brick and stucco walls of its one-storey buildings. A rickety arcade of small shops, known as the *Recova Vieja* separated the two open squares that made up the city centre. This arcade contained a few pastry shops and tailoring establishments and boasted a wealth of shoemakers: thirty-two cobblers lived and worked there. The Plaza de Mayo was little more than a dusty (or muddy, depending on the weather) field, and was mainly used as a parade ground for soldiers from the fort which doubled as presidential and government headquarters.[1]

Here and there a few new buildings had arisen in the 1860s. Recently constructed from red sandstone was the Casa Rosada. Beyond this was a five-storey semicircular Customs House. On the south side of the Plaza, just across from the Casa Rosada, another new construction contained the Senate and Chamber of Deputies: the two houses of the National Congress met on alternate days. On the north side of the Plaza was the city's cynosure – the newly completed 2,500-seater Colón theatre, where leading companies from Europe played during the winter months of June, July and August. Here Burton saw many of the most recent Italian operas, while deploring the noisy philistinism of the *porteño* audience.

To the west of the Plaza de Mayo was the Plaza Victoria, which later disappeared in the renovation of the city.[2] Its nodal point was a small brick pillar commemorating Argentina's independence in 1810. A few benches and trees made a pathetic obeisance to European notions of a city square. On the west of the Plaza stood the two-storey whitewashed and columned *Cabildo*, housing the Supreme Court, Municipal Council and Police Headquarters. Behind the *Cabildo* was the city jail (capacity 200). To the north broad steps led to the low-domed Cathedral, with the archbishop's residence at the side. The numerous shops which made up the arcade separating the two plazas also spilled out to fill in the southern side of the Plaza Victoria.

Buenos Aires was badly paved, ill-drained and dearer to live in than London or Paris. As such it cut a poor figure after Rio.[3] There was piped water in just a handful of houses belonging to the richest members of the élite. It was 1870 before horse-drawn cars ran on streetcar rails and later before an adequate sewage and water system was introduced. The inauguration of Domingo Sarmiento as President saw priority given instead to a massive docks modernization scheme which, however, was criticized by Burton as a rushed job.[4] The annoying narrow sidewalks, built by individual property owners to raise the pedestrian above the street's dust, mud or raging torrent, presented a variety of surfaces and heights. Hemmed in on one side by the street, this 'pavement' provided no elbow room on the other, as the plastered or whitewashed walls crowded to its edge and to the very corner of each block. By this era cobblestones or rough paving stones covered almost all the streets within a mile of the Plaza de Mayo. But since the stones were usually set in sand and dirt, they tended to work themselves loose and leave a pitted or irregular road surface, complete with mud holes and stagnant pools.

Burton left a memorable description of this state of affairs:

The streets are long, narrow, and ill ventilated; and the tramway of modern progress is as yet unknown to them. The pavement, even after Monte Video, strikes us as truly detestable. It is like a fiumana-bed, bestrewn with accidentally disposed boulders, gapped with dreadful chasms and manholes, bounded on both sides by the *trottoirs*, narrow ledges of flattish stone, like natural rock 'benches', flood-levelled on each side of the torrent. In many parts the sidewalks are raised three and even five feet above the modern street plane, and flush with the doors, which are as high as that of the Kaabah. These *trottoirs* covered, like the pavement with rain, with a viscid mud, sliding as a ship's deck, dangerous as a freshly waxed parquet for the noble savage, often end at the corners with three or four rude steps, rounded slabs, greasy and slippery by the tread, as though spread with orange peel, and ascended and descended with the aid of an open-mouthed carronade, or a filthy post blacked by the hand of toil . . . More than one street . . . must be crossed by a drawbridge after rains which drown men, and carry off carts and horses. Before the days of pavements . . . the earth was converted by showers into slush, and swept down into the general reservoir, the river bed – hence the sunken ways. The crossings are nowhere swept; being slightly raised above the general level they soon dry and cut up the line into deep puddles which lie long, or into segments and parallelograms of mire. The thoroughfares are macadamized with the soil of the suburbs, which cakes under the sun, and crumbles before the wind, dirtying the hands like London smoke. Drainage is left to those Brazilian engineers, Messrs Sun and Wind. The only washing is by rain rushing down the cross streets. There is absolutely no sewage; a pit in the patio is dug by way of cesspool, and is filled up with soil, a fair anticipation of the deodorizing earth closet. The *basura* or sweepings are placed at an early hour in boxes by the doorways to be carried off by the breeze, or to be kicked over by horses driven to water: these offals are used to fill up holes in the road outside the city, and yet the citizens expect 'good airs'. Beyond the town, the unpaved lines thus become quagmires, impasses, and quaking bogs where horses and black cattle are hopelessly fixed.[5]

Inadequate drainage left the city noisome and fetid. Seven blocks south of the Plaza de Mayo, on Calle Chile, which had four-foot-high sidewalks, was a so-called main drain. Here the city's refuse and sewage accumulated. Calle Chile was in effect an open sewer; on hot summer days the smell of human waste and assorted garbage along Chile was overpowering. It takes an effort of imagination to comprehend what Damascus must have been like at this time, since Burton testified a year later that the Syrian city's sewage and hygiene problems far exceeded those of Buenos Aires.[6]

The years of the Paraguayan war brought further horrors. In 1867 soldiers returning from the front brought back cholera to the city; 5,000 persons were affected in April–May 1867, of whom some 1,500 died.[7] Quarantine measures halted the spread of the disease, but in 1869 a typhoid epidemic caused another 500 deaths. Burton reported that the populace of Buenos Aires accepted smallpox, typhoid and diphtheria as periodic killers. Ignorance was the main enemy; for example, the role of the mosquito in the spread of the killer diseases was not understood until the turn of the century. Lack of hygiene and proper sanitation compounded the problem, for mosquitoes bred in the raw sewage. Burton was consul in even more unsanitary Damascus when tropical disease wrought the ultimate tragedy on Buenos Aires. In 1871 a yellow fever epidemic devastated the city: 14,000 people died and another 100,000 fled in terror as the fever raged unabated until halted by the coming of winter in June. In April the death rate was over 300 a day, and on 10 April 1871 a record 563 persons perished.

Burton's perceptions of Buenos Aires were distinguished by his usual acuity and flair, though he seriously underestimated the population both of city and nation.[8] The city was not without its comical side. There is a certain dramatic irony in the fact that Argentines regarded the game of soccer – introduced by the large British expatriate community – as a game for the mentally ill only.[9] Even more indicative of the state of civic consciousness was the delicious anecdote provided by Burton's friend, Consul Hutchinson. The night watchmen or 'charlies' in 1860s Buenos Aires were known as *serenos*. At the corner of Calle Bolmar two of them collided. One was crying out 'Half past eleven and cloudless'. The other was calling 'Twelve o'clock and windy'. Each demanded to know what the other meant by this blatant contradiction of the facts. The upshot was blows and fisticuffs. The two ended up locked in combat and rolling around in the mud, where they 'acquired some real estate'. When a passer-by intervened, they agreed to abide by his arbitration. He at once pointed out that they were both wrong, as it was four o'clock in the morning and nearly as bright as day.[10]

All in all, Burton developed a grudging admiration for the inaptly named city of good airs. 'Buenos Aires is evidently a city ... the first glance tells us that it is not, like Montevideo, a town.' He knew enough from his Santos experience of the way railways transformed societies to see that this fact alone made Argentina a potential El Dorado in the future. The pilot track was that from Buenos Aires to the suburb of Flores in 1857, but by 1864 a twenty-mile slice of railroad along the estuary had been completed, followed by a seventy-mile stretch south to Chascomas. The agricultural towns of Merlo, Luján, Mercedes and Chivilcoy were already linked by rail to the city, while La Boca and Barracas could be reached in twenty minutes from the terminus at Plaza Constitución across marshy land which was previously a major barrier to stagecoaches. The Retiro terminus linked Belgrano, San Isidro, San Fernando and the delta area of the Paraná river with the city centre, while in 1870 a 400-mile track to Rosario and Córdoba at last made feasible the dream of an integrated economy.[11] Burton was aware of the city's great potential and admired its swagger and ambition to ape its 'betters' in Europe. 'The weeks that I passed at Buenos Aires will ever be remembered by me with that pleasure with which on a wintry day we recall to mind the sweet savour of perfumed spring.'[12]

In Buenos Aires Burton was in frequent contact with the British Minister Gould, from whose vociferous pro-Brazilian sentiments he decisively dissented. But Burton was able to temper his deprecation of the Triple Alliance with appreciation of the personal qualities of its architect, Bartolomé Mitre, who had just yielded the presidency to Domingo Sarmiento. Mitre was a deeply cultured man, well versed in European literature and history. He knew of Burton's travels and, when introduced by Gould, greeted him as an old acquaintance. He also presented him with a classic of sociology of the kind dear to Burton: Martin de Moussy's three-volume *Description géographique et statistique de la Confédération Argentine*.

Burton found the ex-President profoundly admirable, with a fine memory like that of Pedro II and – wonder of wonders among Latin American politicians – staunchly incorruptible, as evidenced by the fact that after a six-year presidency his friends had had to club together to buy him a house. Writing in this very same year, Burton's friend Consul Hutchinson also pointed up this Aristides-like aspect of Mitre. 'Negligent of dress, but of strict morals . . . he has a childish faith in his lucky star. His countenance is without movement, like a statue. Sparing of words and flattery, upright and honest.'[13] But Burton did not allow his admiration to blind him to Mitre's deep political flaws and diplomatic delinquency. If Mitre had not launched the *colorado* General Flores against Uruguay in 1863, Brazil would not have been sucked into the River Plate. As it was, the war made Buenos Aires a prefecture of Rio. Argentina *vis-à-vis* Brazil seemed to Burton analogous to Britain in relation to France during the Crimean War, namely a second-rate power doing the bidding of a first-rate one. 'My admiration of General Mitre does not blind me to the fact that his later career bears upon it the stain of a profound political immorality in having caused, for party ways, for personal and for egotistic purposes, a military alliance, whose result is the present disastrous and by no means honourable war.'[14]

A little later Burton had an audience with the new president Domingo Sarmiento. Burton likewise found him impressive, though in very different ways from Mitre, and ended by dedicating his *Letters from the Battlefields of Paraguay* to him. But he was sceptical of Sarmiento's ability to solve the manifold problems confronting Argentina. 'Don Domingo has a stiff task before him. He has campaigned but he is rather a civilian than a soldier. The later rule of Spain has familiarized generations to the sway of generals not doctors, and his only bourgeois predecessor, Dr Derqui, lasted about a year. He is pledged by the promise of all his career to make sacrifices in the cause of extended popular education. He must honourably terminate the present state of things and devote to European immigration the energies and expenditures lavished upon a disastrous war. He must reform his fleet, create an army and repress the wild Indians.'[15]

In the end, Burton found the contrast and comparison between Sarmiento and his rival Mitre so fascinating that he drew up a list of each man's qualities, making them representatives of a putative empiricist/rationalist divide. Thus Sarmiento was

studious, prosaic, matter-of-fact, with classically male temperament and the sensibility of a gaucho; fond of work and indifferent to pleasure, he did not reflect on what he had learned but
instead took up the stance of the sturdy popular magistrate and
heaven-born democrat. Mitre, on the other hand, had a feminine
temperament, was a natural aristocrat and intriguer, was in-
stinctive, poetic, imaginative and hedonistic, with a yen for
wine, women and song.[16] It is tempting to see Burton as engaged
here on externalization: imputing to the two great Argentine
statesmen the divergent and contradictory characteristics of his
own self-confessedly dual personality.

But if Mitre had a vinous and bibulous side, he was clearly not
the only one. For it was in Buenos Aires that his British admirer
most clearly indulged the penchant for strong liquor that never
left him. The young Wilfred Scawen Blunt, who had met Isabel
in Rio on his way out to post in Argentina, left a telling portrait
of Burton at this time:

> Burton was at that time at the lowest point I fancy of his
> whole career, and in point of respectability at his very
> worst. His consular life at Santos, without any interesting
> work to his hand or proper vent for his energies, had thrown
> him into a habit of drink he afterwards cured himself of,
> and he seldom went to bed sober . . . His dress and appear-
> ance were those suggesting a released convict rather than
> anything of more repute. He wore, habitually, a rusty black
> coat with a crumpled black silk stock, his throat destitute of
> collar, a costume which his muscular frame and immense
> chest made singularly and incongruously hideous, above it a
> countenance the most sinister I have ever seen, dark, cruel,
> treacherous, with eyes like a wild beast's. He reminded me
> by turns of a black leopard caged, but unforgiving, and
> again with his close cut poll and iron frame of that wonder-
> ful creation of Balzac's, the ex-gallerien Vautrin, hiding his
> grim identity under an abbé's cassock.[17]

Burton talked to Blunt on a wide variety of matters: religion,
philosophy, politics, travel. The older man professed outright
materialism, but Blunt found him deeply credulous and superstitious. Burton would become progressively drunker and more

dangerous in his cups until finally he staggered off to bed, revolver in hand. His ultra-conservative opinions were distasteful to the radical Blunt. Blunt had a Thaddeus Stevens-like reverence (the leader of the Radical Republicans in the House of Representatives) for the black man, while Burton was a convinced negrophobe. Blunt was also *the* great anti-imperialist, who later summed up his distaste for Burton's creed as follows:

> Their poets who write big of the White Burden, Trash!
> The white man's burden, lord, is the burden of his cash.[18]

Blunt later recalled their talks, evidently with some bitter regrets that he had not stood up to Burton:

> In his talk he affected an extreme brutality, and if one could have believed the whole of what he said, he had indulged in every vice and committed every crime. I soon found, however, that most of these recitals were indulged in *pour épater le bourgeois* and that his inhumanity was more pretended than real. Even the ferocity of his countenance gave place at times to more agreeable expressions, and I can just understand the infatuated fancy of his wife that in spite of his ugliness he was the most beautiful man alive . . . I came at last to look upon him as less dangerous than he seemed, and even in certain aspects of his mind, a 'sheep in wolf's clothing'. The clothing, however, was a very complete disguise, and as I have said he was not a man to play with, sitting alone with him far into the night, especially in such an atmosphere of violence as Buenos Aires could then boast, when men were shot almost nightly in the streets. Burton was a grim being to be with at the end of his second bottle, with a gaucho's *navaja* handy to his hand.[19]

So dissolute did Burton appear at the time that Blunt thought Burton looked more criminal than the man he claimed was constantly in his company in Buenos Aires: the notorious Tichborne claimant, who also had 'a very forbidding face, not unlike Burton's'.[20] The Tichbornes were a pre-Conquest Catholic family of Hampshire that had received a baronetcy in 1626. After the death of Sir Alfred Joseph Tichborne (1839-66), eleventh baronet, a butcher from Wagga-Wagga in New South Wales, one Thomas Castro, otherwise Arthur Orton of Wapping, came forward as the pretender to the baronetcy. He claimed to be the elder brother, Roger Charles Tichborne (1829-54), who had been lost at sea off the American coast. In the nineteenth century the 'Tichborne Claimant's imposture was as sensational as that of Anastasia in the twentieth'.[21]

But in 1868-9 the Tichborne claimant's credentials looked impressive. Burton believed his story completely – possibly because the Tichbornes were, like his wife's family, the Arundells, one of the old Catholic recusant dynasties – as did Blunt. The 'will to believe' was also sharpened by the fact that Burton had been at school with Guildford Onslow, the claimant's best friend.[22] Later Burton recanted and in 1872 at the hearing in London to determine the truth of the claimant's case his evidence was unhelpful, not to say hostile, to his former companion.[23] He also attempted to rewrite history by alleging that he had spent just one evening in the company of the bogus 'Sir Roger Tichborne'. Blunt, however, stated that the two men were frequently seen together over a period of weeks and that Burton intended to take the claimant with him on his trans-Andine travels. Even Isabel, who frequently rewrote the historical record to show Richard in a more favourable light, admitted that the two were boon companions for a week.[24]

Burton's forsaking of his old comrade in 1872 was shrewd. On 6 March of that year, on the 103rd day of a trial to assert his claims, 'Sir Roger's' case collapsed. He was committed for perjury then, after a 188-day trial for perjury (which ended on 28 February 1874) which absorbed £55,315 in costs, was sentenced to fourteen years' hard labour for criminal imposture. Released in 1884, the claimant died in 1898, having confessed three years earlier that he was an impostor.[25]

This was the man in whose company Burton at first proposed to explore Patagonia and the western pampas – a journey which would include an ascent of Aconcagua, then a virgin peak. But the bibulous 47-year-old explorer was no longer in good enough physical shape for such arduous enterprises, so the idea soon lapsed. Instead, Burton turned to William Maxwell, the man he had met on the *Yi*.[26] Together they planned a less physically demanding but ultimately more rewarding journey. They went first to Argentina's second city, Córdoba, in the 1860s a veritable cockpit of political factionalism and instability.[27] December 1868 saw the travellers at the city of Mendoza at the foot of the Andes, and scene of a devastating earthquake in 1861, whose ruins Burton picked over with his usual archaeological skill.[28] Then Burton and Maxwell made a sustained exploration of the virtually unknown Sierra de San Luis. This was unquestionably Burton's major contribution to geographical knowledge during his long sojourn in Spanish America.[29]

During his journey across the pampas the acute Burton missed nothing and stored away a wealth of knowledge on the gaucho and his culture which he would later unpack in the notes to his translation of the *Arabian Nights*. At one moment he would be making detailed botanical notes on the coarse growth of *pasto fuerte* on the pampa. Next he would be examining the semiotic significance of the gaucho's stirrups and spurs. For example, he noted that the gaucho's spurs were in some sense a talisman of class. The *vaqueiro* removed them when entering the presence of his *patrón*, while railway clerks mentally graded their passengers by the size of spurs – the larger they were, the lower in the pecking order you went.[30] Burton was well aware that his friend Domingo Sarmiento had posed the values of the city as against those of the pampa in his famous formula 'civilization against barbarism' but he was sceptical that a mere transition from horses to carriages as a mode of conveyance could extirpate a deeply rooted autochthonous culture.[31] Burton also mastered the idiosyncrasies of Argentine horses and horsemanship. He cautioned future travellers from Europe that if one tried to make Argentine nags back, they tangled their legs and fell. On the other hand, gaucho lore had to be taken with a pinch of salt. He believed it when told that Argentine mustangs did not kick and ended by having the breath knocked out of him by a hoof as a result.[32]

The gaucho resembled Burton's beloved Bedouin in one respect: after three days on the pampa a stranger became a friend and was expected to do a friend's duty, including taking part in the host's many quarrels and vendettas. Irritated by this 'guest requirement', Burton consoled himself with the thought that in Argentina's great open spaces, one could eat the best meat in the world. The gaucho with his *asado* method had perfected the art of roasting. The flesh was broiled while it was still quivering and before the fibre had time to set. This method produced meat of a rare tenderness, far superior to European roasts or the kebabs of the East.[33]

Burton was less impressed with the human qualities of the gaucho. He complained that Argentine xenophobia placed gauchos above the law. If one of them shot a foreigner, nothing happened. If a foreigner shot one of *them*, the full weight of the law descended on the '*gringo*'. In every way the martial quality of the pampa *vaqueiros* was overrated, as evidenced by their behaviour in Paraguay. 'Gaucho warfare consists of scattering before the fight, galloping about, banging guns and pistols in the air, shouting the Redskin "slogans" and foully abusing one another's feminine relatives. The infantry take shelter, and advance under cover so as to steal a march upon the enemy. Both cavalry and infantry retire when a few men have been wounded or killed; and, after the battle, the throats of all prisoners are cut, according to the fashion of the Mohawks.'[34] Burton had reservations, too, about *caudillismo*, or the way in which the absolute rule of a charismatic figure was deeply entrenched in the Latin culture and mentality. 'Few men and no woman can resist the temptations of absolute command. The daughter of a certain dictator all powerful in the Argentine republic was once seen on horseback with a white bridle of peculiar leather; it was made of the skin of a man who had boasted of her favours.'[35]

It was the relationship between man and landscape that fascinated Burton more than the gaucho's negligible fighting qualities. He could see the force of the image, already a cliché in the nineteenth century, of the gaucho standing on his horse and gazing out over a limitless plain, the monotony of which was broken solely by the occasional *ombú* tree. 'Man feels comparatively helpless in the tropical forest and in the sub-tropical valley, on the jungly mountain, and on the stony or icy hill. Mounted on his pampa horse, however, he is master of space.'[36]

From San Luis and San Juan, the travellers took their mules through the Upsallata pass, enjoying breathtaking views as they went.[37] This was the occasion for one of Burton's tall stories. He later told his friend Luke Ionides that he had spent Christmas Day 1868 in a running battle with bandits, during which he had killed four men and was badly wounded himself. In his evidence to the Tichborne trial Burton repeated the story and spoke of the shootout as 'a very near thing'. In yet another after-dinner version of the story, the brush was with Araucanian Indians.[38] We may take leave to doubt the story, on several grounds. In the first place, neither Burton in his *Letters from the Battlefields of Paraguay* nor Isabel in her *Life* mentions the story of derring-do. The narration at the Tichborne trial looks superficially more impressive, until we remember the contemptuous way Burton toyed with the barristers at that trial. When questioned about his African wounds – a hideous striating cicatrice across the cheek whose provenance must have been clear to everyone – Burton arrogantly replied that he had sustained them while running away. Most telling of all is this remark to Ambassador Elliott of Turkey in 1871, hidden away in the Foreign Office archives. 'During the four years which I passed in the Brazil [*sic*], the Argentine Republic, Chile, Peru and Paraguay, often travelling through the wildest parts of somewhat lawless regions, I cannot call to mind having had a single dispute.'[39]

Burton and Maxwell at length arrived in Santiago, where to his joy he found that the waiters attended diners at the gallop, as distinct from Buenos Aires where they served at a snail's pace; Burton spent most of his life in a sustained battle against the 'insolence' of waiters.[40] From Santiago they proceeded to the port of Valparaiso to take ship to the northern Chilean ports. Burton did not like his first glimpse of the Pacific: 'that drab-coloured wooden abomination, Valparaiso, where fire or ruin by earthquake is purely a question of time'.[41] But he added a further detail to his comparative geography by likening the south Pacific coast, with its parallel *cordilleras* and flanking waterless deserts, to the eastern Mediterranean coast.[42]

The reference to earthquakes was timely, for Burton was bound for the port of Arica, utterly devastated in a gigantic earthquake in August 1868. This particular seismic convulsion was experienced over a range of 2,000 miles, from Casma in Peru to Valdivia in Chile; Arica was thus virtually at the epicentre of the quake. Arequipa in Peru, with a population of 40,000, was utterly destroyed, with thousands dead. Of Arica itself the only traces left were a half-ruined church tower and two sections of what used to be the Hotel de Europa. Burton's friend F.J. Stevenson, who visited the site shortly before Maxwell and Burton, asked a local where the town was. *'Arica, hombre, Arica no hay'* was the doleful response. Stevenson himself could not believe his eyes. 'I was amazed by the tremendous amount of wreckage resulting from the destruction of so small a town.'[43]

The Pacific coast there was littered with thousands of dead silver-scaled fish, stunned by the submarine volcanic explosion and then cast on shore by fifty-foot-high tidal waves that battered the coast for two hours. All ships at anchor in the harbour were overwhelmed. Among them were the English bark *Chanarcillo*, the Peruvian corvette *America* and the US paddlewheel gunboat *Wateree*. The bodies of dead sailors rolled around in the heavy surf. The only beneficiaries were the country peasants who flocked to the former site of Arica to loot with immunity.[44]

Stunned by what he saw, Burton soon embarked for the northward run to Lima. Peru had two main associations for Burton. One was personal: his fellow officer in the Bashi-Bazouks in the Crimea, 'Blakeley of the Gun', who had retired to Chorillos, a suburb of Lima, and died there of yellow fever.[45] The other related to his anthropological and sexological interests. He was fascinated by Peru's *pages* – the southern hemisphere's shamans. Even more intriguing were the sexual customs of the Incas and other ancient Peruvian tribes. South American Indians looked on female virginity as a reproach; it meant the girl had never inspired love. Among the priestly castes sodomy was commonplace – a means of creating *esprit de corps* as among the Companions of Alexander the Great. Burton also uncovered the ancient Peruvian belief that syphilis was the product of intercourse between man and alpaca, which was why an ancient law forbade bachelors to have domestic animals in their house.[46]

It was while he was sitting in a café in Peru's capital one day in February 1869 that an acquaintance from the British embassy approached him and congratulated him on the 'good news'. What good news was that, asked Burton. Why, said his friend, he surely could not be unaware that he had been appointed consul in Damascus?[47] Burton jumped up with alacrity. This was an old dream come true. He booked passage on the first ship bound for the River Plate.

The return trip was via the Straits of Magellan, which as a spectacle Burton thought easily dwarfed Rio. It was 'a splendid novelty, a wonder, a delight that electrified the most jaded of fellow-travellers.'[48] He was still reeling from the sensuous impact of this trip six months later, as he acknowledged. 'My eyes were still full of the might and majesty of the Chilian Andes, and of the grace and grandeur of Magellan's straits – memories which fashionable Vichy and foul Brindisi had strengthened not effaced – as I landed upon the Syrian shore on Friday October 1st, 1869.'[49] Burton was back in Buenos Aires on 29 March 1869. But instead of hastening on to the consulate of his dreams, he took the extraordinary decision to revisit the battlefields of Paraguay.[50]

Much had happened since Burton's last visit. After the fall of Humaitá, Solano López retired to prepared positions at Lomas Valentinas. In December 1868 was fought the final great set-piece battle of the war – what Burton called the 'Waterloo' of the Paraguayan conflict.[51] Defeat here and the subsequent invest-ment of the fortress of Angostura opened the way to Asunción itself. On 5 January 1869 Brazilian armies entered the capital and sacked it; they were left to the plunder undisturbed, since the Argentine forces remained in their camp at Trinidad and took no part in the pillage.[52] This was only the most dramatic sign of the worsening relationship between the Allies. Sarmiento had been elected in 1868 to end the war on almost any terms. There was war-weariness in Brazil too, but Pedro II scuppered the chance of peace on terms by threatening to abdicate if his goal of uncon-ditional surrender by Paraguay was not achieved.

On 4 April 1869 Burton embarked on the *Proveedor*, which contained a complement of passengers Burton described as 'the veriest ruffians, riffraff, ragamuffins, that I had seen in South America, even at Montevideo.' To assuage this he had two genial Americans as company (Messrs Curtis and Palmer) and, best of all, his old friend from Bahia, Charles Williams – the man whose life Isabel had saved after the bite from the rattlesnake.[53]

The Paraná was swollen by floods. The ship spent just three hours at Rosario – just long enough for Burton to renew acquain-tance with Consul Hutchinson – then continued north, past Bur-ton's old stamping grounds at Corrientes and Humaitá and up the river Tebicuari into territory that had been held by the Para-guayans during his last visit. This area teemed with game. The red ibis and the vampire bat were common, though not the rhea. Jaguars, otters, opossums and armadillos abounded, though the tapir had already been made extinct by hunters. Fowl were plentiful: not just the royal duck (*pato real*) but the *palmeada cornuda* – a kind of turkey or bustard. Burton's companions shot several large caymans or *jacarés* and some warthogs.[54]

Burton made a microscopic inspection of the battlefield of Lomas Valentinas and combed through the abandoned Paraguayan batteries. It seemed impossible that Solano López could have escaped after such a disaster, and that he did Burton could attribute only to the incompetence of Commander-in-chief Marshal Caxias. 'Any service in the world would have called upon Marshal Caxias to justify himself before a court martial, and a strict service like the French or the Austrian would probably have condemned him to be shot. In Brazil he was created a duke.'[55] The true explanation for this fiasco was almost certainly that Caxias acted under orders from Rio. Pedro II wanted the entire Paraguayan nation exterminated. The inference is strengthened from the further inexplicable fact that Caxias, having failed to net López after the battle,' sent the infantry, not the cavalry, in pursuit of him. If the Brazilian emperor's goal was genocide, he came close to achieving his aim. Total war dead in the Paraguayan war amounted to 350,000 – equal to the combined populations of Rio and Montevideo in 1864 or twice that of Buenos Aires at the same date. 220,000 of these fatalities were Paraguayan; at the end of the war only 28,700 males were left alive.[56]

Neither López nor Burton had expected such a terrible end to the war. But the disaster of LomasValentinas threw up its own Grouchy in the form of the Paraguayan general, Caminos. Burton quoted López's mistress Eliza Lynch as saying: 'We have had a terrible disaster; we owe it to M.Caminos.' Caminos had been detailed by López to fall upon the Brazilians who landed on his flank from the Chaco; instead Caminos retreated to Cerro Léon.

From 13 to 15 April Burton was in Asunción. He found the Paraguayan capital a hotbed of pro-López espionage. The Hungarian Colonel Wisner von Morgenstern, one of López's adventurers, had been allowed to reside in Asunción after his capture by the Allies. Here 'he kept a small *pulpería* at the street corner, where officers came for their periodic dram, and visited a pretty "daughter" who was reported to reward important intelligence.'

Two other colonels, Iturburu and Paez, while supposedly heading a force of anti-López Paraguayans, were in fact spying for him.

Burton interviewed Marshal de Souza and the new commander-in-chief, 27-year-old Comte d'Eu, whom he knew from Pedro II's receptions in Petrópolis. While he was in Asunción, the Paraguayans reopened hostilities with a newly gathered army of between 6,000 and 12,000. López sent the first armoured train in South American history careering down the rails to attack the Allies. 'The Paraguayans, after doing damage, leisurely retired, and stopped the train to pick up two of their wounded who had fallen out of it.' Once again Burton wanted to get into the thick of the fighting at the front, but the Brazilians vetoed his bid. He had no choice but to acquiesce. The Brazilians had, in the main, been good to him, and in any case his 'sick leave' had been granted with the proviso that he exercised due caution. Burton rationalized his disappointment with grumbling at the behaviour of the imperial subalterns, which he contrasted with the courtesy of the senior officers. As he said to his readers: 'I have before warned you not to confound this *negraille* – these sweepings of second- and third-class negroes and negroids – with the noble Brazilian nation.'[57]

While Burton lodged at a French-run hotel – where he was delighted to get everything for $3.50 a day – he investigated closely the two main Allied charges against Solano López. One was that the Paraguayan dictator had committed war crimes, especially against foreign nationals. The other was that he had massacred large numbers of his own people in a frenzy of bloodletting, masking his homicidal fury under trumped-up allegations of treason and plotting against his person.

Burton found the charge of war crimes singularly unconvincing. It seemed to him that British sources had tried to bracket López with Emperor Theodore of Abyssinia, who the year before genuinely *had* detained British nationals in his capital. Burton showed that the comparison was facile. Minister Gould in 1868 headed a mission to Asunción which took away those 'captives' whose contracts had already expired. 'But many had voluntarily renewed their engagements, and all were in an exceptional position. It was hardly reasonable to expect that the Marshal-President should dismiss a score of men – of whom sundry were in his confidence and knew every detail which it was most important to conceal from the enemy.'[58]

The allegations that López had committed war crimes against British and other foreign nationals derived entirely from unsubstantiated reports from George Thompson and US Minister Washburne.[59] Burton pointed out that Thompson admitted he had seen no atrocities but claimed to have been 'converted' by material in Allied possession. Burton's close analysis of Thompson's 'proofs' revealed them as a rehash of Washburne, himself the most unreliable of sources, whose every allegation 'savours of want of truth . . . I regret to say that Lieutenant-Colonel Thompson had largely quoted from a document which breathes in every line a spirit of fierce hatred against a quondam friend.' Washburne had piled on insensate accusations that López had killed or would kill every foreigner in his power! Burton attributed the statements to Washburne's nervous breakdown. He had met the US Minister in Buenos Aires and found him 'living in a state of nervous excitement, in an atmosphere of terror and suspicion . . . many of his assertions were those of a man who was hardly responsible for his actions'.

Even more wildly inaccurate, Burton thought, was the Allied propaganda to the effect that a blood-soaked López had massacred large numbers of his own people under pretext that there had been a treasonable conspiracy against him. Burton's refutation of this proposition was twofold. In the first place, he was sceptical of all Allied claims relating to the alleged purge and holocaust ('the conspiracy that has been so fiercely asserted and denied, the new Reign of Terror called by some the Reign of Rigour'). A list of the executed, said to be taken from the captured diaries of the Paraguayan General Resquin, was published in the Argentine press.[60] But, as Burton pointed out: 'even this paper was looked upon with suspicion. It might, after all, be nothing but a *ruse de guerre*.' Burton took the story with a pinch of salt, adding that the Argentines, less credulous than the Brazilians, did not believe a word of it. When he was embarking to return to Buenos Aires he was told of the discovery of 'six corpses, laid out straight, with their feet towards the enemy, and each bearing pinned to his breast a paper inscribed "thus perish the traitors"'. By the time he reached Buenos Aires, 'the victims were killed and brought to life again half a dozen times . . . the figure of six had grown to sixty-seven, and included women and children: it there advanced, temporarily halting at sixty-four . . . at seventy, and at 400 to 800 victims.'

Burton's scholarly scepticism was in strong contrast to the credulity of another famous British traveller in nineteenth-century South America. R.B. Cunninghame Graham swallowed the myth whole and absurdly claimed that by 1869 López had dispatched 8,000 victims.[61] Burton summed up the situation sardonically by saying he would be in a better position to know the truth if Thompson had been more explicit. But this worthy constantly reiterated that he knew nothing on the subject except what the Allies told him. Other US citizens who claimed to have been put to the torture in Asunción (such as Bliss and Masterman) were later exposed as liars by Admiral Davis of the US Navy and by a Committee of the Congress.[62] Burton's summing-up was a judicious analysis of the likely truth of the matter. 'The suspicion of treason, and the firm resolve to fight to his last man, seems to have acted unfavourably upon the Marshal President.' Before this, López 'had preserved a certain character for moderation . . . despite the reports set on foot . . . he could not be accused of cruelty . . . If they [the executions] really took place . . . the most fatal of necessities . . . the dementia preceding the destruction'. Burton confirmed that López 'had become addicted to port-wine and piety; to mass going and hard drinking' but he pointed to reports 'which show the heart of a softer stuff'.

The principal evidence Burton adduced to show that López had been grossly maligned was his treatment of women. No more absurd report was ever current than that bruited by Washburne that the dictator had imprisoned, flogged and tortured his own mother and sisters. Here Burton was able to refute Washburne by internal evidence. He simply quoted from an intercepted letter from López to his mother on 10 September 1868 – when, according to Washburne, his mother was already on the rack. Moreover, López's treatment of Eliza Lynch was never less than exemplary. Eliza was the heroine of Burton's piece and he was wholly on her side against the many vile calumnies spread by the Allies. 'All are agreed that during the war Madame Lynch has done her utmost to mitigate the miseries of the captives and to make the so-called *detenus* comfortable.'

As the final phase in his closely-argued rebuttal of Allied propaganda, Burton gave his opinion that, so far from there having been a massacre following a bogus conspiracy, in fact there had been leniency by López following a *real* conspiracy. 'It would appear that shortly after 22 February 1868, when the Brazilian ironclads had fired into Asunción, many Paraguayans began to despair of the cause. General Bruguez . . . others say the Minister of Foreign Affairs, was deputed by the citizens to perform the pleasant operation which is popularly called "belling the cat".'

Having completed his dossier on the war, and unable to reach the front, Burton set off down river with his companions in the *Osorio* for Corrientes, where they transferred to the *Goya* for the run to Buenos Aires. On the way down the Paraná the *Goya* was in collison with a hit-and-run steamer. Burton was thrown from his bunk by the violence of the impact, which could have been disastrous had it pierced the bulkheads.[63] He did not tarry in Buenos Aires, but at once (26 April) took ship on the *Arno* for Rio. He was satisfied with the fortnight spent in Paraguay. It had given him the material for one of his better books and had enabled him to report the truth to a British public grown used to the bromides of Allied propaganda. Burton retained his admiration for López. When the dictator was killed early in 1870 while making a last-ditch stand in the Paraguayan jungle, Burton paid his tribute to 'the heroic death of President López'.[64]

At Rio Burton boarded the *Douro* for Southampton. Everything about the passage home irritated him. There were 365 fellow-travellers, but eighty-six of them, to his horror, were shrieking, ill-disciplined children. 'The passengers were mainly Portuguese, whose main characteristic was expectoration.' He consoled himself with long conversations with fellow-countryman Arthur Rowbottom on the fortunes to be made from sulphur mines and boracic acid. It was a weary and dispirited Burton who disembarked at Southampton on the first day of June 1869.[65] And yet something had been achieved. Fawn Brodie sums it up like this: 'By tarrying in Paraguay he risked censure and even the loss of the Damascus post that his wife had won for him. But there was something important to be regained in Paraguay – his self-respect.'[66]

Chapter Twelve

The Literary Legacy

For Burton the Americas were always a *pis-aller*. In his next consular posting in Syria he graphically underlined the difference between the Old World and the New. 'We find hardly a mile without a ruin, hardly a ruin that would not be held deeply interesting between Hudson's Bay and Tierra del Fuego.' For all that, Burton adapted so well to South America that he experienced profound culture shock when returning to his beloved Arab world. The impact of Syria 'took me back half a dozen centuries and made me feel six times farther away from home than when living in Brazil'.[1]

What made South America bearable for Burton was the extended leisure it gave him for his translations. It was here that he first made serious inroads on the *Arabian Nights*, hailed as his literary masterpiece when it finally appeared in 1885. The enchanted world of Harun-al-Rashid, Sinbad and old Baghdad acted as a tonic against the tedium of consular life in Brazil. 'During my long years of official banishment . . . to the dull and dreary half-clearings of South America, it proved itself a charm, a talisman against *ennui* and despondency . . . from my dull and commonplace "respectable surroundings", the Jinn bore me at once to the land of my predilection, Arabia, a region so familiar to my mind that even at far sight, it seemed a reminiscence of some bygone metempsychic life in the distant past.'[2]

Burton's friendly rivalry with the railway superintendent J.J. Aubertin over a proposed English version of Camoens's *Lusiads* was another spur to translation. Santos was always associated in Burton's mind with the first steps taken on this venture. As it turned out, Aubertin beat him to the punch both as regards time (Aubertin's translation appeared in 1878, Burton's in 1880) and the respective quality of the versions. By common consent, Burton's poetic ear was inferior to his friend's. He made up for this defect by the sheer massiveness of his scholarship. He followed his translation in 1881 by two volumes of biography and commentary on Camoens as well as a two-volume translation of the *Lyricks* in 1884.

Polymath, polyglot and linguist extraordinary, Burton did not confine his efforts to works done into English from his two favourite languages, Arabic and Portuguese. He also grappled with Sanskrit and in particular the vast collection of folk tales known as the *Katha Sarit Sagara*, dating from the eleventh century. Burton focused his attention on the section entitled *Vetala-pancha-Vinshati* or *Twenty-Five Tales of a Demon*, which had been translated into Hindi in 1799. Making use of both the original Sanskrit and the Hindi version, Burton produced a sharp edition of ironic and amoral tales of the sex war. In their use of fantasy and magic, the stories were obvious precursors of Burton's later work on the *Arabian Nights* and the *Il Pentamerone*. He worked assiduously on them and was able to send back his completed version to London from Syria in early 1870, together with *Letters from the Battlefields of Paraguay*.[3]

Published as *Vikram and the Vampire*, this collection of folk tales tells of the capture of a vampire by Vikram, the Hindu equivalent of King Arthur, Frederick Barbarossa or Harun-al-Rashid. The vampire then relates the garish fables. At their best, the tales are amusing oddities, as in 'Showing that a Man's Wife Belongs not to his Body but to his Head', which tells of a wife who transposes the heads of husband and lover so that each is on the wrong body. The conundrum is then posed (without answer): 'To which does she belong, the head or the body of her husband?' But at their worst, as indeed the individual titles – 'In which a Man Deceives a Woman', 'On the Relative Villainy of Men and Women', 'Of a Woman who Told the Truth', etc. – indicate, the fairy tales become the excuse for a pessimistic account of the sex war, suffused with the kind of oriental misogyny Burton himself endorsed. Vikram routinely executes women for familiarity without enquiring into the circumstances or provocation and cuts off their noses for adultery. Only extensive quotation could do justice to this dark side of the world of Sanskrit moralists but some representative citations will convey the drift:

Women . . . are worse than we are; a man, however depraved he may be, ever retains some notion of right and wrong but a woman does not. She has no regard whatever . . . Enlarging, as women are apt to do, upon everything but the truth . . . In nine times out of ten, a woman's 'no' is a distinct 'yes' . . . with respect to the young woman, I have only to say that she was a young woman, and thereby of necessity a possible murderess . . . One should put no confidence in a changeful mind, a black serpent, or an armed enemy, and one should dread a woman's doings . . . A woman, whether she love or hate, will be a source of pain. For there are few things which a woman will not do. She never brings to her tongue what is in her heart, she never speaks out what is in her tongue, and she never tells what she is doing. Truly the deity has created woman a strange creature in this world . . . In this world women are a mine of grief, a poisonous root, the abode of solicitude, the destroyers of resolution, the occasioners of fascination, and the plunderers of all virtuous qualities.'[4]

Not surprisingly, perhaps, the bulk of Burton's translations in Brazil were from the Portuguese, which was in any case his second favourite language. He was keen to proselytize for the language in general and in particular to bring before a British audience the best of Brazilian literature.[5] His choice of subjects was surprising, though suitably exotic. *Lands of the Cazembe* (published 1873) dealt with early Portuguese penetration of East Africa and was a translation of the Brazilian explorer Lacerda's journey to Cazembe. This fitted with a favourite Burton theme: the homology of Brazil and East Africa. Lacerda had completed the circle started when Pedro Alvares Cabral, the discoverer of Brazil, made landfall at Zanzibar.[6] *The Captivity of Hans Stade of Hesse* (1874) was actually translated by Burton's collaborator Albert Tootal. It dealt with the captivity of a German sailor among the wild tribes of Brazil's eastern seaboard in the year

1547-55. But Burton contributed a valuable 94-page preface; indeed his 250 notes are longer than the autobiographical tale of the German captured by cannibals. Both this and the notes to *Captivity* and *Lands of the Cazembe* are indispensable sources for Burton as Americanist and for detail of his life in Brazil.[7]

Burton also undertook two translations of works by contemporary Brazilian writers, J.M. Pereira da Silva's *Manuel de Moraes* dealt with a seventeenth-century scholar who had been condemned by the Tribunal of the Holy Office. When in Rio the Burtons had made several attempts to meet the author and secure his approval for the translation, but da Silva refused to meet them. Burton gave short shrift to such fastidious or antisocial souls. He made a token apology for translating the tale without permission but added about da Silva: 'He has himself courted this injury: *tous les droits sont réservés* would have saved him from the liberty thus taken by a stranger.'[8]

In the same year (1886), Burton published the translation of José de Alencar's *Iracéma* which he subtitled *The Honey-Lips, a legend of Brazil*. This was a novel which had first appeared in the year of Burton's arrival in Brazil (1865) and had caught his imagination immediately. Alencar was a more substantial figure than da Silva: he was Brazil's most famous novelist at the mid-century and as 'father of the Brazilian novel' acted as 'prodromos' for the greater and more famous Machado de Assis. Politican and author, Alencar specialized in novels of bourgeois life, but his real significance was as a Romantic and the founder of an indigenous Brazilian prose tradition. His readers preferred the exotic worlds of *Iracéma* and *O Guaraní* (1857), with its evocation of the savage Tupis and the mysteries of the jungle to the quotidian banality of high society and bourgeois Rio, centred on the *corte* at Petrópolis or the bustle of Rio.[9] An invalid when his versions of these two novels appeared, Burton allowed himself to be persuaded into a 'white lie' by his wife Isabel, who fancied herself as a serious literary figure. Accordingly, though Isabel scarcely mastered enough Portuguese to give efficient orders in her own household, Burton allowed his own work to go out under her name. *Iracéma* was billed as having been translated by Isabel alone, while in *Manuel de Moraes* she was credited with joint authorship with Richard. This pretension, absurd to anyone who knows the Burtons' life in close-up, was peddled by

Wilkins in his hagiographic 'Life' of Isabel, and has been accepted uncritically since, even by serious students.[10]

But Burton's most significant translation from the Portuguese was not published in his lifetime, nor indeed until nearly a hundred years after his death. *O Uruguai* ('The Uruguay') was an epic poem by José Basilio da Gama (1741-95), first published in 1769; 1,400 lines long, this historical romance dealt with a subject now firmly in popular consciousness, following the Hollywood film *The Mission*. The War of the Seven Reductions (1754-9) was waged between the forces of Portugal and Spain on one side, and the Tupi-Guaraní Indians and their Catholic missionaries on the other. Its genesis was the 1750 Treaty of Limits between Spain and Portugal, which abandoned the papal division of the New World between the two nations in the Treaty of Tordesillas (1492) in favour of the principle of *uti possidetis* (actual possession). By the 1750 compact Portugal granted to Spain Colonia del Sacramento, which the Spanish regarded as a menace to their colonies; in return, Spain gave Portugal the *Sete Povos das Missãoes* – Spanish Jesuit reductions along the left or eastern bank of the river Uruguay – which seemed to the Portuguese to threaten their control of Rio Grande do Sul. The treaty also required the priests and Indians of the missions to move to lands under Spanish rule. The Jesuits and Tupi-Guaranís had no reason to love the Portuguese and were in any case reluctant to leave their cattle, churches and tilled soil. With their Jesuit leaders, the Indians decided to fight. The ensuing war lasted five years. On 10 February 1756, in a battle lasting just one hour and fifteen minutes, Gomes Freire de Andrade, leading a mixed force of Portuguese and Spaniards, routed the Indians at the battle of Caaibate. The slaughter prefigured the colonial wars of Burton's own lifetime. At a cost of four killed and forty wounded, the allies left 1,500 Indians dead on the battlefield. For the next three years the Guaraní sustained their forlorn hopes by guerrilla warfare.[11]

Burton had a fellow-feeling for da Gama, since both men were bitterly hostile towards the Jesuits. Da Gama had been brought up by the Jesuits, but then turned on them and denounced them, thus winning the patronage of the Marqués de Pombal. As for Burton, one of his favourite tags was *si cum Jesuitis no cum Jesu itis*.[12] It was his strictures on the Society of Jesus, as much as his apparent advocacy of polygamy, that led Isabel to publish her famous 'rebuttal' in the introduction to *The Highlands of Brazil*. Despite his partiality for Solano López, Burton thought that eighteenth-century Paraguay under the Jesuits was a mere 'sterile, theocratic despotism'.[13]

Da Gama also presented Burton with material perfectly attuned to his sensibility. The aesthetic vision of the New World and its native peoples presented in *O Uruguai* brimmed with the sort of exotic detail Burton found irresistible. The poem's images make an immediate visual impact: plumed Guaranís facing European artillery; flooded rivers with troops bivouacked in treetops; an Indian warrior crossing the Uruguay by night and setting fire to the enemy's camp; the ululations and prophecies of a dusky sorceress; the Cleopatra-like suicide of an Indian maiden; vultures wheeling in the sky over hummocked plains scarlet with blood and crisscrossed with corpses. Burton's interest in exotic literature and peoples was an expression of the same impulse that drove him to explore virgin lands. At a deeper level the quest for the exotic and the primitive was a 'solution' to the conundrum of industrialization faced by all the great Victorians. Carlyle, Disraeli, Dickens, Ruskin, Matthew Arnold and William Morris were all preoccupied with the resulting extremes of wealth and poverty. While Dickens and Disraeli tried to solve the problem of the 'two nations' by plunging into the internal 'Dark Continent' of the slums (a strategy perfected in France by Zola), Ruskin and Morris tried to integrate the problems of the new by a partial return to the imagined aesthetic 'golden age' of medieval times. Burton's strategy was to escape the horrors of the dark Satanic mills by seeking out the exotic, much as the Pre-Raphaelites sought an escape in fifteenth-century Italy and FitzGerald in the cult of Omar Khayyám. Burton drew attention to the fact that da Gama's poem was closer to a romance in verse than the traditional epic. Modern scholarship endorses the judgment. *The Uruguay* has been called 'a romance of exotic adventures'.[14]

Da Gama took a more ruthless attitude towards the stereotypes of epic poetry than Burton's beloved Camoens. One of the jarring aspects of *The Lusiads* is the way Age of Discovery material relating to the early Portuguese explorers has to be fitted into a traditional matrix of gods, goddesses and all the other gallimaufry of the supernatural. Da Gama jettisoned all this ballast. As Burton explained: 'He despised the pen worn subjects of remote antiquity . . . the Trojan clique, the . . . exhausted subjects of Portuguese discovery and the romantic tales made their own by Ariosto and Tasso.'[15] Instead he fashioned a tale that looked to the future; his Indian warrior became an inspiration to Brazilian writers looking for national symbols.

O Uruguai, with its five cantos, instead of the traditional ten, twelve or more, approached the form of a five-act tragedy, a similarity reinforced by its Aristotelian unities. Da Gama purged his language of rhyme and archaic rhetorical devices. The structure of the poem resembles a linear chronicle rather than a classical epic. In other words, Da Gama begins at the beginning; in the epic proper, the author begins *in medias res*, and indeed Horace in the *Ars Poetica* explicitly praised Homer for not beginning his story *ab ovo* (with Leda's egg from which Helen hatched). Formally, *The Uruguay* is ten-syllable blank verse, with no strophic divisions. A typical example is the couplet quoted by Burton in *Zanzibar* to underline the ancient lure of the Nile:

> The sombre range virginal, ne'er by foot of man profaned,
> Where rise the Nile's fountains, if such fountains be.[16]

The first two cantos consist of historical scene-setting. In the first canto the hero Andrade tells how in previous campaigns the Portuguese troops had been forced to bivouack in trees during the flooding of the Jacuí river:

> My tents in sylvan trunks at first I pitcht
> Then on lofty branches: step by step
> High in the windy realm we clomb to seek
> Houses and homes amid the buoyant birds.

In the second canto the troops confront the enemy on an open plain. Andrade argues that the public good must prevail over private interests, and anyway the king has commanded it. The Indians reply in effect, 'America for the Americans':

> Ye sons of Europe, would that ne'er the wind

And wave had borne you hither. Not in vain
Nature between ourselves and you hath spread
The water-wilderness, this vasty deep.

Thereupon the uneven fight between artillery and spears and arrows begins.

If the first two cantos are historical, the third, the cornerstone of the whole poem, is symbolic. As Andrade marches closer to the Guaraní settlements, the Indian chief Cacambo has a dream. The image of the slain Sepe urges him to fire the Hispanic camp in revenge. The Indian hero then swims across the river Uruguay in darkness to carry out this mission:

From the tall head and in the inky waves
Diving another time with downward plunge
He sinks to seek the sands that floor the streams.

When he returns, Cacambo is poisoned by the Jesuit Balda. His widow Lindoia then commits suicide. Before doing so, she experiences a vision, under the influence of the sorceress Tanajura. She sees scenes of seismic destruction that obviously refer to the great Lisbon earthquake of 1755. Here da Gama is at his most sycophantic, for the vision contains scenes of the rebuilding of the city under the leadership of 'the great Pombal'. This is intended by the poet as an allegory for the destruction of the Guaraní villages and their rebirth as Luso-Brazilian civilization.

The fourth canto sees Andrade putting out the fire in his own camp and marching on to find the Indian villages abandoned and gutted by order of the Jesuits:

The flames devoured the wretched hovel-homes
Of poor redskins and upon the ground
Smouldered and smoked each nobler edifice
Delightful dwellings of the Reverend Men.

Later he sees the spot in the forest where Lindoia killed herself by snakebite:

This spot, most beautiful, most melancholy
Had chosen weary of her wretched life

Hopeless Lindoia for her bed of death
Reclined, as lulled in drowsy sleep, the Bride
Upon the verdant turf and varied flowers,
Hard-propped her cheek, the while her arm was wound
Round the funereal cypress glooming earth
With black lugubrious shades. A nearer view
Shows that around her body is enrolled
A green-hued serpent that now glides now coils
O'er neck and arms and licks her lovely breasts
While still preserve her feathers wan and fixt
A something telling of a boundless woe,
A voiceless grief that melts the stoniest heart;
So beautiful upon her face was death.

In the fifth canto the victorious troops see frescos on the ceiling of the mission church depicting the nefarious history of the Jesuit order. This is a palpable absurdity. Ever since the poem first appeared, critics have made the obvious point that the Society of Jesus would hardly portray itself in this light. The fifth canto is in fact a serious blemish on the whole. It is pure propaganda, put in to truckle to Pombal, and wholly extrinsic to the subject matter of the poem. With typical perversity, however, Burton chose to defend da Gama against this charge, arguing that this absurd scene had an 'organic purpose'.[17]

Da Gama is at one with Burton in his simultaneous hatred of missionaries and glorification of the 'noble savage'. As a recent scholarly commentary has remarked: 'In a contradiction typical of Enlightenment thought, Gama exalted natural men while insisting on the need to integrate them within the rational world of civilization.'[18] This is not da Gama's only fault. The dramatic tension is wrong, since his hero Andrade is wooden when compared with the Indian Cacambo and Lindoia. Moreover, as documentary *O Uruguai* is deficient: it is not a good source for the War of the Seven Reductions. Its great strength is in the power of its imagery.

What of Burton as translator? *O Uruguai* reveals Burton in much the same light as *The Lusiads*, with the same strengths and weaknesses. His strength was in his integrity; his abiding concern was to avoid the *traditore, tradutore* trap. This meant that the scholar prevailed over the communicator. Lack of readability was the commonest indictment brought against Burton's translations. In his determination to remain faithful to the original he often used uncommon or anachronistic words or resorted to slang and neologism. The result was a linguistic pot-pourri in which archaism and pedantry predominated. As one wag remarked: ' Captain Burton knows dozens of languages; unfortunately English is not among them.'

In the case of *O Uruguai* all these faults can be detected, plus a tendency to use English cognates for Portuguese words. 'Margent' is preferred to 'edge' or 'bank'. Portuguese *sem* is translated by the Shakespearian 'sans'. *Ninho* becomes 'natal nide' instead of 'nest'. He had a wealth of Anglo-Saxon and Chaucerian verse at his fingertips, which gave him a taste for alliteration. So in the fourth canto:

> Brother Patusca, bearing keys in belt,
> By weight of vastest paunch to earth attached

Sometimes the alliteration approximates to the 'kennings' of the Norse sagas he elsewhere deplored:

> Now with a sheaf of shafts anew supplied
> He hies once more to fight anew the fight.

Very occasionally Burton improves on the original, as when '*tropel confuso de cavalaria*' becomes:

> A jostling troop of savage chivalry.

But in general his notion of loyalty to da Gama led him away from the poet's idiomatic tone into preciosity. The usual judgment of those who know both languages is that the Burton translation has worn less well than the Portuguese original. An additional strike against Burton is that he piled on the denigration of the Jesuits by larding his version with vituperative adjectives not found in da Gama's poem.

Burton completed his critical preface to *The Uruguay* at Santos on 23 April 1867, and signed it 'Frank Baker' – his usual pseudonym. It is a typical piece of Burton extravaganza: polemical, argumentative, pedantic, oddball, quizzical, ironic.[19] By

1872 he was able to inform the *Athenaeum* that his translation was complete. There is evidence that he put the finishing touches to his work in late 1878. Unfortunately, he left it to Isabel to find a publisher while he was in Trieste as HM Consul. Isabel, angry at the animadversions on the Jesuits, killed it by neglect; it was a case of failure to find a publisher through nonfeasance. It is likely that after Burton's death Isabel, as part of her general holocaust of her husband's writings, burned all his and da Gama's anti-Catholic fulminations. Her sister Mrs Fitzgerald 'mopped up' after Isabel's death in 1896 with a second round of burning. The miracle is that the translation survived.[20]

Burton's experiences in the Paraguayan war increased his resolve to bring da Gama's work before the British public. As has been well said, 'Burton had a need to relate his literary work to a vital existential concern; he believed that he was reliving the events of da Gama's poem one century later in the Paraguayan war.'[21] There was the same clash of cultures and ideologies, the same hopeless struggle of the Guaraní against superior numbers and technology.

It was this convergence of conscious and unconscious impulses that made *Letters from the Battlefields of Paraguay* one of Burton's best books, far superior to the rather anodyne *Highlands of Brazil*. *Battlefields* has been absurdly underrated *vis-à-vis* the established classics by Burton on his journeys to Mecca, Harar and Lake Tanganyika, but it can only improve in reputation as it is rediscovered. Burton may have been inferior to Stanley as an African explorer but he was fully his equal as war correspondent. His Paraguayan despatches caught the imagination of Conrad, already deeply impressed by Burton's Arabian lore, and it has been speculated that the Martin Decoud of *Nostromo* owes much to the Decoud of *Battlefields*.[22]

The Paraguayan war experience, because it enabled Burton to reassert himself at the correct level of creative energy, also accounts for the softening in attitude of Burton towards Latin America. When he arrived in Brazil in 1865, Burton was obsessed with the thought that he had been consigned to a 'wretched hole . . . a government crumb.'[23] He saw Latin America primarily as a land of benighted savagery: 'men wish they had a gold ounce for every throat that has been cut in this place.'[24] But by the time he boarded the *Douro* for England, a more nuanced attitude is in evidence. Although he continued to regard South America as a risky place for financial investment, and later presciently advised Isabel to withdraw her funds from Argentine bonds (and was proved right, against the advice of her broker), he could see the splendid opportunities there for making individual fortunes and later advised his young cousin Frederick that the best place to make a quick million was the River Plate.[25] The change in attitude is clear from the opinions he expressed when consul in Damascus: Syria, he claimed, if properly cultivated and adminstered, 'has a future as promising as that of Mexico or the Argentine republic.'[26]

Back in England, he found the level of ignorance about South America irritating. There was the occasion when his careful pronunciation of Maipú, Tupungato and Aconcagua drew groans at the anniversary dinner of the Alpine Club.[27] There was the confusion about his career when someone mistook Fernando Po, where he had been consul during 1861-4, with Juan Fernandez (the 'Robinson Crusoe' island) off the Pacific coast of Chile.[28] Burton always worked hard to overcome this wall of prejudice and ignorance. It may have been unpardonable hyperbole for Isabel to claim, as she did in 1869 when lobbying Sir Roderick Murchison, that Burton's work in Brazil and the River Plate merited a knighthood.[29] But in his translations of Brazilian classics and his vivid journalism from Argentina he surely deserves greater accolades from Americanists than he has received to date.

Conclusion

Burton is of course best known as Arabist and African explorer. To this extent his years in the Americas form a kind of coda to his main achievements. Yet in his years in North and South America, at his prime, he achieved enough to merit an entry in a dictionary of Victorian travellers even if he had not been 'Captain Burton, the famous traveller'.

Apart from Gerstäcker, no other European traveller visited both North and South America at the height of the frontier era. Burton's time in the West in 1860 provides a very good contrast with the roughly equal period of time spent on the plains in 1867 by his rival in African exploration, Henry Morton Stanley. This contrast in general engenders its own paradoxes, for Burton the professional soldier through sheer ill-luck never saw a single day of front-line service, even though he was a captain of irregulars in the Crimea and was in the Indian Army at the time of the two Sikh wars and the Indian mutiny. The nearest he came to a theatre of war was at the Paraguayan front, where again by ill-luck he missed the fighting. Stanley, by contrast, though a journalist, saw bloody hand-to-hand fighting in Spain, Ethiopia and the Gold Coast and was taken prisoner at the Battle of Shiloh in the American Civil War.

Stanley was perhaps the greater war correspondent, though there are passages in *Battlefields of Paraguay* which show that if Burton could ever have curbed his natural propensity towards scholarship in favour of racy journalism, he would have been no mean competitor for the mantle of W.H. Russell. But as a traveller (as opposed to explorer) Burton was Stanley's superior. He missed nothing, and had an intuitive understanding of every society he encountered. Stanley was uninterested in tribal cultures and local folkways except in so far as they helped or hindered towards the goal of his explorations. For him the end was all-important; for Burton the means had equal validity. Burton was clearly one of those who preferred travelling hopefully to arriving.

It is a pity that Burton had no real talent as historian or political scientist, for he might then have made more of the unique historical moment in which he undertook his travels. It was not just that he was one of the few to experience the open frontier in both North and South America, so that he was acquainted with both prairie and pampa, cowboy and gaucho, Sioux Indians *and* Araucanians. The virtual coincidence of the American Civil War, which he had predicted, with the dreadful Paraguayan conflict, might have alerted him to the possibility that momentous historical changes were afoot, denoted also by the French invasion of Mexico, the Maori uprisings, the Indian mutiny and the Taiping rebellion in China – all of these wars the product of a single decade 1857-67. In retrospect we can see all these convulsions as co-existent manifestations of a single impulse: the stress of integration of backward societies into a global economic system. Some contemporary observers discerned this vaguely, but Burton was not one of them. His talent for broad sociological generalizations, so evident in his anthropological work, deserted him when it came to historical process.

Yet Burton is never less than a stimulating companion, whether in the Rockies or the Andes, on the Missouri or the São Francisco, in Rio or in California. We may sometimes question the eclecticism of his sympathies – it is far from clear, for instance, how one and the same man can admire both Pedro II *and* Francisco Solano López – but this protean aspect of Burton is itself part of the dazzling and contradictory array of talents that entitles him to be considered something of a genius. It is appropriate that the Americas took up some of the best years of the life of a man best known for his exploits in Arabia and Africa for, as Charles Churchill reminds us in *The Rosciad*:

CONCLUSION

Genius is of no country; her pure ray
Spreads all abroad, as general as the day.

Notes on Sources

All unattributed books are by Burton.

Abbreviations used in notes: Add. MSS. Additional Manuscripts, British Library; A.M. Archivo del General Mitre, 27 Vols (Buenos Aires, 1911-3); F.O. Foreign Reports in Public Record Office, London; F.O.C.P. Foreign Office Confidential Print; Huntington MSS. Burton Manuscripts at the Huntington Library, San Marino, California; NLS. National Library of Scotland; RGS. Royal Geographical Society Archives.

CHAPTER ONE

1. Burton to Shaw, 5,19 January, 1,7,10,16 February 1860; Royal Geographical Society archives
2. Burton to Shaw, 16 March 1860; Richards to Shaw, 16 May 1860, RGS
3. Burton to Shaw, April 1860, RGS
4. Isabel Burton, *Life of Captain Sir Richard F. Burton,* 2 vols (1893) (hereinafter *Life),* i. pp.337-8
5. Burton to Shaw, 22 April 1860, RGS
6. The public version is in *The City of the Saints* and *Across the Rocky Mountains to California* (1861). The private version is in one of the few Burton diaries to survive Isabel's pyromania (Add.MSS.49,380 K ff.54-5)
7. *Zanzibar: City, Island and Coast,* 2 vols (1872) i. pp.14-15
8. ibid. ii. pp.389-90
9. Add. MSS.49, 380 K f.56

10. Diary entries, 24 April, 1,2 May 1860, ibid. ff.58-60
11. ibid. ff.58-60
12. ibid. f.62
13. Isabel Burton, *Inner Life of Syria, Palestine and the Holy Land,* 2 vols (1877), ii.p.141
14. *Life,* i. p.26
15. Speke to *Blackwood's,* 1 February 1861, NLS 4731
16. *The Highlands of Brazil,* 2 vols (1861), ii. p.446
17. ibid. i. pp.6,410
18. 'Whilst at Washington I had resolved – as has already been intimated – when the reports of war in the West were waxing loud, to enjoy a little Indian fighting', *City of the Saints* p.52
19. *Wanderings in West Africa: From Liverpool to Fernando Po,* 2 vols (1863), i. p.292
20. *Highlands of Brazil,* i. p.42
21. *A Plain and Literal Translation of the Arabian Nights' Entertainments,* 16 vols (1885-88) (hereinafter *Arabian Nights*) v.p.103; iii. p.105; xi. p.85
22. See Burton's attack in *Stone-Talk* (1865) pp.51-4. For his general views on slavery see Frank McLynn, *Burton: Snow Upon the Desert* (1990)
23. *Wanderings in West Africa,* i. p.300
24. *A Mission to Gelele, King of Dahome,* 2 vols (1864), ii.pp.185-6
25. *To the Gold Coast for Gold,* 2 vols (1883), ii.p.36
26. *Stone-Talk* p.113
27. *City of the Saints* pp.41-2
28. Burton to Monkton Milnes, 1 December 1861, Houghton MSS, Trinity College, Cambridge
29. *Life,* ii. p.497
30. *Stone-Talk* p.113
31. The Mormon newspaper *Deseret News,* 29 August 1860, gives a full list of all who arrived on the stage with Burton. Steinhaeuser was not among them (see Fawn Brodie, *The Devil Drives* (1967) p.179)
32. *Wanderings in Three Continents* (1901) p.150
33. *City of the Saints* p.54
34. ibid. p.20
35. 'Its muddiness is beyond all description; its colour and consistency are those of thick milk porridge; you could not discern an egg in a glass of it. A fly floating in a teacup of this dubious fluid an eighth of an inch below the surface would be quite invisible . . . I have not yet learned to like it.' (Horace Greeley, *An Overland Journey from New York to San Francisco . . . in 1859* (1860) p.13

36. Conversely, when in the Arabian desert he remembered his journey across the prairie. See *The Land of Midian Revisited,* 2 vols (1879), i. p.45

37. *City of the Saints* p.21

38. *Wanderings in Three Continents* p.159. These adverse comments on American cooking have been deeply resented by modern Americans. See Athearn's introduction to his abridged version of *City of the Saints* (1977) p.vii, where he comments, 'The British, of all people!'

39. *Wanderings in Three Continents* pp.161-2

40. For the best description of the Pony Express see Mark Twain, *Roughing It*(1872) pp.70-4

41. *Wanderings in Three Continents* p.158

42. *City of the Saints* p.102

43. Richard Walden Hale, *Sir Richard F. Burton at Salt Lake City 1860* (1930) p.7

44. Burton mentions the sketching incident and the encounter with peevish Arapaho in two separate accounts: *City of the Saints* pp.178-9 and *Wanderings in Three Continents* p.163, but says nothing about the attack. For Wild Bill Hickok's movements at this time see Joseph G. Rosa, *They Called him Wild Bill: the life and adventures of James Butler Hickok* (Norman, Oklahoma 1974) pp. 28-33

45. For the 'Grattan massacre' see J.P. Dunn, *Massacres of the Mountains* (New York 1886)

46. For Carson see Thelma S. Guild, *Kit Carson: a pattern for heroes* (Lincoln, Nebraska 1986)

47. *City of the Saints* p.193

48. ibid, pp.236-7

49. *Wanderings in Three Continents* p.169. Burton was not the only traveller to notice this aspect of Salt Lake City. See Charles F. Browne, *Artemus Ward: His Travels among the Mormons* p.xix: 'The crescent crowned dome and the minaret for the muezzin are all that are wanted to give Salt Lake City the aspect of the Asiatic Orient.'

50. *City of the Saints* pp.240-1

CHAPTER TWO

1. For Joseph Smith and the early history of the Mormons see Fawn Brodie, *No Man Knows my History: The Life of Joseph Smith the Mormon Prophet* (New York 1945); Richard L. Bushman, *Joseph*

Smith and the beginnings of Mormonism (Chicago 1984); Scott H. Faulring, ed., *An American Prophet's record: The Diaries and Journals of Joseph Smith* (Salt Lake City 1988)

2. M.R.Hunter, *Brigham Young, the Colonizer* (Salt Lake City 1940); Marvin S. Hill, *Quest for Refuge: The Mormon Flight from American Pluralism* (Salt Lake City 1988)

3. Brigham Young, *Journal of Discourses,* iv. p.344 quoted in P.A.M. Taylor, *Expectations Westward: The Mormons and the Emigration of their British converts in the nineteenth century* (Edinburgh 1965)

4. 'Extracts from the private journal of Orson Pratt', in *Utah Genealogical and Historical Magazine* 15 (Salt Lake City 1924)

5. L.J. Arrington, *Great Basin Kingdom: An Economic History of the Latter-Day Saints 1830-1900* (Cambridge, Mass. 1958) p.26

6. ibid. pp.52-3

7. See C.H. Brough, *Irrigation in Utah* (Baltimore 1898)

8. See Andrew L.Neff, *History of Utah, 1847-60* (Salt Lake City 1949); Nels Anderson, *Desert Saints: the Mormon Frontier in Utah* (Chicago 1942); Wallace Stegner, *The Gathering of Zion: the story of the Mormon Trail* (1966). It is also interesting to compare the progress made between the visits of the very earliest 'gentile' writers on Mormonism (C.Mackay, *The Mormons: or latter-day Saints in the valley of the Great Salt Lake* (Philadelphia 1852) and those of travellers immediately before Burton (e.g. William Chandless, *A Visit to Salt Lake: being a journey across the plains and a residence in the Mormon settlements at Utah* (1857)

9. Arrington op. cit. pp.167-8

10. G.E. Larson, *Prelude to the Kingdom: Mormon Desert Conquest – a Chapter in American Cooperative Experience* (Francetown, New Hampshire 1947) pp.235-6

11. Horace Greeley, *An Overland Journey* (ed. Charles T. Duncan 1965) pp.208-9

12. ibid. p.215

13. Jules Rémy, *Voyage au pays des Mormons,* 2 vols (Paris 1860). For the preference for this tome over Burton's on the ground that Rémy was not so gullible as Burton see Browne, *Artemus Ward: His Travels among the Mormons,* op. cit. p.vi

14. Norman F. Furniss, *The Mormon Conflict 1850-1859* (Yale 1960) p.208

15. For this see Browne, *Artemus Ward,* op. cit. p.xviii

16. See Brodie, *Devil Drives,* op. cit. p.356. Cf also *City of the Saints* p.509: 'One of my favourite places of visiting was the Historian and Recorder's office, opposite Mr Brigham Young's block.'

17. *Wanderings in Three Continents* p.184

18. Browne, *Artemus Ward*, op. cit. pp.42,59
19. *Wanderings* p.178; *City of the Saints* p.277
20. See Juanita Brooks, *The Mountain Meadows Massacre* (Stanford 1950). There is a graphic impression of the massacre in Jack London's novel *The Star Rover*
21. *City of the Saints* pp.411-14
22. *Wanderings in West Africa,* i. p.37. Cf. his comment on the B'albak mountains in Syria in 1870: 'It wants only a Brigham Young to order the planting of a round million of trees.' *Unexplored Syria,* ii. p.91
23. *City of the Saints* p.326. 'Gentile' was the name applied by the 'Saints' to all non-Mormons. As John Gunther remarked in *Inside USA* (1947): 'Jews in Utah, being non-Mormons, are theoretically subject to classification as Gentiles, which gives rise to the well-known remark that 'Utah is the only place in the world where Jews are Gentiles.'
24. *City of the Saints* pp.426-7
25. The prophecy that the end of the world would occur in 1890 can be found in B.H. Roberts's edition of Joseph Smith's official *History of the Church* (Salt Lake City, 1902-12), ii. p.182
26. *City of the Saints* p.497
27. *Wanderings in Three Continents* p.194. Some of the apostates wrote books denouncing the evils of the Church they had abandoned. See T.B.H. Stenhouse, *The Rocky Mountain Saint* (New York 1873); Fanny Stenhouse, *Tell it All: the story of a Life's Experience in Mormonism* (Hartford, Connecticut 1874)
28. Browne, *Artemus Ward*, op. cit. pp.xviii-xix
29. *City of the Saints* pp.304,306
30. ibid. pp.274,434,517. The first work to describe the Danites and their depredations was Anon, *History of the Saints, or an Exposé of Joe Smith and Mormonism* (Boston 1842)
31. Burton eventually made the overt charge of physical cowardice in *Letters from the Battlefields of Paraguay* p.72
32. *City of the Saints* p.276
33. ibid. pp.358,431-2
34. ibid. p.377
35. ibid. p.380
36. Greeley, *Overland Journey*, op. cit. pp.179-80
37. Eccentric pronunciation seems a feature of American religious prophets. Billy Graham is notorious for pronouncing 'logos' as if it rhymed with 'bogus'.
38. As Browne archly commented: 'Smith did a more flourishing business in the prophet line than Brigham Young does. Smith used

to have his little Revelations almost every day – sometimes two
before dinner. Brigham Young only takes one once in a while.'
Artemus Ward, op. cit.p.52

39. Burton's interview with Brigham Young is treated extensively in
City of the Saints pp.290-303 and in *Wanderings in Three
Continents* pp.180-3
40. Browne, *Artemus Ward*, op. cit. p.54
41. *Life*, i. p.338
42. Thomas Wright, *Life of Sir Richard Burton*, 2 vols (1906), i.
pp.163-4
43. *City of the Saints* p.443; *Wanderings* p.185
44. Mark Twain, *Roughing It* p.127
45. R.G. Cleland & Juanita Brooks, eds. *John D. Lee: A Mormon
Chronicle*, 2 vols (San Marino, California 1955), i. p.83
46. For full accounts of the service in the Bowery see *City of the Saints*
pp.315-18; *Wanderings* pp.186-90
47. Greeley, *Overland Journey* p.187
48. *Wanderings* p.189
49. Burton to Shaw, 7 September 1860, *Proceedings of the Royal
Geographical Society* 5 (1860) pp.1-2
50. Quoted in Brodie, *Devil Drives* p.184. Hale's version (see Hale op.
cit.) runs as follows: 'His friends were kept busy hunting up
influence with Bishop Lee, Orson Pratt, Tom Kane and others of
the Avenging Angels to keep Burton out of the caboose.' From her
close study of Mormon sources Brodie easily pointed up the
absurdity of this story. Briefly, Kane was not a Danite and Lee was
not living in Salt Lake City at the time (see Brodie's introduction
to her edition of *City of the Saints* (New York 1963). For the facts
in the case of Bishop Lee see Juanita Brooks, *John D. Lee*
(Glendale, California 1962)
51. *City of the Saints* pp.409-10
52. See, for example, the witty account in Kipling's *From Sea to Sea*
(1889)
53. *City of the Saints* p.399
54. *Ultima Thule; or a Summer in Iceland*, 2 vols (1875), ii.
pp.147,183. He comforted himself by visiting Steamboat Springs in
the Californian Sierra Nevada (*Abeokuta and the Cameroon
Mountains*), 2 vols (1863), ii. p.206
55. Mark Twain, *Roughing It* p.158
56. Browne, *Artemus Ward* p.22
57. *City of the Saints* p.597
58. For their description of the town as Burton would have seen it see
Twain, *Roughing It* p.378; Browne, *Artemus Ward* p.24. For a

detailed study of everyday life in California at this time see Robert
M. Senkewicz, *Vigilantes in Gold Rush California* (Stanford 1985)
59. *City of the Saints* p.604
60. Hale, *Sir Richard Burton at Salt Lake City,* op. cit.
61. *City of the Saints* p.606

CHAPTER THREE

1. *City of the Saints* pp.68-9
2. *Arabian Nights*, ii. p.265
3. *Personal Narrative of a Pilgrimage to El-Medinah and Meccah,*
   2 vols (1893), ii. pp.118-19
4. *Arabian Nights*, x. p.241
5. *Abeokuta*, i. p.46; *Gelele*, ii. p.124; *Arabian Nights*, i. pp.283,300;
   v. p.135; x. pp.240-1
6. For Burton's analysis see *City of the Saints* pp.116-26. For
   confirmation of his findings by modern scholars see George E.
   Hyde, *Spotted Tail's Folk: A History of the Brûlé Sioux* (Norman,
   Oklahoma 1961); *Red Cloud's Folk: A History of the Oglala Sioux
   Indians* (Norman 1937). See also James C. Olson, *Red Cloud and
   the Sioux Problem* (Lincoln, Nebraska 1965)
7. Francis Parkman, *La Salle and the Discovery of the Great West*
   (New York 1963)
8. *City of the Saints* pp.62-5,91
9. *Stone-Talk* p.35
10. Stanley Ivins, 'Notes on Mormon Polygamy', *Western Humanities
    Review* 10 (1956) pp.229-39 (at p.233). See also Richard S. Van
    Wagoner, *Mormon Polygamy* (Salt Lake City 1988)
11. Jules Rémy, *A Journey to Great Salt Lake City*, 2 vols (1861), ii.
    p.60
12. *City of the Saints* p.520
13. *Wanderings in Three Continents* p.178. Mark Twain did not agree
    that Mormon women were pretty: 'I was touched. My heart was
    wiser than my head. I warmed towards these poor ungainly and
    pathetically homely creatures, and as I turned to hide the generous
    moisture in my eyes, I said, "No" – the man that marries one of
    them has done an act of Christian charity which entitles him to the
    kindly applause of mankind, not their harsh censure – and the man
    that marries sixty of them has done a deed of open-handed
    generosity so sublime that the nations should stand uncovered in
    his presence and worship in silence.' *Roughing It* pp.117-18
14. *Wanderings* pp.192-3

15. *City of the Saints* pp.523-5
16. ibid. p.523
17. ibid. pp.522-3
18. William Chandless, *A Visit to Salt Lake* (1857) pp.191-2
19. Jules Rémy, *A Journey to Great Salt Lake City*, 2 vols (1861), i. p.201; ii. p.156
20. Browne, *Artemus Ward*, op. cit. pp.xxiv-xxv
21. Greeley, *Overland Journey* pp.184-5
22. *Wanderings* pp.164-5
23. *City of the Saints* p.524
24. ibid. p.520
25. 'A plurality of wives is the natural condition of man in thinly populated countries where he who has the largest family is the greatest benefactor of mankind.' *First Footsteps in East Africa* (1856) p.121
26. *City of the Saints* p.524
27. *The Lake Regions of Central Africa*, 2 vols (1860)
28. *Abeokuta*, i. p.216
29. *Personal Narrative*, ii. p.90
30. ibid. p.91. The reference is to Harriet Martineau's *Eastern Life: present and past*, 2 vols (1848)
31. *The Captivity of Hans Stade of Hesse in A.D. 1547-1555, Among the Wild Tribes of Eastern Brazil* (1874) p.143
32. *The Jew, the Gypsy and El-Islam* (1898) p.327
33. Wright, *Burton*, i. p.133
34. *First Footsteps* p.120. For an extended discussion of Burton's misogyny see Frank McLynn, *Burton: Snow Upon the Desert*
35. *Highlands of Brazil*, i. p.115
36. *Athenaeum*, 30 November 1861, 1179 pp.723-5
37. Monkton Milnes reviewed the *City of the Saints* for the *Edinburgh Review* and regretted that he did not have the space to include all the stories about the Mormons. A favourite tale was of one 'Saint', angry with his 'brother', who said to him: 'Sir, if you was Mr Jesus Christ, or Mr Joseph Smith himself sitting there, with your halo hanging above your head, I would pull your nose at any rate.' T. Wemyss Reid, *Life, Letters and Friendships of Richard Monkton Milnes, First Lord Houghton*, 2 vols (1886), ii. p.77
38. *Arabian Nights*, ii. p.11
39. *The Jew, the Gypsy and El-Islam* pp.344-5
40. *Wanderings in West Africa*, i. p.300
41. See Appendix
42. See Harriet Martineau, *Society in America*, 2 vols (1839), ii. Chapter 5; Fanny Kemble, *Journal of a Residence on a Georgian*

Plantation in 1838-39(1863) pp.188-94

43. *City of the Saints* p.78
44. See Frederick Marryat, *A Diary in America with remarks on its Institutions*, 2 vols (Philadelphia 1839), ii. Chapters 31,32
45. Captain Basil Hall, *Travels in North America in the Years 1827 and 1828*, 2 vols (Edinburgh 1829), i. Chapter 4
46. *Highlands of Brazil*, i. p.51. There is a classic description of the perils posed by tobacco when travelling 'on the cars' in Mackay, *The Western World, or, Travels in the US in 1846-47*, 2 vols (1850), ii. Chapter 7
47. G.A. Sala, *My Diary in America in the Midst of War* (1865)
48. Alexis de Tocqueville, *Democracy in America, the Second Part* (1840)
49. Marryat, *A Diary in America*. op. cit. See also the remarks of William Cobbett, who in most things was pro-American: 'There is one thing in the Americans which . . . I have . . . kept back to the last moment. It has presented itself several times, but I have turned from the thought, as men do from thinking of any mortal disease that is at work in their frame. It is not covetousness; it is not niggardliness; it is not insincerity; it is not enviousness; it is not cowardice, above all things; it is DRINKING. Aye, and that too, amongst but too many men, who, one would think, would loathe it. You can go into hardly any man's house without being asked to drink wine or spirits even *in the morning*. They are quick at meals, are little eaters, seem to care little about what they eat and never talk about it . . . Nor do the Americans *sit and tope much after dinner*, and talk on till they get into nonsense and smut, which last is a sure mark of a silly, and, pretty generally, even of a base mind. But they *tipple*; and the infernal spirits they tipple too! . . . the Americans preserve their gravity and quietness and good humour even in their drink; and so much the worse. It were far better for them to be as noisy and quarrelsome as the English drunkards; for then the odiousness of the vice would be more visible, and the vice itself might become less frequent.' *A Year's Residence in the United States of America* (1817-9)
50. Ruskin's remark is in *Praeterita* (1885-9). Matthew Arnold's comes in a letter to Sir Mountstuart Grant Duff, 29 July 1886. James's is in Henry James to Mrs Henry James Sr, 15 October 1869
51. Frances Trollope, *Domestic Manners of the Americans* (1832). The philistinism and prudery is dealt with in Chapter 9, the inability to pronounce in Chapter 5, religion in Chapter 15 and inquisitiveness in Chapter 14
52. ibid, Chapter 28

53. *Arabian Nights*, xv. p.224
54. James Silk Buckingham, *America: Historical, Statistical and Descriptive* (1841); William E. Baxter, *America and the Americans* (1855)
55. Anthony Trollope, *North America* (1862)
56. Dickens to Jane Welsh Carlyle, 7 January 1844; Dickens to John Forster, 24 February 1842. For a convenient collection of relevant documents see Michael Slater, ed., *Dickens on America and the Americans* (Austin, Texas 1978)
57. De Tocqueville, *Democracy in America*, First Part (1835). For other examples of American prickliness and vainglory see Mackay, *The Western World*, op. cit. and Captain Basil Hall, *Travels in North America* (1829)
58. *Arabian Nights*, xvi p.445; i. p.450
59. See de Tocqueville, passim, and George Combe, *Notes during a Phrenological Visit 1838-40* (1841)
60. *Arabian Nights*, i. p.449
61. ibid. p.448
62. John Keats to George Keats, 31 October 1818
63. Samuel Butler, *Notebooks* (1890)
64. *Arabian Nights*, xvi. p.425
65. *City of the Saints* p.57
66. *Arabian Nights*, x. p.425
67. *The Economist*, 28 September 1861
68. *Stone-Talk* p.96
69. As for instance Emerson in his essay 'Success' in *Society and Solitude* (1870): 'I hate this shallow Americanism which hopes to get rich by credit, to get knowledge by raps on midnight tables, to learn the economy of the mind by phrenology, or skill without study, or mastery without apprenticeship.' And who can forget Ambrose Bierce's dismissal: 'A great broad blackness with two or three small points of light struggling and flickering in the universal black of ignorance, crudity, conceit, tobacco-chewing, ill-dressing, unmannerly manners and general barbarity' quoted in W. Blair & Hamlin Hill, eds. *America's Humour* (1978)
70. *City of the Saints* p.377

CHAPTER FOUR

1. See Burton to Russell, 17 April 1865, F.O.13/432; Russell's minute of 19 April 1865, F.O.84/1244; F.O. to Burton, 21 April 1865, F.O.84/1244

2. 'Farewell dinner to Captain Burton on his departure to Santos', *Anthropological Review* 23 (1865) pp.167-82
3. Burton to F.O., 16 May 1865, F.O.97/438
4. *Life*, i. p.416
5. *To the Gold Coast for Gold*, op. cit., i. p.18
6. 'From London to Rio de Janeiro: letters to a friend', *Fraser's Magazine* 430,433,436 (1865-6) pp.492-503, pp.78-92 and 496-510 respectively
7. *Highlands of Brazil*, i. p.1
8. Burton to F.O., 13 July 1865; F.O. minute, 3 August 1865, F.O.13/432
9. M.G. and E.T. Mulhall, *Handbook of Brazil* (Buenos Aires 1877) p.76; William Hadfield, *Brazil and the River Plate in 1868* (1869) p.33. For a (naturally) more favourable impression of Rio see the official publication prepared for the Vienna Exhibition of 1873, which the Burtons attended: *The Empire of Brazil at the Vienna Universal Exhibition of 1873* (Rio 1873)
10. Burton to F.O., 8 September 1865, F.O.13/432
11. *Life*, i. p.418
12. Wilkins, *Romance*, i. pp.247-8
13. *Life*, i. p.419
14. Burton had already visited São Sebastião with Commander Napier of the *Triton* on his way up from Santos to Rio in September; *Captivity of Hans Stade of Hesse*, op. cit. p.xxxix
15. For Pedro II see H.Lyra, *Historia de Dom Pedro*, 3 vols (Rio 1938-40); Harry Bernstein, *Pedro II* (New York 1973). For a close-up on the years of the Paraguayan war see Mary Wilhelmine Williams, *Dom Pedro the Magnanimous* (Chapel Hill, (North Carolina 1937) pp.111-27
16. Leslie Bethell, *Britain and the Abolition of the Brazilian Slave Trade* (Cambridge 1970) p.375
17. For detail see Mary C. Karasch, *Slave Life in Rio de Janeiro 1808-1850* (Princeton 1987)
18. On Brazilian slavery and its abolition see Richard Graham, 'Causes for the Abolition of Negro Slavery in Brazil: an interpretive essay', *Hispanic American Historical Review* 46 (1966) pp.123-37; 'Brazilian slavery re-examined: a review article', *Journal of Social History* 3 (1970) pp.431-53; Robert Conrad, *The Destruction of Brazilian Slavery 1850-1888* (Berkeley 1972); *Brazilian Slavery* (Boston 1977)
19. *Highlands of Brazil*, i.p.5,7. For Brazilian appreciation of Burton's stance see Lyra, op. cit., i. p.324
20. For Pedro's die-hard, jingoistic, 'unconditional surrender' posture

see the many letters from the Emperor to the Condessa de Barral (especially that of 9 October 1866) reproduced in Alcindo Sodre, *Abrindo um cofre* (Rio 1956). For a detailed explanation of how Brazil entered the war see Efraím Cardozo, *El Imperio del Brasil en el Rio de la Plata* (Buenos Aires 1961); Ricardo Caillet-Bois, *Un año crítico en la política exterior de la presidencia de Mitre* (Buenos Aires 1946)

21. Percy A. Martin, 'Slavery and Abolition in Brazil', *Hispanic American Historical Review* 13 (1933) p.173
22. Thornton to Clarendon, 5 January 1866, F.O.84/1259
23. See Anyda Marchant, *Viscount Mauá and the Empire of Brazil* (Berkeley 1965); Lydia Besouchet, *Mauá y su época* (Buenos Aires 1952); Alberto de Fario, *Ireneo Evangelista de Souza, barão e visconde de Mauá, 1813-1889* (São Paulo 1973)
24. *Letters from the Battlefields of Paraguay* p.xiii
25. ibid. p.388
26. *Highlands of Brazil*, i. pp.271-3

CHAPTER FIVE

1. Wilkins, *Romance*, i. p.249
2. ibid. p.250
3. *Life*, i. p.422; Wilkins, i. p.252
4. H.G. and E.T. Mulhall, *Handbook of Brazil* (Buenos Aires 1977) pp.224-5. For an illuminating history of São Paulo see R.M. Morse, *From Community to Metropolis; a biography of São Paulo* (Gainesville 1958)
5. Isabel Burton, *A.E.I. Arabia, Egypt, India* (1879) p.22
6. William Hadfield, *Brazil and the River Plate in 1868* (1869) p.70
7. *Zanzibar*, i. p.323. Brazil was expensive because much of its food was imported
8. *Life*, i. p.596
9. Wilkins, i. pp.253,255
10. *Ultima Thule*, ii. p.300; *Life*, i. p.371; *AEI* pp.207-9
11. *Life*, i. p.423
12. ibid. i. pp.429-30
13. *Captivity of Hans Stade of Hesse* p.vi
14. ibid. pp.x-xi
15. *Camoens: His Life and His Lusiads*, 2 vols (1881), i. p.363
16. *The Jew, the Gypsy and El-Islam* p.284. Selina was the pretty gypsy girl whose favours Burton and other undergraduates of 1840 enjoyed

17. Wilkins, i. p.258
18. *Camoens: His Life and His Lusiads* i. pp.167-74
19. *Life*, i. p.421
20. Burton to F.O., 2 April 1866; F.O. minute, 8 May 1866; F.O. to Burton, 8 May 1866, F.O.13/442
21. Wilkins, i. p.260
22. *Life*, i. pp.438-9
23. The two-part lecture is reproduced in *Trans. Royal Soc.of Literature* 20 (1899) pp.197-235. See also *Wanderings in Three Continents* pp.35-69
24. Wilkins, i. pp.260-1
25. *Captivity of Hans Stade of Hesse,* p.61
26. *Arabian Nights*, x.p.246
27. He left São Paulo on 1 June 1866 and was back by 7 July (Burton to F.O. 23 June, 7 July 1866, F.O.13/442)
28. *Zanzibar*, i. p.29
29. Wilkins, i. p.262
30. *Captivity of Hans Stade* p.xxiii.
31. *The Times* 10,14,23,26,30 October, 2,10,14,21 November 1848; Bernard Heuvelmans, *In the Wake of true Sea Serpents* (1968). A monster of the deep was reported at Pernambuco in 1640 as having taken both men and dogs. In all probability the incident was an attack by a giant squid.
32. *Captivity of Hans Stade of Hesse*, pp.xxvi-xxviii; *Zanzibar*, i. p.250
33. *Captivity of Hans Stade of Hesse*, pp.xxix-xlii
34. Wilkins, i. p.263
35. *Life*, i. pp.424,433
36. Wilkins, i. pp.265-6
37. ibid. i. p.264
38. *Life*,i. pp.430-1; Wilkins, i. p.265
39. Wilkins, i. pp.256,267; ii. p.634
40. *Life*, i. p.436; ii. p.264
41. *Arabian Nights*, v. p.294; *Zanzibar*, i. p.185
42. For the snakes of Brazil see especially Charles Waterton, *Wanderings in South America*, ed. L.Harrison Matthews (1973) pp.65,107 and James W. Weeks, *Three Thousand Miles Through Brazil*, 2 vols (1886),i. p.244. Waterton was able to pull off the trick Burton found so dangerous – that of grabbing a venomous snake round the neck. But Waterton, as his famous alligator-riding exploit (*Wanderings*, op. cit. pp.133-4) demonstrated, was fearless almost to the point of folly. One had to treat with caution, then, his firm asseveration that snakes never attack first: 'Time and

experience have convinced me that there is not much danger in roving amongst snakes and wild beasts provided only that you have self-command.' (*Wanderings* p.106)

43. *Zanzibar*, i. p.210, ii. p.170; *Sindh Revisited*, 2 vols (1877), ii. p.279; *Two Trips to Gorilla Land and the Cataracts of the Congo*, 2 vols (1876), i. p.168
44. *Arabian Nights*, vi. p.205
45. *Life*, i. pp.427-8
46. Wilkins, i. p.267; *Life*, i. p.425
47. *Lacerda's Journey to Cazembe in 1798* (1873) p.99; *Highlands of Brazil*, i. p.72
48. *Two Trips to Gorilla Land*, i. p.204, ii. pp.22-5,129
49. *Zanzibar*, i. p.151
50. *Ultima Thule*, i. p.48; *Zanzibar*, i. p.121
51. *Zanzibar*, i. pp.150-76, esp. pp.156,163,165,167
52. *Unexplored Syria*, i. p.3
53. *Two Trips to Gorilla Land*, i. p.215
54. *Captivity of Hans Stade of Hesse*, pp.1xi-xciv,22,156; *Arabian Nights*, x. p.210; *Two Trips to Gorilla Land*, i. pp.98,164; *Zanzibar*,ii. p.244
55. *Zanzibar*, ii. p.45; *Ultima Thule*, ii. pp.33,35,46; *Captivity of Hans Stade of Hesse*, pp.98-9,103
56. *Ultima Thule*, ii. pp.46,89; *Zanzibar*, i. p.216; *Arabian Nights*, viii. p.90,ix. p.181
57. Burton to Bates, 9 December 1872, 19 November 1873, 20 December 1880, RGS; *Lacerda's Journey to Cazembe* p.90; *Two Trips to Gorilla Land*, i. p.163
58. *Arabian Nights*, i. p.221; *Zanzibar*, i. p.129; *Two Trips to Gorilla Land*, ii. p.21
59. *Zanzibar*, i. p.227,247-48; *Arabian Nights*, ii. p.123
60. *Zanzibar* i. pp.213,229,235-36,238; *Ultima Thule*, i. p.294; *Lacerda's Journey to Cazembe* pp.16,42,59,71; *Arabian Nights*, i. pp.448-9
61. *Zanzibar*, i. pp.29,149,223,362
62. Alan Moorehead, introduction to his 1960 edition of *Lake Regions*
63. *Ultima Thule*, ii. pp.34,38,41,261; *Zanzibar*, i. p.322; ii. p.198
64. *Two Trips to Gorilla Land*, i. p.136; *Ultima Thule*, i. p.367; *Arabian Nights*, i. p.264, vii. p.168; *Zanzibar*, i. p.33; *Sindh Revisited*, ii. p.120; *Life*, i. p.359
65. *Zanzibar*, i. p.380
66. *Life*, i. p.424. Steinhaeuser died in Berne. Burton also recalled the incident in *Zanzibar*, i. p.15: 'At that time I was wandering about the Brazil [*sic*], and I well remember dreaming on what proved to

be the date of his death, that a tooth suddenly fell to the ground, followed by a crash of blood.'

CHAPTER SIX

1. Burton to F.O., 18 August, 18 September, 7,19 October 1866, F.O.13/442
2. *Highlands of Brazil*, i. pp.9-10
3. Wilkins, i. p.265
4. Many of the Foreign Office minutes of rebuke and exasperation are undated. But see in particular F.O. minute of 5 January 1866 and F.O. to Burton, 20 January, 20 October 1866, F.O.13/450
5. F.O. to Burton, 18 October 1866, F.O.13/442; Burton to F.O., 6 January 1867, F.O.13/450
6. Francis Hitchman, *Richard F. Burton*, 2 vols (1887), ii. p.254
7. Burton to Thornton, 2 November 1865, F.O.84/1244; 1 October 1866, F.O.84/1259; Thornton to Russell, 5 October 1866; Russell to Thornton, 7 November 1866, F.O.84/1259
8. For a general survey see F.Goldman, *Os pioneros americanos no Brasil* (São Paulo 1959). See also *Highlands of Brazil*, i. pp.5-6,421; T.P. Bigg-Wither, *Pioneering in Southern Brazil*, 2 vols (1878); L. Waibel, 'European Colonisation in Southern Brazil', *Geographical Review* 15 (1950); P. Monbeig, *Pionniers et planteurs de São Paulo* (Paris 1952)
9. Hitchman,op.cit., ii. p.257
10. Burton to F.O., 15 April 1867; F.O. to Burton, 27 May 1867, F.O.13/450
11. Thornton to Russell, 4 October 1866; F.O. minute, 13 November 1866; Russell to Thornton, 17 November 1866, F.O.13/438
12. F.O. to Thornton, 7 March 1867, F.O.13/447
13. F.O. to Burton, 14 August 1865, F.O.13/432
14. For a discussion of the affair in the context of West African politics see Christopher Fyfe, *A History of Sierra Leone* (Oxford 1962) p.342
15. Burton to F.O., 8,16 May 1865; F.O. to Burton, 23 May 1865, F.O.97/438
16. Report of 12 November 1866, F.O.97/438
17. Robinson to Stanley, 1 April 1867, F.O.97/438
18. F.O. to Burton, 31 January, 4 June 1867, F.O.13/450
19. Burton to Stanley, 5 June 1867, F.O.97/438
20. F.O. minute to Stanley, 23 July 1867, F.O.97/438

CHAPTER SEVEN

1. *Life*, i. p.425
2. *Highlands of Brazil*, i. p.31
3. Burton to F.O., 10 January 1867, F.O.13/450; *Life*, i.pp.436,439
4. Wilkins, i. p.268
5. ibid., i. p.269, ii. p.597; *AEI* pp.299,301,304
6. Bates to Burton, 5 April 1867, RGS; *PRGS* 13 (1868-9) p.311; Burton to F.O., 15 April 1867, F.O.13/450
7. Swinburne to Lord Houghton (Monkton Milnes), 11 July 1865; Swinburne to Hotten, 2 January 1867, in Cecil Y. Lang, ed. *The Swinburne Letters* (Yale 1959), i. pp.124,219
8. ibid. i. pp.223-5
9. Burton to Swinburne, 5 April 1867, B.L.Ashley MSS.297
10. Swinburne to Houghton, 8 August 1867, *Swinburne Letters*, i. p.258
11. Thornton to Clarendon, 23 June 1866; Stanley to Thornton, 23 July 1866, F.O.13/438
12. *Letters from the Battlefields of Paraguay* p.296
13. Thornton to Burton, 20 August 1866; Burton to Thornton, 27 August 1866; Thornton to Stanley, 3 Sept. 1866, F.O.13/438
14. Burton to F.O., 13 June 1867, F.O.13/450
15. Wright, *Life*, i. p.199; *Highlands of Brazil*, i. p.19; 'The Extinction of Slavery in Brazil', Burton to Anthropological Society, 1 June 1867, *Anthropological Review* (1868) pp.56-63; *Athenaeum*, 27 July 1867, No.2074 p.115
16. Wilkins, i. p.273; *Life*, i. p.440
17. *Highlands of Brazil*, i. pp.34,57; Wilkins, i. pp.275-6; *Life*, i. p.440
18. For Agassiz in Juiz de Fora see *A Journey in Brazil* (1868) pp.75-9
19. Wilkins, i. pp.278-80
20. ibid. pp.282-3; *Highlands*, i. p.107
21. *Highlands*, i. pp.38,113; Wilkins, 1. p.284
22. Wilkins, i. p.285
23. *Wanderings in Three Continents* p.262; *Highlands*, i. p.155; Wilkins, i. pp.268-9
24. *Life*, i. p.441; *Highlands*, i. p.161; Wilkins, i. pp.290-1
25. *Life*, i. p.441
26. ibid. ii. p.294
27. *Highlands*, i. pp.435-53; Wilkins, i. pp.295-9
28. Wilkins, i. pp.300-4; *Highlands*, i. p.227
29. *Life*, i. p.442; *Highlands*, i. p.279
30. For a contemporary description of Ouro Prêto see M.G. and E.T.

Mulhall, *Handbook of the Brazil* (Buenos Aires 1877) pp.109,221. For Gardner's description twenty years earlier see George Gardner, *Travels in the Interior of Brazil* (1846) pp.509-12. For a description of the town fifty years *after* Burton's visit see Paul Wallé, *Au Brésil de l'Uruguay au Rio Sao Francisco*, 2 vols (Paris 1910), i. pp.394-402

31. Wilkins, i. p.305; *Highlands*, i. p.358
32. *Highlands*, i. pp.373-4,402-3
33. Wilkins, i. pp.306-7
34. For descents of the Morro Velho mine by other nineteenth-century travellers see Gardner, *Travels in the Interior*, op. cit. pp.495-9; Frank Vincent, *About South America* (1890) pp.277-81
35. *Life*, i. pp.443-5; Wilkins, i. pp.309-13; *Highlands*, i. pp.245-52
36. *Wanderings in Three Continents* pp.265-6; *Highlands*, i. pp.428-34, ii. p.1
37. *Wanderings* p.266; *Highlands*, ii. p.2; Wilkins, i. p.317
38. *Life*, i. pp.446-7
39. ibid. pp.447-9; Wilkins, i. pp.322-41

CHAPTER EIGHT

1. *Wanderings in Three Continents* p.267
2. *Two Trips to Gorilla Land*, ii. p.293
3. *Wanderings* p.268
4. ibid. p.270
5. *Highlands of Brazil*, ii. p.234
6. See Roosevelt's sensational presentation of piranha in *Through the Brazilian Wilderness* (1914) pp.49-51
7. *Highlands*, ii. p.42
8. ibid. ii. p.62
9. *Wanderings* pp.271-3
10. ibid. p.274
11. Agassiz, *A Journey in Brazil*, op. cit. pp.515-16
12. *Highlands* ii. p.98
13. ibid. pp.98-100,119,126-7
14. ibid. pp.102,117
15. For stories of encounters with alligators see Henry Walter Bates, *The Naturalist on the River Amazon* (1910) pp.299-301, 306 et seq.; Charles Waterton, *Wanderings in South America*, ed. L. Harrison Matthews (1973) pp.133-5; Baron von Humboldt, *Personal narrative of a voyage to the equinoctial regions of America* 7 vols (1829); Richard Spruce, *Notes of a Botanist on the Amazon*

and Andes 2 vols (1908) i. pp.170,172

16. Bates, op. cit. pp.51,150-1, 316. Bates reckoned the *fer-de-lance* to be both aggressive and highly venomous, and claimed that the only man he knew who survived its bite was maimed for life (ibid. p.316). Waterton claimed that snakes never attacked first and pooh-poohed the threat from the *fer-de-lance*. (*Wanderings in South America* p.106.) Weeks, who followed closely in Burton's footsteps a few years later, reported a narrow escape by one of his men from the fangs of a *jararaca-assu*, which when killed pegged out at 8'4" long (James W. Weeks, *Three Thousand Miles through Brazil*, 2 vols (1886), i. p.331. Interestingly, in view of Burton's translation, the rattlesnake occurs in Alencar's *Honey-Lips* as a prize pest (*Honey-Lips* p.11)

17. Bates, op. cit. p.51; S.A.S. Maximilien, *Voyage au Brésil dans les années 1815,1816 & 1817,* 2 vols (Paris 1821), ii. p.294

18. Waterton, op. cit. pp.115-20,198

19. *Highlands*, ii. p.180

20. Bates,op. cit. pp.214-15

21. Bates pp.215-16; Waterton p.34; Weeks, op. cit. ii. p.167

22. G.M. Dyott, *Man Hunting in the Jungle* (1930) p.105

23. P.H. Fawcett, *Exploration Fawcett* (1953) pp.85-6

24. *Lacerda's Journey to Cazembe* p.2; *Ultima Thule*, ii. p.239

25. Marston Bates, *The Land and Wildlife of South America*, op. cit.

26. James Weeks commented when he went in Burton's wake seven years later: 'My craft was not a first-class ship like Captain Burton's *Eliza* (Weeks, ii. p.35)

27. *Highlands*, ii. p.185

28. *Wanderings* p.275. For other accounts of Pirapora see Paul Wallé, *Au Brésil*, op. cit., i. pp.430-2. Weeks, who came here in 1874, said proudly: 'I am now again on the track of Captain Burton.' (Weeks, i. p.341)

29. *Highlands*, ii. pp.192-3

30. Weeks, ii. p.29

31. *Highlands*, ii. p.209

32. The three South American rivers incontestably longer than the São Francisco are the Amazon, the Paraná and the Madeira (itself a tributary of the mighty Amazon). There is an academic controversy over whether the São Francisco or the Purus (both about 1,850 miles long) should occupy fourth position. The world's 'top twenty' rivers in point of length are: the Nile, Amazon, Mississippi-Missouri, the Russian quartet of Ob-Irtysh, Lena, Yenisey and Volga, the Yangtze and Hwang-Ho (Yellow River) in China, the Congo and Niger in Africa, the Mackenzie and St Lawrence in

Canada (plus the Yukon in Alaska), the Murray-Darling in Australia, the Amur, Mekong and Indus in Asia, plus the aforementioned Paraná and Madeira in South America. Thereafter the situation becomes a little confused. The Rio Grande, Purus, Brahmaputra, Orinoco and São Francisco all have their supporters. At best, then, the São Francisco is the twenty-first longest in the world; at worst it occupies twenty-fourth place.

33. *Highlands*, ii. p.214. Modern scholars have questioned Burton's model and tried to construct homologies between North and South America. Some of these efforts simply compound the confusion. Alistair Hennessy, for example, at various times compares the São Francisco with the Mississippi, the St Lawrence and the Cumberland Gap. Hennessy, *The Frontier in Latin American History* (1978) pp.18,51,142

34. *Highlands*, ii. pp.238-41

35. *Two Trips to Gorilla Land*, ii. p.78

36. *Wanderings*, p.277

37. Weeks travelled down at the height of the rainy season seven years later and ruefully commented: 'Captain Burton should congratulate himself upon having chosen another season of the year, whereby he avoided the horrible night of misery we had to undergo' (Weeks, ii. p.42). For Gardner's journey on this stretch of the São Francisco see *Travels in the Interior of Brazil* (1846) pp.113-37

38. *Highlands* ii. pp.257-67

39. John Hemming, *Amazon Frontier* (1987) p.505

40. This stretch of the São Francisco was exhaustively travelled by Weeks in 1874-5. His report on those who met Burton at Carunhanha is in Weeks, ii. pp.25-9. At nearby Pedras de Maria da Cruz he recorded: 'At this place I again entered upon Captain Burton's tracks . . . apparently little alteration had taken place in the village since Captain Burton's visit seven years previously.' (ibid., i. pp.404-5)

41. *Highlands*, ii. pp.281-2

42. See Henrique Guilherme Fernando Halfeld, *Atlas e relatorio concernante a Exploração do Rio de São Francisco desde a Cachoeira da Pirapora ate O Oceano Atlántico, levantado por ordem do Governo de S.M.I.O. Senhor dom Pedro II en 1852,1853 e 1854* (Rio 1860)

43. Burton's translation of Camoens, *The Lusiads*, 2 vols (1880), Canto 6, Stanza 95

44. *Highlands*, ii. pp.297-319

45. ibid. pp.347-57

46. *Two Trips to Gorilla Land*, ii. p.303

47. *Arabian Nights*, ix. p.253
48. *Highlands*, ii. pp.366-9
49. *Two Trips to Gorilla Land*, ii. p.200
50. *Highlands*, ii. pp.380-5
51. ibid. ii. pp.390-1, 401
52. ibid, ii. pp.393-405
53. Douglas Timmins, ed. *A Traveller of the Sixties: The Journals of F.J. Stevenson* (1929) p.89. The particular reason Stevenson wanted to meet Burton was that Senhor Campos, agent of the Bahia Steam Navigation Company, 'entrusted me with official letters to deliver to Captain Burton, the celebrated traveller in India, Arabia and Africa, now British consul at Santos. He is expected to arrive at Piranha in a day or two from the almost unknown interior, where he has been making some important explorations for the Brazilian government, with the consent and at the instance of the British government.' (ibid. p.76)
54. *Highlands*, ii. pp.410-15
55. *Wanderings*, p.279
56. *Highlands*, ii. p.433
57. *Wanderings*, p.279
58. *Highlands*, ii. p.437
59. *Two Trips*, ii. pp.287-9
60. For other nineteenth-century travellers' impressions of the Falls see Timmins, *F.J. Stevenson*, op. cit. p.85-9; Frank Vincent, *Round and About South America* (1890) pp.328-30. Cf. also *The Times*, 20 September 1880; *The Graphic*, 7 May 1881
61. Gardner, *Travels in the Interior of Brazil* (1846) p.138
62. *Wanderings*, pp.279-80; *Highlands*, ii. pp.444-6
63. *Wanderings*, p.281; *Highlands*, i. p.12, ii. p.457

CHAPTER NINE

1. Wilkins, i. p.343
2. Wilfred Scawen Blunt, *My Diaries*, 2 vols (New York 1921), ii. p.128. For an assessment of Blunt see Elizabeth Longford, *A Pilgrimage of Passion: The Life of Wilfred Scawen Blunt* (1979)
3. Timmins, *Journals of F.J. Stevenson*. op. cit. p.95
4. *Life*, i. p.449
5. See Burton to F.O., 7,19 January, 1,21 February, 18 May 1868, F.O.13/457
6. Burton's weatherbook, RGS archives
7. *Highlands of Brazil*, i. p.119

8. Mulhall, *Handbook of Brazil*, op. cit. pp.24-5
9. William Hadfield, *Brazil and the River Plate in 1868* (1869) p.54
10. ibid. pp.56-61,77,84
11. ibid. p.69
12. ibid. p.68; *Life*, i. p.434
13. Wilkins, i. pp.344-45
14. ibid; *Life*, i. p.450
15. Wilkins, i. p.346; *Life*, i. p.453
16. Burton to F.O., 22,23 July 1868, F.O.13/457
17. F.O. to Burton 22 July 1868; Burton to F.O. 23 July 1868, F.O. 13/457
18. Wilkins, i. p.348
19. ibid. p.349
20. *Highlands*, i. pp.v-vi
21. ibid. p.viii. Burton's advocacy of polygamy is at ibid. i. p.115
22. *Life*, i. p.454
23. ibid. i. p.591
24. See the *Athenaeum* 2151, 16 January 1869, pp.83-4; *Anthropological Review* 12 No.25 (1869) pp.170-6
25. Roosevelt, *Through the Brazilian Wilderness* (1914) p.333
26. *Life*, i. p.58
27. 'Primordial Inhabitants of Minas Gerais and the occupations of the present Inhabitants', *Journal of the Anthropological Institute* 2 (1873) pp.407-23; 'Notes on the Kitchen-Middens of São Paulo, Brazil, and the Footprints of St Thomas, alias Zome', *Anthropologia* 1 (1873) pp.44-59. See also *Journal of the Anthropological Society* 4 (1866) pp.cxciii-cxiv; *Anthropological Review* 6 (1868) pp.462-3
28. Burton to RGS, 18 December 1871, RGS provides a glowing recommendation for a paper on Minas Gerais by Henrique Gerber. The translation by Burton appeared as 'Geographical Notes on the Province of Minas Gerais', in *JRGS* 44 (1874) pp.262-300
29. *Sindh Revisited*, ii. p.229
30. Compare Stevenson in Timmins, op. cit. pp.336-7 with *Life*, i. p.45. For the ticks see W.H.Hudson, *The Naturalist in La Plata* (1892) p.141. For the soil erosion see Harold Blakemore and Clifford T. Smith, eds, *Latin America: Geographical Perspectives* (1971) p.364
31. *Arabian Nights*, xiv. p.57
32. *Captivity of Hans Stade of Hesse*, p.146
33. Isabel Burton, *Inner Life of Syria*, i. p.3; *Unexplored Syria*, i. p.3; *Life*, i. p.496
34. *To the Gold Coast for Gold*, i. p.53

35. *The Gold Mines of Midian* (1878) p.215

CHAPTER TEN

1. A.J. Kennedy, *La Plata, Brazil and Paraguay during the Present War* (1869) pp.8-19
2. *Life*, i. p.51
3. *Letters from the Battlefields of Paraguay*, p.110
4. See especially the copious reports from Thornton in Argentina in F.O.6/250,251,255,256 during the year 1864
5. Harry Bernstein, *Dom Pedro II* (New York 1973) pp.93-6
6. See Juan Bautista Alberdi, *Obras Completas* (Buenos Aires 1886), v. pp.30,64-5. Alberdi's view was taken over uncritically by P.H. Box, *The Origins of the Paraguayan War* (Illinois 1929) p.112
7. For a detailed argument along these lines see F.J. McLynn, 'The Causes of the War of Triple Alliance', *InterAmerican Economic Affairs* 33 (1979) pp.21-43. See also John Hoyt Williams, *The Rise and Fall of the Paraguayan Republic 1800-1870* (Austin 1979)
8. For detail on this see Ricardo Caillet Bois, *Un año crítico en la política exterior de la Presidencia de Mitre* (Buenos Aires 1946); Efraím Cardozo, *El Imperio del Brasil en el Rio de la Plata* (Asunción 1961)
9. See also F.J. McLynn, 'Consequences for Argentina of the War of Triple Alliance', *The Americas* 41 (1984) pp.81-98
10. *Letters from the Battlefields of Paraguay* p.58
11. ibid. p.xii
12. For the cholera epidemics see Matthew to Stanley, 26 April, 28 May 1867, F.O.6/267; Gould to Stanley, 11,25, January, 4 March 1868, F.O.6/273
13. A.J. Kennedy, op. cit. p.51
14. For full details on this complex affair see F.J. McLynn, 'The Corrientes Crisis of 1868', *North Dakota Quarterly* 47 (1979) pp.45-58
15. *Letters from the Battlefields of Paraguay*, pp.165-6,276
16. ibid. pp.292-4
17. For Paso de la Patria see Ford to Clarendon, 15 February 1866, F.O.6/262. For Mitre's boast see *El Nacional* (Buenos Aires), 17 April 1865
18. See *Archivo del General Mitre*, 27 vols (Buenos Aires 1911-13), vi. pp.76-142 for detail on Tuyutí and its consequences
19. The most graphic accounts of Curupaití are in *La Tribuna* (Buenos Aires), 29,30 September 1866

20. *Letters from the Battlefields of Paraguay*, p.307
21. Quoted in Gilbert Phelps, *Tragedy of Paraguay*, (1975) p.196
22. Charles J. Kolinsky, *Independence or Death: the story of the Paraguayan war* (Gainesville 1965)
23. *Letters from the Battlefields of Paraguay*, p.295
24. For Reclus's description see *Revue des Deux Mondes*, 15 October 1866, 15 August 1868
25. *Letters from the Battlefields of Paraguay*, p.321
26. ibid. p.349
27. ibid. pp.379-81,386
28. ibid. p.322
29. ibid. p.383
30. Stuart to Clarendon, 26 April 1869, F.O.6/282. This compared with an estimated £9 million spent on the war by Argentina in the years 1865-9 (Stuart to Clarendon, 13 Nov 1869, F.O.6/284)
31. For another visit to Urquiza by a Briton in 1868 see A.J. Kennedy, *La Plata* etc., op. cit. pp.195-217
32. For Urquiza in general see Beatriz Bosch, *Urquiza y su tiempo* (Buenos Aires 1971). For his humiliation in the election see F.J. McLynn, 'The Argentine Presidential Election of 1868', *Journal of Latin American Studies* 11 (1979) pp.303-23
33. *Letters from the Battlefields of Paraguay*, p.199
34. A.P. Castro, *Nueva historia de Urquiza, industrial, comerciante, ganadero* (Buenos Aires 1953) pp.22-3, 71-2. It is difficult to give an exact sterling equivalent for Urquiza's fortune because of wild fluctuations of the Argentine peso. But an estimate of his total wealth in the 1860s produced a figure of 347,412,500 gold pesos, with the real estate alone accounting for 184,625,000 pesos (Castro,op. cit.) This means he was easily a sterling millionaire. For Urquiza's diversification see Manuel Macchi, *Urquiza el saladerista* (Buenos Aires 1971)
35. *Letters from the Battlefields of Paraguay*, pp.200-6.

CHAPTER ELEVEN

1. For this and other details see the copious material in M.G. and E.T. Mulhall, *Handbook of the River Plate* (Buenos Aires 1869)
2. The Plaza Victoria and the Plaza 25 de Mayo were united in the 1880s to form the new Plaza de Mayo and the shops were removed.
3. Hadfield, op. cit. pp.104-5
4. Stuart to Clarendon, 25 April 1869, F.O.6/282
5. *Letters from the Battlefields of Paraguay*, pp.160-1

6. Burton to Elliott, 8 August 1871, F.O.195/976
7. For the cholera epidemic see additionally A.M. v. pp.121-42
8. Burton estimated that Buenos Aires contained 110,000 inhabitants and Argentina itself about 1,500,000 (*Letters from the Battlefields of Paraguay*, p.158). The true figures, recorded in the first national census of 1869, were, respectively, 180,000 and 1,836,490 (see Ernesto J. Maéder, *Evolución demográfica Argentina de 1810 a 1869* (Buenos Aires 1869).
9. J.R. Scobie, *Buenos Aires: Plaza to Suburb 1870-1910* (New York 1974) p.49
10. Thomas J. Hutchinson, *Buenos Aires and Argentine Gleanings* (1865)
11. R. Scalabrini Ortiz, *Historia de los ferrocarriles argentinos* (Buenos Aires 1957)
12. *Letters from the Battlefields of Paraguay*, p.188
13. Thomas J. Hutchinson, *The Paraná* (1868) p.147-8
14. *Letters from the Battlefields of Paraguay*, p.168
15. ibid. p.164. For Sarmiento in general see A.W. Bunkley, *Life of D.F. Sarmiento* (Princeton 1952); José S. Campobassi, *Sarmiento y su época*, 2 vols (Buenos Aires 1975)
16. *Letters from the Battlefields of Paraguay*, p.169
17. Blunt, *My Dairies*, op. cit., ii. p.129
18. Blunt, *Satan Absolved: A Victorian Mystery* (1899) p.19
19. Blunt, *My Diaries*, ii. p.131
20. ibid. i. p.141
21. See Sir Alex Cockburn, *Charge*, 2 vols (1875)
22. Blunt, *My Diaries*, i. p.360; *Life*, i. p.30
23. Burton's evidence is reproduced in Byron Farwell, *Burton* (1963) pp.292-5
24. *Life*, i. pp.453,593,596
25. See Douglas Woodruff, *The Tichborne Claimant: a Victorian Mystery* (1957); J.B. Atlay, *The Tichborne Case* (1917)
26. *Letters from the Battlefields of Paraguay*, p.136
27. See F.J. McLynn, 'Political Instability in Cordoba Province in the 1860s', *Ibero-Amerikanische Archiv* (1980) pp.251-69
28. For details of the earthquake see Thornton to Russell, 8 April 1861, F.O.6/233
29. Burton rated this and his exploration of the São Francisco river in Brazil as major exploits and waxed indignant at any attempt to belittle his achievements. 'A president of the RGS wrote that I had done nothing for geography in South America, after having, in one of my half-a-dozen journeys through the almost unexplored Sierra de San Luís in the Argentine Republic, inspected and described

1,300 miles of a river certainly unknown to him ten years ago. This meagre idea of geography, reducing a journey to a skeleton of perfectly uninteresting "crucial stations", carefully laid down by human occulations and other observations, and fitted only for the humblest professional map-maker, seems to have taken route in the RGS's brain, since the days when that learned body was presided over by Admiral Smyth. Volney never handled sextant; yet see what Gibbon says of his labours.' *Zanzibar,* ii. p.224

30. *Ultima Thule,* ii. pp.109,266; *Arabian Nights,* xi. p.115; xiii. p.478

31. *Sindh Revisited,* i. p.88. Burton's observations on the Argentine gaucho can be verified from a wealth of contemporary sources. See Thomas J. Hutchinson, *Argentine Gleanings,* op. cit. pp.49-54; *The Paraná* pp.86-102; cf.also Friedrich Gerstäcker, *Gerstäcker's Travels* (1854) p.73 and John Walker, ed. *The South American Sketches of R.B.Cunninghame Graham* (Norman, Oklahoma, 1978). For the gauchos in general, apart from Sarmiento's own *Facundo* (1872) and epics like José Hernandez's *Martin Fierro* see Madeline W. Nichols, *The Gaucho: Cattle Hunter, Cavalryman, Ideal of Romance* (Durham, North Carolina 1942); Ricardo Rodriguez Molas, *Historia social del gaucho* (Buenos Aires 1968)

32. *Ultima Thule,* ii. pp.36-7

33. *Arabian Nights,* vi. p.225; vii. p.121

34. *Letters from the Battlefields of Paraguay,* pp.92,466

35. *Arabian Nights,* vii. p.254

36. ibid. p.167

37. For other early nineteenth-century crossings of the difficult Andine passes between Argentina and Chile see Robert Crawford, *Across the Pampas and the Andes* (1884); *Gerstäcker's Travels* op. cit. pp.96-115; Hutchinson, *The Paraná* pp.205-21

38. For the story see Luke Ionides, 'Memories of Richard Burton', *Transatlantic Review,* March 1924; Farwell, *Burton,* op. cit. p.294. For the Araucanian Indians in general see Juan Carlos Werther, *La conquista del desierto* (Buenos Aires 1970); J. Rossignol, 'Chiliens et Indiens Araucanos au milieu du XIXème siècle', *Caravelle* 20(1973). For a brief popular account see F.J. McLynn, 'The Frontier Problem in Nineteenth-Century Argentina', *History Today,* January 1980 pp.28-32. For accounts of encounters with the Araucanians see Hutchinson, *The Paraná* pp.52-60; *Gerstäcker's Travels* p.73

39. Burton to Elliott, 18 June 1871, F.O.C.P.2148 (F.O.406/12) p.56

40. *Letters from the Battlefields of Paraguay,* p.170

41. ibid. p.74

42. *Unexplored Syria,* i. pp.1-3

43. Timmins, *F.J. Stevenson* op. cit. p.192
44. See the copious detail in ibid. pp.185-206
45. *Life*, i. p.236
46. *Arabian Nights*, iv. p.57; x. p.89,227,242-5; *Zanzibar*, ii. p.213
47. *Life*, i. p.455. The official letter of appointment was dated 3 December 1868 (Stanley to Burton, F.O.C.P.2148 p.1)
48. *Life and Lusiads* p.453; *Letters from the Battlefields of Paraguay*, p.414. Consul Hutchinson did not agree with Burton's hyperbolic estimate of the straits. See Hutchinson, *Two Years in Peru*, 2 vols (1873), i Chapter 1
49. *Unexplored Syria*, i. p.1
50. Burton to Hammond, 30 March 1869; Burton to Clarendon, 1 June 1869, F.O.C.P.2148 pp.1-2
51. Stuart to Stanley, 13 October, 26 December 1868, F.O.6/275; same to same 12 January 1869, F.O.6/282
52. *La Tribuna* (Buenos Aires), 19,20 January 1869
53. And whom Burton later escorted around Syria (*Unexplored Syria*, i. pp.137-8)
54. *Letters from the Battlefields of Paraguay*, pp.392-7
55. ibid. p.420
56. Max von Versen, 'Historia da Guerra do Paraguai', *Revista do Instituto Histórico e Geográfico Brasileiro* 76 (1913) p.57
57. *Letters from the Battlefields of Paraguay*, p.447
58. ibid. p.329
59. For full details of British nationals working in Paraguay at this period see Josefina Pla, *The British in Paraguay 1850-70* (1976)
60. *La Tribuna* 20 February 1869
61. See R.B. Cunninghame Graham, *Portrait of a Dictator* (1933)
62. US House of Representatives Report No.65, 41st Congress, 2nd session, 28,29 October 1869
63. *Letters from the Battlefields of Paraguay*, pp.471-2
64. *Captivity of Hans Stade*, p.35
65. *Ultima Thule*, ii. p.202; F.O.C.P.2148 p.2
66. Brodie, *Devil Drives* p.246

CHAPTER TWELVE

1. *Unexplored Syria*, i. pp.4,20. 'The New World, which had been my latest scene of action, wearies with its want of history, of association, and consequently of romance.' (ibid. p.3)
2. Burton's foreword to the *Arabian Nights*, i. p.vii; cf. also xvi. p.396

3. *Vikram and the Vampire*, (1870) pp.18,32,69,95,133,138,164,272
4. *Life*, i. p.499. For a tepid review of *Letters from the Battlefields of Paraguay* see *Athenaeum* 2214, 2 April 1870 p.447
5. 'Translation', *Athenaeum* 2313, 24 February 1872, pp.241-3
6. *Zanzibar*, ii. p.363
7. See the review in *Athenaeum*, 2392, 30 August 1873, p.276
8. *Manuel de Moraes: A Chronicle of the Seventeenth Century* (1886) p.vii
9. For José de Alencar see Raimundo Magalhaes Junior, p*José de Alencar e sua época* (Rio 1977)
10. As, for instance, Brodie, *Devil Drives* p.242
11. Frederick C.H. García, 'Richard Francis Burton and Basilio da Gama: the translator and the poet', *Luso-Brazilian Review* 12 (1975) pp.34-57
12. *Two Trips to Gorilla Land*, ii. p.315
13. *Letters from the Battlefields of Paraguay*, p.27
14. Antonio Candido, *Varios escritos* (São Paulo 1970) p.175
15. Huntington MSS 27954 f.89
16. *Zanzibar*, i. p.7
17. Huntington MSS.27954f.96
18. Frederick C.H. García and Edward F. Stanton, *The Uruguay by José Basilio da Gama, translated by Richard F. Burton* (Berkeley 1982) p.19
19. Huntington MSS.27954 f.97; *Life*, i. p.436
20. Norman Penzer, *An Annotated Bibliography of Sir Richard Francis Burton* (1923) pp.184-5; García and Stanton, op. cit. pp.33-4
21. García and Stanton p.25
22. For the Arabian influence see Hans Van Marle, 'Conrad and Richard Burton on Islam', *Conradiana: A Journal of Joseph Conrad Studies* (Lubbock, Texas) 17 (1985) pp.137-42. For the influence of *Letters from the Battlefields of Paraguay*, on *Nostromo* see Norman Sherry, *Conrad's Western World* (Cambridge 1971) pp.165-6
23. Burton to Monkton Milnes, 23 October 1865, Houghton MSS,TCC
24. *Letters from the Battlefields of Paraguay*, p.144
25. *Life*, ii. pp.270,542; Wright, i. p.238
26. *Life*, i. p.496
27. *Unexplored Syria*, i. p.2
28. *Wanderings in West Africa*, ii. p.295
29. *Life*, ii. p.46

Appendix

Burton and the American critics of his *Arabian Nights* translation

(From the concluding volume of his translation)

The Critic in Anglo-America

The *Boston Daily Advertiser* (26 January 1886) contains the following choice *morceau* which went the round of the Transatlantic Press:

G. W. S. writes from London to the *New York Tribune* in regard to Captain Burton's notorious translation of the *Arabian Nights*. Of Captain Burton's translation of the *Arabian Nights*, two volumes have now appeared. Before anything had been seen of them, I gave some account of this scheme, and of the material on which he had worked, with a statement of the reasons which made all existing versions unsatisfactory to the student, and incomplete. Captain Burton saw fit to reprint these desultory paragraphs as a kind of circular or advertisement on his forthcoming book. He did not think it necessary to ask leave to do this, nor did I know to what use my letter had been put till it was too late to object. In any ordinary case it would have been of no consequence, but Captain Burton's version is of such a character that I wish to state the facts, and to say that when I wrote my letter I had never seen a line of his translation, and had no idea that what I said of his plans would be used for the purpose it has been, or for any purpose except to be printed in your columns. As it is, I am made to seem to give some sort of approval to a book which I think offensive, and not only offensive, but grossly and needlessly offensive. If anybody has been induced to subscribe for it by what I wrote I regret it, and both to him and to myself I think this explanation due.

Mr Smalley is the London correspondent of the *New York Tribune*, which represents Jupiter Tonans in the Western World. He may be unable to write with independent tone – few Anglo-Americans can afford to confront the crass and compound ignorance of a 'free and independent majority' – but even he is not called upon solemnly to state an untruth. Before using Mr Smalley's article as a circular, my representative made a point of applying to him for permission, as he indeed was bound to do by the simplest rules of courtesy. Mr Smalley replied at once, willingly granting me the favour, as I can prove by the note still in my possession; and presently, frightened by the puny yelping of a few critical curs at home, he has the effrontery to deny the fact.

In my last volumes I have been materially aided by two Anglo-American friends MM. Thayer and Cotheal and I have often had cause to thank the *Tribune* and the *Herald* of New York for generously appreciating my labours. But no gratitude from me is due to the small fry of the Transatlantic Press which has welcomed me with spiteful little pars., mostly borrowed from unfriends in England and mainly touching upon style and dollars. In the *Mail Express* of New York (7 September 1885) I read, 'Captain Richard Burton, traveller and translator, intends to make all the money that there may be in his translation of the *Arabian Nights*. . . If he only fill his list, and collects his money he will be in easy circumstances for the remainder of his days.' In a subsequent issue (24 Oct.) readers are told that I have been requested not to publish the rest of the series under pain of legal prosecution. In the same paper (31 October 1885: see also 7 November 1885) I find:

> The authorities have discovered where Capt. Burton's *Thousand and One Nights* is being printed, despite the author's efforts to keep the place a secret, but are undecided whether to suppress it or to permit the publication of the coming volumes. Burton's own footnotes are so voluminous they exceed the letterpress of the text proper, and make up the bulk of the work.[1] The foulness of the second volume of his translation places it at a much higher premium in the market than the first.

The *Tribune* of Chicago (26 October 1885) honours me by declaring, 'It has been resolved to request Captain Burton not to publish the rest of his translation of the *Thousand and One Nights*, which is really foul and slipshod as to style.' The *New York Times* (17 October and 9 November 1885) merely echoes the spite of its English confrère:

Capt. Burton's translation of the *Arabian Nights* bears the imprint 'Benares'. Of course the work never saw Benares. America, France, Belgium and Germany have all been suggested as the place of printing, and now the *Pall Mall Gazette* affirms that the work was done 'north of the Tweed'. There is, without a doubt, on British soil, it says, 'a press which year after year produces scores of obscene publications'.

And the same is the case with the *St Louis Post Dispatch* (11 November 1885); the *Mail Express* of New York (23 November 1886); the *Weekly Post* of Boston (27 November 1885) which again revives a false report and with the *Boston Herald* (16 December 1885). The *Chicago Daily News (30 January 1886)* contains a malicious sneer at the Kamashastra Society. The *American Register* (25 July 1886) informs its *clientèle*, 'If, as is generally supposed, Captain Burton's book is printed abroad, the probability is that every copy will on arrival be confiscated as "indecent" by the Customhouse.' And to curtail a long list of similar *fadaises* I will quote the *Bookmart* (of Pittsburg, PA., USA, October 1886): 'Sir Richard Burton's *Nights* are terribly in want of the fig leaf if anything less than a cabbage leaf will do, before they can be fit (fitted?) for family reading. It is not possible (is it not possible?) that by the time a household selection has been sifted out of the great work, everything which makes the originality and the value – such as it is – of Richard's series of volumes will have disappeared, and nothing will remain but his diverting lunacies of style.' The *Bookmart*, I am informed, is edited by one Halkett Lord, an unnaturalized Englishman who finds it pays best to abuse everything and everyone English. And lastly the *Springfield Republican* (5 April 1886) assures me that I have published 'fully as much as the (his?) world wants of the *Nights*.'

In the case of the *Nights*, I am exposed to that peculiar Protestant form of hypocrisy, so different from the Tartuffean original of Catholicism, and still as mighty a motor force, throughout the length and breadth of the North-American continent, as within the narrow limits of England. There also as here it goes hand in hand with 'Respectability' to blind judgment and good sense.

A great surgeon of our day said (or is said to have said) in addressing his students: 'Never forget, gentlemen, that you have to deal with an ignorant public.' The dictum may fairly be extended from medical knowledge to general information amongst the many-headed of England; and the publisher, when rejecting a too recondite book, will repeat parrot-fashion, 'The English public is not a learned body'. Equally valid is the statement in the case of the Anglo-American community which is still half-educated and very far from being erudite. The vast country has produced a few men of great and original genius, such as Emerson and Theodore Parker, Edgar Allan Poe and Walt Whitman; but the sum total is yet too small to leaven the mighty mass which learns its rudiments at school and college and which finishes its education with the newspaper and the lecture. When Emerson died it was said that the intellectual glory of a continent had departed; but Edgar A. Poe, the peculiar poetic glory of the States, the first Transatlantic who dared be himself and who disdained to borrow from Schiller and Byron, the outlander poet who, as Edgar Allan Poe, is now the prime favourite in France, appears to be still under ban because he separated like Byron from his spouse, and he led a manner of so-called 'Bohemian' life. Indeed the wide diffusion of letters in the States, that favourite theme for boasting and bragging over the unenlightened and analphabetic Old World, has tended only to exaggerate the defective and disagreeable side of a national character lacking geniality and bristling with prickly individuality. This disposition of mind, whose favourable and laudable presentations are love of liberty and self-reliance, began with the beginnings of American history. The 'Fathers', Pilgrim and Puritan, who left their country for their country's good and their own, fled from lay tyranny and clerkly oppression only to oppress and tyrannize over others in new and distant homes. Hardly had a century and a half elapsed before the sturdy colonists, who did not claim freedom but determined to keep it, formally revolted and fought their way to absolute independence – not, by the by, a feat whereof to be overproud when a whole country rose un-animously against a handful of troops. The movement, however, reacted powerfully upon the politics of Europe which stood agape for change, and undoubtedly precipitated the great French Revolution. As soon as the States became an empire, their democratic and republican institutions at once attracted hosts of emigrants from the Old World, thus peopling the land with a selection of species: the active and the adventurous, the mal-content and the malefactor readily expatriate themselves while the *pauvre diable* remains at home. The potato famine in Ireland (1848) gave an over-whelming impetus to the exodus of a race which had never known a racial baptism; and, lastly, the Germans flying from the conscription, the blood tax of the Fatherland, carried with them over the ocean a transcendentalism which has engendered the wildest theories of socialism and communism. And the emigration process still continues. Whole regions, like the rugged Bocche di Cattaro in Dalmatia and pauper Iceland, are becoming depopulated: to me the wonder is that a poor man ever consents to live out of America or a rich man to live in it.

The result of such selection has been twofold. The first appears in a splendid self-esteem, a complacency, a confidence which passes all bounds of the golden mean. 'I am engrossed in calmly contemplating the grandeur of my native country and her miraculous growth,' writes to me an old literary friend. The feeling normally breaks out in the grossest laudation of everything American. The ultra-provincial twang which we still hear amongst the servant classes of Lancashire and Yorkshire, and which is so notable in the *nouveau riche*, modified by traditional nasalization and, as in Australia, by climatic influences, is American and, therefore, the purest of English utterances. The obsolete vocabulary – often obsolete in England without just reasons – contrasting with a modern disfigured etymology which strips vocables of their genealogy and history, is American and *ergo* admirably progressive. The spurious facetiousness which deals mainly in mere jargon, words ill-spelt and worse pronounced; in bizarre contrast of ideas, and in ultra-Rabelaisian exaggeration, is American wit and humour – therefore unsurpassable. The Newspaper Press, that great reflector of nationalities, that prime expression of popular taste, too often of an *écoeurant* vulgarity, personal beyond all bounds of common decency, sensational as a transpontine drama, is American; America is the greatest nation upon earth's face; *ergo* the daily sheet is setting up the standard of English speech and forming the language of the Future, good and too good for all the world. This low standard of the Press is the more regrettable as its exalted duty is at present to solve the highest problems social and industrial, such as co-operation in labour, the development of fisheries, direct taxation versus indirect and a host of enigmas which the young world, unencumbered by the burdens of the Old World, alone shall unravel.

The second result is still more prejudicial and perilous. This is the glorification of mediocrity, of the average man and woman whose low standard must be a norm to statesman and publicist. Such cult of the common and the ignoble is the more prejudicial because it 'wars against all distinction and against the sense of elevation to be gained by respecting and admiring superiority'. Its characteristic predominance in a race which, true to its

Anglo-Saxon origin, bases and builds the strongest opinions upon the weakest foundations, hinders the higher Avatars of genius and interferes with the 'chief duty of a nation which is to produce great men'. It accounts for the ever-encroaching reign of women in literature – meaning as a rule cheap work and second-rate. And the main lack is not so much the 'thrill of awe', which Goethe pronounces to be the best thing humanity possesses, but that discipline of respect, that sense of loyalty, not in its confined meaning of attachment to royalty, but in a far higher and nobler signification, the recognizing and welcoming elevation and distinction whatever be the guise they may assume. 'The soul lives by admiration and hope and love.'

And here we see the shady side of the educational process, the diffusion of elementary and superficial knowledge, of the veneer and polish which mask, until chipped off, the raw and unpolished material lying hidden beneath them. A little learning is a dangerous thing because it knows all and consequently it stands in the way of learning more or much. Hence it is sorely impatient of novelty, of improvement, of originality. It is intolerant of contradiction, irritable, thin-skinned, and impatient of criticism, of a word spoken against it. It is chargeable with the Law of Copyright, which is not only legalised plunder of the foreigner, but is unfair, unjust and ungenerous to native talent for the exclusive benefit of the short-sighted many-headed. I am far from charging the United States with the abomination called 'International Copyright'; the English publisher is as sturdy an enemy to 'protection' as the Transatlantic statesman; but we expect better things from a new people which enjoys the heritage of European civilization without the sufferings accompanying the winning of it. This mediocrity has the furious, unpardoning hatred of *l'amour propre offensé*. Even a word in favour of my old friends the Mormons is an unpardonable offence: the dwarfish and dwarfing demon 'Respectability' has made their barbarous treatment a burning shame to a so-called 'free' country: they are subjected to slights and wrongs only for practising polygamy, an institution never condemned by Christ or the early Christians. The calm and dispassionate judgments of Sir Lepel Griffin and the late Matthew Arnold, who ventured to state, in guarded language, that the boasted civilization of the United States was not quite perfect, resulted in the former being called a snob and the latter a liar. English stolidity would only have smiled at the criticism even had it been couched in the language of *persiflage*. And when Mr Max O'Rell traverses the statements of the two Englishmen and exaggerates American civilization, we must bear in mind first that *la vulgarité ne se traduit pas*, and secondly, that the foes of our foemen are our friends. Woe be to the man who refuses to fall down and do worship before that brazen-faced idol (*Eidolon Novi Mundi*), Public Opinion in the States; unless, indeed, his name be Brown and he hail from Briggsville.

Some years ago I proposed to write a paper upon the reflex action of Anglo-America upon England, using as a base the last edition of Mrs Trollope, who was compelled to confess that almost every peculiarity which she had abused in her first issue had become naturalized at home. Yankee cuteness has already displaced in a marvellous way old English rectitude and plain dealing; gambling on the Stock Exchange, cornering, booms and trusts have invaded the trading classes from merchant princes to shopkeepers and threaten, at their actual rate of progress, not to leave us an honest man. But now the student's attention will be called to the great and ever-growing influence of the New World upon the Old, and notably upon Europe. Some 550,000 Americans annually visit the continent, they are rapidly becoming the important item of the floating population, and in a few years they will number 500,000. Meanwhile they are revolutionizing all the old institutions; they are abolishing the classical cicerone whose occupation is gone amongst a herd which wants only to see streets and people; they greatly increase the cost of travelling; they pay dollars in lieu of francs, and they are satisfied with inferior treatment at superior prices: hence the American hotel abroad is carefully shunned by Englishmen and natives. At home the 'well-to-do class' began by regarding their kinsmen *d'outre-mer* with contemptuous dislike; then they looked upon them as a country squire would regard a junior branch which has emigrated and has thriven by emigration; and now they are welcomed in Society because they amuse and startle and stir up the duller depths. But however warm may be private friendship between Englishmen and Anglo-Americans there is no public sympathy nor is any to be expected from the present generation. 'New England does not understand Old England and never will,' the reverse being equally the fact. 'The Millennium must come', says Darwin, 'before nations love each other': I add that first *Homo alalus seu Pithecanthropus* must become *Homo Sapiens* and cast off his moral slough – egoism and ignorance. Mr Cleveland, in order to efface the foul stigma of being the 'English President', found it necessary to adopt the strongest measures in the matter of 'Fisheries'; and the 'Irish vote' must quadrennially be bought at the grave risk of national complications. Despite the much-bewritten 'brotherhood of the two great English-speaking races of the world', the old leaven of cousinly ill-feeling, the jealousy which embitters the Pole against his Russian congener, is still rampant. Uncle Sam actively dislikes John Bull and dispraises England. An Anglo-American who has lived years amongst us and in private intimacy must, when he returns home, speak disparagingly of the old country unless he can afford the expensive luxury of telling unpopular truths and of affronting Demos, the hydra-headed.

But there are even now signs of better things in the Great Republic. Mr James R. Lowell, an authority (if there be any) upon the subject of Democracy, after displaying its fine points and favourable aspects in his addresses to English audiences, has at length had the uncommon courage to discuss family affairs, and to teach Boston and New York what 'weaknesses and perils there may be in the practical working of a system never before set in motion under such favourable circumstances, nor on so grand a scale'. He is emboldened to say firmly and aloud, despite the storming of false and hollow self-praise, that American civilization, so strong on the material side, is sadly wanting on the other, and still lacks much to make it morally acceptable or satisfactory. And we have home truths concerning that Fool's Paradise the glorification of the 'average man'. Every citizen of the world must wish full success to the 'Independents' (in politics) who sit at the feet of so wise and patriotic a teacher.

1. Quite untrue: the critic as usual never read and probably never saw the subject of his criticism. In this case I may invert one of my mottoes and write 'To the foul all things are foul'.

Index

Acapulco, 44
Agassiz, Jean Louis Rodolphe, 104, 125,
   143, 239n
Alencar, José de, 212, 241n, 250n
alligators, 144-5, 150, 152
Amazon, River, 149, 153, 163, 170, 241n
American Civil War (1861-65), 8, 9, 10, 11,
   34, 182, 184, 221, 222
ants, 103
Arapaho Indians, 19, 226n
Arabian Nights, Burton's translation of,
   209, 210
Araucanian Indians, 201, 222, 248n
Arkansas River, 149, 184
Arnold, Matthew, 62, 214, 232n, 256
Assis, Machado de, 81, 212
Asunción, 178, 179, 181, 203, 205
Aubertin, J.J., 91, 94, 120, 165, 209-10

Bagehot, Walter, 68
Balzac, Honoré de, 56, 123, 188, 196
Bates, Henry Walter, 104, 146, 240n
Bermejo River, 149, 183, 184, 185
Bierce, Ambrose, 233n
Blunt, Wilfred Scawen, 162, 169, 196, 243n
Bolívar, Simon, 178
Borrow, George, 61
Brazil: political state of: 78-84
   slavery in, 78-80, 81-82
Browne, Charles, alias Artemus Ward,
   31-32, 43, 44, 55, 226n, 227n, 228n,
   229n
Buchanan, James, 26
Buenos Aires, 176, 181, 187, 189, 190-94,
   206
Burton, Edward, 12
Burton, Isabel, 3-5, 12, 73, 76, 114, 118,

123, 171, 196, 198, 201, 203, 212-3,
   214, 219, 220
   in Lisbon, 74-5
   in Rio de Janeiro, 77-8, 95-7, 119, 124,
      162-64
   at Santos, 86-7, 92, 120-1, 138, 167-8
   in Sao Paulo, 87-92, 93-5, 99-100, 101-2,
      104, 109, 111, 120, 121, 165-6
   at Petrópolis, 95-6, 125
   accompanies Richard to Sabara, 125-35
   descent into Morro Velho mine, 133-5
   returns to Rio from Sabará, 136-8
   parting from Richard, 168-9
Burton, Richard Francis, Captain (later
      Sir),
   as consul, 110-18
   literary work of, 94, 124, 209-220
   travels of: to lake Tanganyika, 3, 56-7,
      159, 170, 219
   crossing the Atlantic, 5-7
   in Canada, 7
   at Niagara Falls, 7
   in New York, 7-8
   in Washington, 8
   in the South, 9-12
   in New Orleans, 12
   in Missouri, 13
   from Missouri to Salt Lake City, 13-20
   in Salt Lake City, 20-40
   from Salt Lake to Carson City, 40-3
   in California, 44, 222
   in Panama, 44-5
   crosses Atlantic to England, 44-5
   in West Africa, 73-4
   on holiday in Ireland (1864), 74
   in Lisbon, 74-5
   at Pernambuco, 76

259

in Rio, 76-8, 95-7, 124, 162-4, 208, 212, 222
in Santos, 78, 92, 120-1, 161, 164-5, 167-8, 210
in Sao Paulo, 87-92, 93-5, 99-100, 119-200, 119-20, 121, 165-6
in interior of Brazil, 92-3, 98-9, 100-1, 123
at Petrópolis, 95-6, 119, 125, 131, 205
in Minas Gerais, 125-9
at Morro Velho, 129-31, 133-5
at Ouro Preto, 131-3
at Sabará, 135-6
begins river journey on Rio das Velhas, 136-8
down Rio Sao Francisco, 139-59
at Paulo Afonso falls, 159-61
departs for River Plate, 168-9
in Montevideo, 175-6
up Paraná river, 178-81
at fortress of Humaitá, 184-5
in Buenos Aires, 187, 190-7, 204, 208
on River Uruguay, 187-9
across Andes to Chile, 198-201
in Chile and Peru, 201-2
returns to Argentina via Straits of Magellan, 202-2
revisits Paraguayan war battlefields, 203-8
Butler, Samuel, 67, 233n

California, 28
Camoens (Camões), Luis de, 94, 124, 153, 209, 214, 242n
Captivity of Hans Stade of Hesse, The, 211-12
Carlyle, Thomas, 214
Carson, Kit, 20, 226n
Caxias, Marques de, 83, 204
Chandless, William, 28, 54, 227n, 231n
Chaucer, Geoffrey, 218
Cheyenne Indians, 13
Chile, 105, 201, 203, 220
Churchill, Charles, 222-3
Clarendon, George William Frederick Villiers, 4th Earl of, 95, 97
Cobbett, William, 232n
Comanche Indians, 13
Confederation of Southern States (see also: American Civil War; slavery), emigrants from to Brazil, 93, 112-3, 133, 139, 142
Congo River, 138, 150, 241n
Conrad, Joseph, 219
Cooper, Fenimore, 46, 105
Cunninghame Graham, Robert Bontine, 207
Curupaití, battle of, 151, 182, 183

Custer, George Armstrong, 14

Damascus, 118, 169-70, 171, 193, 202, 208, 220
Danites, 21, 33, 43, 228n
Darwin, Charles, 104
Derby, Edward Geoffrey Smith Stanley, 14th Earl of, 74
Dickens, Charles, 65, 214, 233n
Disraeli, Benjamin, 214
Dyott, George, 146, 241n

Emerson, Ralph Waldo, 28, 67, 233n, 254
Engels, Friedrich, 47
Eu, Comte d', 96, 205

Fawcett, Percy, 147, 241n
FitzGerald, Edward, 214
Francia, José Gaspar Rodriguez, 178
freemasonry, 31
Fremont, John Charles, 14, 20, 49
Freud, Sigmund, 60, 104

Gama, José Basilio de, 213-9
Gardner, George, 104, 146, 160, 240n
Gerstäcker, Friedrich, 221, 248n
Gosh-Utah Indians, 42, 43
Glennie, Charles Archibald, 111-2, 124, 164, 168
Graham, Billy, 228n
Grant, Ulysses S., 112
Grattan massacre, 19
Greely, Horace, 14, 27-8, 34, 39, 55, 225n, 227n, 228n
Gunther, John, 228n

Hadfield, William, 165-6
Halifax (Canada), 7
Harar, Burton's journey to, 170, 187, 219
Hickok, Wild Bill, 19, 226n
Hudson, W.H., 171
Humaitá, fortress of 151, 176, 181, 182-4, 185, 203
Humboldt, Friedrich Heinrich Alexander, Baron von, 104, 108, 240n
Hutchinson, Thomas, 179, 195, 203

Indians, Native American (see also under individual tribes), 17, 19, 33, 42-3, 46-51, 97, 105-6, 152, 170, 171, 201, 202, 212-7
Iracéma (Burton's translation of), 212

James, Henry, 62, 232n
Jesuits, 157, 177-8, 213-4, 216, 217,218, 219
jiggers, 103, 171
Jordán, Ricardo López, 177
Jung, Carl Gustav, 60

Kansas, 14, 27
Kasidah, the, 140
Keats, John, 67, 233n
Kimball, Heber, 39-40
Kiowa Indians, 13
Kipling, Rudyard, 28, 229n

Lacerda, Francisco José Maria de, 147, 211
Lands of the Cazembe (Burton's translation of), 211-2
Lawrence, D.H., 172
Lee, Robert Edward, 112
Lima, 202
Lincoln, Abraham, 81
Little Big Horn, battle of, 47
Livingstone, David, 35, 124
Lomas Valentinas, battle of, 203, 204
London, Jack, 172
Longfellow, Henry Wadsworth, 48
López, Carlos Antonio, 178
López, Francisco Solano, 81, 176, 177, 179, 182, 183, 184, 185, 186, 188, 203, 204, 205, 206, 207, 208, 214, 222
Lusiads, the (Burton's translation of), 209-10, 214-5, 217, 242n
Lynch, Eliza, 2045, 207-08

Magdalena, River, 150
Malinowski, Bronislaw, 104
Mao-tse-tung, 32
Marryat, Frederick, 61, 62, 231n, 232n
Martineau, Harriet, 57, 65, 231n
Marx, Karl, 26
Mauá, baron (Ireno Evangelista de Souza), 82, 235n
Maxwell, William, 198-9
Mecca, Burton's journey to, 97, 170, 219
Melville, Herman, 158, 172
Milnes, Richard Monkton, 1st Baron Houghton, 11, 59, 121, 123, 231
Mission, The (film), 213
Mississippi, River, 14, 50, 51, 149, 150, 241n, 242n
Missouri River, 14, 50, 149, 222, 241n
Missouri (state), 13
Mitre, Bartolomé, 83, 177, 179, 180, 181, 182, 187, 195-6, 245n
Montesquieu, Charles de Secondat, baron de, 47, 104, 108, 149
Montevideo, 175-6, 194, 203
Montreal, 7
Moorehead, Alan, 108
Moraes Manuel de (Burton's translation of), 212
Morgan, Lewis, 47
Mormons,
 Burton's attitude to, 30-2, 35-7, 39-40, 51-9, 256

early history of, 23-5
early farming and irrigation in Salt Lake City, 25-8
and polygamy, 29, 37, 51-9
and Mountain Meadow massacre, 30
crime and punishment among, 32-3
theology of, 30-1, 37-8, 39
and *Book of Mormon*, 23, 37-8
attitude to women (see also polygamy), 40, 52-6
and Indians, 19, 30, 33, 38
and relations with the U.S.A., 24-5, 26, 27-8, 34, 38
Morris, William, 214
Murchison, Sir Roderick, 220

Nebraska, 14
New Mexico, 33
New Orleans, 11-2
New York, 7-8, 258
Niagara Falls, 7
Nietzche, Friedrich, 58
Niger, River, 138, 149, 241n
Nile, River, 138, 150, 215, 241n

Ohio, River, 149, 184

Panama, 44-5
Parkman, Francis, 49-50
Pará, 169-70
Paraguay, 107, 160, 177, 178, 179-80, 181-2, 185, 200
Paraguay River, 149, 183, 184
Paraguayan War (1864-70), 80-4, 111, 124, 127, 151, 165-6, 176-81, 193, 203-8, 219, 221-2
Paraná, River, 149, 163, 178, 179, 184, 187, 203, 241n
Paulo Afonso Falls, 129, 149, 150, 157, 159-61, 163
Pedro II, 78, 79, 83-4, 94, 96, 124, 156, 176, 186, 188-9, 194, 203, 204, 222, 234n
Pentamerone, II, Burton's translation of, 210
Peru, 105, 201
Pilcomayo River, 149, 184
piranha, 141-2
Plate, River, 17, 149, 184
Poe, Edgar Allan, 67, 254
Polygamy, Burton on, 8, 29, 37, 46, 48, 51-9
Pony Express, 17-18, 26
railway construction, 94-5, 100, 113, 114, 120, 127, 139, 164-5, 194

Rank, Otto, 60
rattlesnakes, 20, 43, 103, 106, 169, 203, 241n

Reclus, Elisée, 184, 246n
Red River, 149, 184
Rémy, Jules, 28, 51, 54, 227n, 230n
Rio de la Plata (River Plate), 149, 167, 168, 175-6, 202, 220
Rio Grande, 153
Roosevelt, Theodore, 147, 170
Rosas, Juan Manuel de, 79, 187
Ruskin, John, 62, 214, 232n
Russell, John, 1st Earl, 74, 114

Sala, G.A., 28, 61, 232n
St. Lawrence River, 149, 150
Salado River, 149, 184
Salem, 7
Salt Lake, 20, 24, 32, 42
Salt Lake City, 20-2, 25-40, 51, 52, 54
San Francisco, 42, 44
Santiago, 201
São Francisco River, 124, 135, 138, 139-61, 164, 167, 170, 179, 184, 222, 241n, 242n, 247n
Sarmiento, Domingo Faustino, 83, 187, 191, 194-6, 199, 203, 247n
sea serpents, 98-9
Shakers, 39
Shakespeare, William, 218
Shoshone Indians, 43
Silve, J.M. Pereira da, 212
Sioux Indians, 19, 46-51, 58, 170, 222, 230n
slavery, Burton's attitude to, 9-11, 61, 84-5
Smith, Joseph, 23-4, 25, 31, 32, 33, 34, 35, 36, 43, 54, 59, 178, 228n
snakes (see also rattlesnakes), 78, 103, 106, 120, 145-7, 149, 157, 169, 170, 216-7
Speke, John Hanning, 3, 7, 138
Stanley, Edward Henry Smith, 15th Earl of Derby, 74, 114, 117
Stanley, Henry Morton, 219, 221-2
Steinhaeuser, John, 5, 12, 109, 225n
Stevenson, F.J., 157, 163, 171, 201-2, 243n
Summer, Charles, 8

Tebicuari River, 183, 203
Thompson, George, 206
Thornton, Sir Edward, 77, 82, 97, 112, 114, 123, 124, 176, 183

Tichborne Claimant, 197-8, 201
Tocqueville, Alexis de, 62, 63, 65-6, 232n, 233n
Trollope, Anthony, 65, 233n
Trollope, Frances, 63-64, 232n
Tuyutí, battles of, 151, 182, 183
Twain, Mark, 28, 37-38, 43, 44, 226n, 229n, 230n

United States, 81, 84, 93, 149, 168, 188, 206, 207
   Burton's attitude to, 59-60, 62-3, 64, 66-9
   British attitudes to, 60-9
Urquiza, Justo José de, 177, 180, 187-9, 246n
Uruguay, 81, 175-6, 179, 195
O Uruguai (Burton's translation of), 213-9
Uruguay River, 179, 187, 189

Valparaiso, 201
Vera Cruz, 44
Vespucci, Amerigo, 46
Vikram and the Vampire (Burton's translation of), 210-1

Wallace, Alfred Russel, 104
Ward, Artemus (see Browne, Charles)
Washburne, Charles, 206
Washington, 8, 33
Waterton, Charles, 104, 145-6, 236-7n, 240n
Weeks, James W., 146, 241n, 242n
Wegener, Alfred Lothar, 104
Wheelwright, William, 179
Whitman, Walt, 63, 67, 254
Wilde, Oscar, 28, 61
Wordsworth, William, 172
women, Burton's attitude to, 7-8, 16-7, 18-20, 30, 52-3, 58, 64, 130, 133

Young, Brigham, 21, 24-40, 51, 52, 53, 55, 58, 93, 178

Xingu River, 163, 170

Zola, Emile, 214